The Law in Holy Scripture

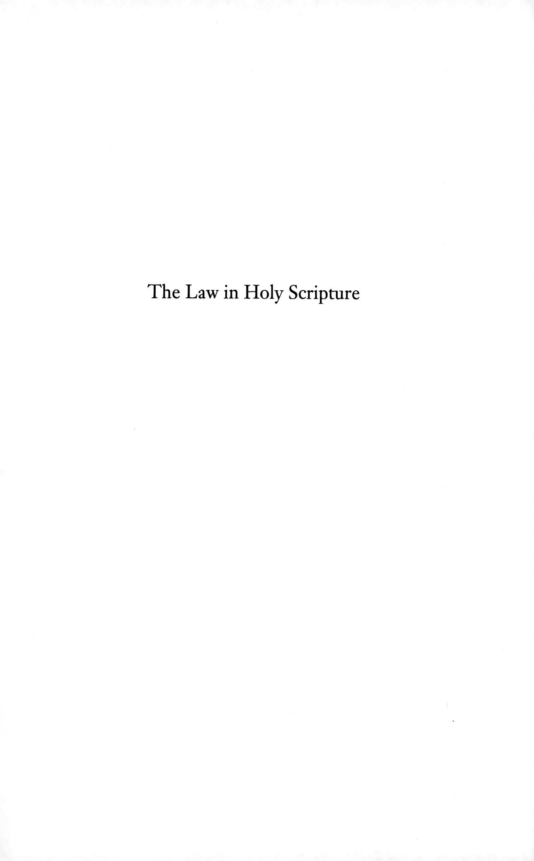

CONCORDIA ACADEMIC PRESS

THE LAW
IN HOLY SCRIPTURE

ESSAYS FROM THE CONCORDIA THEOLOGICAL
SEMINARY SYMPOSIUM ON EXEGETICAL THEOLOGY

EDITED BY
CHARLES A. GIESCHEN

CONCORDIA PUBLISHING HOUSE · SAINT LOUIS

ACADEMIC PRESS

Library of Congress Cataloging-in-Publication Data

Symposium on Exegetical Theology (16th : 2001 : Concordia Theological Seminary)
    The law in Holy Scripture : essays from the Concordia Theological Seminary, Symposium on Exegetical Theology / edited by Charles A. Gieschen.
        p. cm.
    Includes indexes.
    ISBN 978-0-7586-5758-9
    1. Law (Theology)—Biblical teaching—Congresses. I. Gieschen, Charles A. II. Title.
    BS680.L33S96 2001
241'.2—dc22

1 2 3 4 5 6 7 8 9 10   13 12 11 10 09 08 07 06 05 04

CONTENTS

ACKNOWLEDGMENTS

Sometimes a symposium where a variety of biblical scholars gather to speak on a common theme looks better in the planning stage than it sounds in the delivery stage at the podium. The 16th Annual Symposium on Exegetical Theology at Concordia Theological Seminary that took place on January 21–22, 2001, however, delivered beyond expectations. Many of the more than 600 attendees recognized that these essays deserved to be shared with a wider audience and requested their publication. I herewith thank everyone who planned and attended this memorable event.

I especially express my heartfelt appreciation to all the contributors to this volume, many of whom are my esteemed colleagues in the Department of Exegetical Theology at Concordia Theological Seminary. David Scaer's effort to expand his brief response delivered during the symposium into an essay is noteworthy. I thank Andrew Das and the editorial committee of *Concordia Journal* for permission to reprint his essay, which was published in volume 27 (2001): 234–52. Although the masterful essay by Piotr Malysz was not delivered at the symposium, its content complements the other essays in this volume. I thank him and the editorial committee of *Logia* for permission to reprint a slightly revised version of his article, which was published in *Logia* XI:4 (2002): 9–19. I am also indebted to Chad Bird and Mark Braden for help with proofing and Justin Kane for help with the indices. John Klinger and Jason Reed provided invaluable technical support. Finally, I express my sincere gratefulness to the other members of the Concordia Academic Press editorial committee for their acceptance of this project and to the staff of Concordia Publishing House for their careful labor in publishing it.

The Epiphany of Our Lord
Charles A. Gieschen
6 January 2004

ABBREVIATIONS

AB	Anchor Bible
AC	Augsburg Confession
Ap.	Apology of the Augsburg Confession
CJ	*Concordia Journal*
Ep.	Epitome of the Formula of Concord
ESV	English Standard Version
FC	Formula of Concord
ICC	International Critical Commentary
JJS	*Journal of Jewish Studies*
JSNT	*Journal for the Study of the New Testament*
JSNTSup	Journal for the Study of the New Testament: Supplement Series
JSOTSup	Journal for the Study of the Old Testament: Supplement Series
K-W	Kolb, Robert, and Timothy J. Wengert, eds. *The Book of Concord.* Translated by Charles P. Arand et al. Minneapolis: Fortress, 2000.
LC	Large Catechism
LW	Luther, Martin. *Luther's Works.* American Edition. General editors Jaroslav Pelikan and Helmut T. Lehmann. 56 vols. St. Louis: Concordia; Philadelphia: Muhlenberg and Fortress, 1955–1986.
LXX	Septuagint
NASB	New American Standard Bible

NIV	New International Version
NKJV	New King James Version
NovTSup	Novum Testamentum Supplements
NRSV	New Revised Standard Version
NTS	*New Testament Studies*
RSV	Revised Standard Version
SBLDS	Society of Biblical Literature Dissertation Series
SD	Solid Declaration
SNTSMS	Society for New Testament Studies Monograph Series
Tappert	Tappert, Theodore G. ed. *The Book of Concord.* Philadelphia: Fortress, 1959.
WBC	Word Biblical Commentary
WUNT	Wissenschaftliche Untersuchungen zum Alten und Neuen Testament

Abbreviations for other ancient texts, including rabbinic writings and Qumran texts, can be found in *The SBL Handbook of Style* (ed. Partick H. Alexander et al; Peabody, Mass.: Hendrickson, 1990).

LIST OF CONTRIBUTORS

DALE C. ALLISON JR. is Professor of New Testament at Pittsburgh Theological Seminary in Pittsburgh, Pennsylvania.

A. ANDREW DAS is Assistant Professor of Religion at Elmhurst College in Elmhurst, Illinois.

DANIEL L. GARD is Professor of Exegetical Theology and Dean of the School of Graduate Studies at Concordia Theological Seminary in Fort Wayne, Indiana.

CHARLES A. GIESCHEN is Associate Professor of Exegetical Theology and Chairman of the Department of Exegetical Theology at Concordia Theological Seminary in Fort Wayne, Indiana.

ARTHUR A. JUST JR. is Professor of Exegetical Theology and Dean of the Chapel at Concordia Theological Seminary in Fort Wayne, Indiana.

PIOTR J. MALYSZ is the assistant pastor of Our Savior Lutheran Church in Westminster, Massachussetts, and a doctoral student at Harvard University.

PAUL R. RAABE is Professor of Exegetical Theology and Chairman of the Department of Exegetical Theology at Concordia Seminary in St. Louis, Missouri.

DAVID P. SCAER holds the David P. Scaer Chair of Systematic and Biblical Theology and is Chairman of the Department of Systematic Theology at Concordia Theological Seminary in Fort Wayne, Indiana.

PETER J. SCAER is Assistant Professor of Exegetical Theology at Concordia Theological Seminary in Fort Wayne, Indiana.

DEAN O. WENTHE is the President of Concordia Theological Seminary in Fort Wayne, Indiana, and also is Professor of Exegetical Theology.

INTRODUCTION

Those living in the United States during the latter half of the twentieth century and the beginning of the new century have witnessed significant debate on foundational moral issues, both within our wider society and the Christian church. The Supreme Court's *Roe v. Wade* decision in 1973 legalized the killing of unborn children by abortion. Although some Christians continue to march annually in Washington, D.C., or weekly around the local abortion clinic, abortion is no longer a pressing issue in some mainline churches whose members are among those who use such clinics or take the "morning-after pill" to shed themselves of unwanted pregnancies. Meanwhile, the debate about how and when a child's life can be ended, resparked in recent years by ethicist Peter Singer of Princeton University, has moved on to the legitimacy of killing children during the initial weeks after birth in the case of those born with an abnormality. The issue of homosexuality has gone far beyond the need for protective rights for homosexuals in society; now marriage is being redefined by states such as Massachusetts and Vermont, the latter of which gave such unions legal status in 2000, while the former recognized these unions as "marriage" in 2004.[1] Even more shocking is the fact that some pastors are consecrating homosexual unions as marriages blessed by God, even without their state's legal sanction. In addition, some church bodies are ordaining homosexuals to lead their flocks.[2]

---

1. Although registering homosexual partnerships since 1998, the Netherlands became the first country to allow homosexual couples to marry on the same legal terms as heterosexual couples in 2000. Canada followed this trend in 2003 after its courts ruled that laws against homosexual marriages were unconstitutional.

2. The United Church of Christ has the most liberal policy, but homosexual marriage and the ordination of avowed homosexuals have been given serious consideration by recent conventions of the United Methodist Church, the Episcopal Church, the Presbyterian Church U.S.A., and the Evangelical Lutheran Church in America. If policy on such practices is being considered, it is probable that such practice already has begun to various degrees in these denominations. For example, V. Gene Robinson, a priest of the Episcopal Church in New Hampshire, who is publicly known to be in a homosexual relationship, was elected as a bishop in 2003.

Such significant issues within our society, and especially as these issues confront the church from within, have led Christians to search Holy Scripture for answers or—at the very least—justification for the conclusions they have drawn. In the introduction to his significant volume on New Testament ethics, Richard Hays makes this observation: "Christians of all sorts, even those who might not subscribe formally to a 'high' doctrine of biblical inspiration, have always deemed it essential that their ethical teachings and practices stand in continuity with Scripture."[3] Charles Cosgrove has recently contributed a hermeneutical examination of how the interpreters of Scripture have done this in the past.[4]

Appeals to Holy Scripture in a moral debate must address, sooner or later, the issue of the Christian's relationship to "the Law." This has been a topic of controversy from the infancy of Christianity. Jesus debated issues related to the Law with the Pharisees. At the Apostolic Council, the church debated the role of the Law in the Gentile congregations (Acts 15). Two extreme understandings of the Law arose in those early decades of Christianity that exist to this day: those who advocate a complete break with the Law in the church and those who emphasize the complete continuity of the Law in the church. The former position is often labeled antinomianism and is visible already in Marcion, a second-century heretic who sought to excise anything related to the Old Testament or the Law from the Christian Scriptures because, as Marcion asserted, the Old Testament presented a god who was inferior to Jesus Christ, who shows forth God to be love. The latter extreme, sometimes labeled nomianism (more recently nomism) or legalism, is visible in the Judaizers whom Paul attacks in his Epistle to the Galatians.[5] The Ebionites discussed by early heresiologists are another example of this tendency among early Christians.[6]

A significant amount of the confusion among Christian laity concerning what "the Law" means comes from a misunderstanding of the varied usage of this term in Holy Scripture. Some of this con-

---

3. Richard B. Hays, *The Moral Vision of the New Testament: A Contemporary Introduction to New Testament Ethics* (New York: HarperSanFrancisco, 1996), 2.

4. Charles H. Cosgrove, *Appealing to Scripture in the Moral Debate: Five Hermeneutical Rules* (Grand Rapids: Eerdmans, 2002).

5. See the discussion of rising Zealotism in Bo Reicke, *Re-examining Paul's Letters: The History of the Pauline Correspondence* (ed. David P. Moessner and Ingalisa Reicke; Harrisburg, Penn.: Trinity Press International, 2001), 10–15, 45–48.

6. For example, Epiphanius, *Panarion* 30.1.1–30.34.6; see *The Panarion of St. Epiphanius, Bishop of Salamis: Select Passages* (trans. Philip R. Amidon; New York: Oxford University Press, 1990), 94–107.

fusion arises from interpreting the English word *law* to mean the same thing no matter where it is found in the Old and New Testaments.[7] Some Christians, especially Lutherans nurtured on distinguishing between Law and Gospel as they apply in the Scriptures, understand the Law exclusively as demands that accuse and condemn us as sinners.[8] According to this understanding, the Law performs the important function of showing us our sin, but it is not something in which we can delight. Christian laypeople have trouble, therefore, understanding the many portions of Scripture that praise the Law (e.g., Psalm 119). Other Christians argue that Jesus has freed us from the Law, so we should live in the Spirit and not burden people with the Law, especially ethical teaching from the Old Testament.[9] Still others note that Jesus did not come to abolish or set aside the Law (Matt 5:17–18), but then they wonder why the church does not honor a number of the commands that God gave to Israel.

The issue of the Law is also debated among biblical scholars. Some argue against the continuing relevance of ancient Israel's understanding of the Law because it is culturally and ethnically conditioned.[10] Some debate whether Jesus had a coherent and consistent position concerning the Law; sometimes he seems to affirm Jewish interpretation of the Law and other times he challenges it.[11] Some argue that Paul's primary concern with the Law was not that Jews believed that obedience to the Law played a role in their righteous status before God but that he did not want the requirement of circumcision and dietary laws to inhibit the Gentile mission.[12]

---

7. Several of the essays that follow in this volume discuss the various ways of understanding the Hebrew and Greek words for "law" in their given context.

8. Martin Luther emphasized the role of distinguishing properly between Law (Scripture that speaks of what we should or should not do) and Gospel (Scripture that speaks of God's love and forgiveness, especially what he has done in Christ) in preaching. This distinction is often improperly understood as the exegetical method Luther employed to determine the *meaning* of a text. It is more helpful to see this distinction as guiding Luther (and Lutherans) in the *application* of the meaning of a text to people. The classic expression of this Law-Gospel distinction is found in C. F. W. Walther, *The Proper Distinction between Law and Gospel* (trans. W. H. T. Dau; St. Louis: Concordia, 1929).

9. See the helpful discussion by C. E. B. Cranfield, "Has the Old Testament Law a Place in the Christian Life?" in *On Romans and Other New Testament Essays* (ed. C. E. B. Cranfield; Edinburgh: T&T Clark, 1998), 109–24.

10. For an introduction to the subject, see Elmer A. Martens, "How Is the Christian to Construe Old Testament Law?" *Bulletin for Biblical Research* 12 (2002): 199–216.

11. See further the essay by Dale C. Allison Jr. in this book. In more recent decades, scholars have tended to (over)emphasize the continuity between Jesus and first-century Judaism; see E. P. Sanders, *Jesus and Judaism* (London: SCM, 1985).

12. See further the essay by Charles A. Gieschen below.

There is, however, scholarly agreement on the fact that early Christian perspectives toward the Law are not simplistic. Because of the intertextuality between the Old and New Testament ethical texts, Richard Hays advises that we "read the New Testament texts with careful attention to their Old Testament subtexts."[13]

This volume consists of essays that were delivered during the 16th Annual Symposium on Exegetical Theology at Concordia Theological Seminary, Fort Wayne, Indiana, on January 16–17, 2001. The theme for that symposium, which also serves as the title of this volume, was chosen to address some of the serious questions that exist within the church and within biblical scholarship on the matter of the Law. Biblical scholars with expertise in the Old Testament, Jesus and the Gospels, and the Pauline Epistles, were purposely chosen so the essays would offer a wide and representative portrait of the Law in biblical literature. Furthermore, two important concluding essays evaluate and synthesize many of the issues raised by the other essays to present a biblical theology of the Law for the church as she faces the challenges of the twenty-first century. Both the choice of essayists and the context of their original delivery will help the reader to understand the ecclesial focus and reverent tone of the essays.

Each of the three essays dealing with the Old Testament emphasize the importance of understanding the broader meaning of *Torah* ("the Law") as "instruction" or even "revelation" for proper interpretation of this issue. More than the other two essayists, Dean Wenthe stresses the importance of not divorcing *Torah* from the wider gracious narrative of the Old Testament. The narrative, from which *Torah* cannot be dissected, defines our identity. Paul Raabe touches this same theme, but goes much further in helping Christians understand the role of the Law in sanctification, even as Israel was called to delight in a pattern of life distinct from the pagan nations that surrounded her. The essay by Daniel Gard presents *Torah* as the reflection of the character of God in his people because the Law is derived from God's own attributes and essence. As with Wenthe's essay, Gard stresses that the Law identifies who we are in Christ. After reading these three essays, one could easily draw the conclusion that a better title for this volume would have been *The Holy Scriptures as Torah*.

Of the five essays on the Law in the New Testament, two deal with Jesus and three with Paul. Dale Allison, a prominent biblical

---

13. Hays, *Moral Vision of the New Testament*, 309.

scholar from outside the Lutheran circle to which the other essayists belong, has contributed a wide-ranging essay that demonstrates
that Jesus was both in continuity with some Jewish interpretations
of the Law as well as distinctive from others. Although Allison's
exegetical approach is more critical than that of his original audience, his contribution reflects careful historical reflection on the
Gospel accounts of Jesus' teaching and his conclusions resonate
well with those of the other essays.[14] The essay by Peter Scaer is
more focused on Luke's theological portrait of Jesus and the apostles in Luke-Acts. Scaer's foray into Luke's portrait of Paul provides a nice transition to the essays that follow his and address Paul
and the Law. Charles Gieschen provides the uninitiated reader with
a critical introduction to recent scholarship on this issue, with some
attention to how the perspective on Paul and the Law that was pow-
erfully promulgated by Martin Luther has been set aside by many
adherents of the "New Perspective." The essay by Andrew Das continues and deepens the critique of the New Perspective by picking
up on one issue introduced by Gieschen, namely, evidence for the
"perfect obedience" demanded by the Law. Das's essay will,
undoubtedly, whet one's appetite for his books on the subject.[15] The
essay by Arthur Just serves as an apt conclusion to the essays dealing
with Paul because it sidesteps much of the scholarly debate and
plunges us into Paul's most passionate discussion of the Law in light
of Christ, namely, his Epistle to the Galatians.

The two essays on a biblical theology of the Law are written by
scholars who are biblical theologians in the best sense of the term.
Both David Scaer and Piotr Malysz discuss theology with eyes
firmly set on the Scriptures. Scaer's essay was originally a response
to the papers delivered at the symposium. As such, it is a synthetic
reflection on the earlier essays of this volume that discusses their
content in the wider context of biblical theology and the life of the
church. The essay by Malysz is one of the most provocative of the
volume, especially for Lutherans who are at home with traditional

---

14. It is the practice of the planners of the Symposium on Exegetical Theology to invite at
    least one scholar each year from outside The Lutheran Church—Missouri Synod to
    present the central plenary paper. Dale Allison was chosen because of both his schol-
    arly acumen as demonstrated in his research on the Synoptic Gospels and his willing-
    ness to address this topic for an audience that consisted primarily of conservative
    Lutheran pastors. For a more extensive example of his exegetical approach, see the
    three-volume commentary by W. D. Davies and Dale C. Allison Jr., *A Critical and
    Exegetical Commentary on the Gospel according to Saint Matthew*, 3 vols. (ICC; Edin-
    burgh: T&T Clark, 1988–1997).

15. A. Andrew Das, *Paul, the Law, and the Covenant* (Peabody, Mass.: Hendrickson, 2001),
    and *Paul and the Jews* (Peabody, Mass.: Hendrickson, 2003).

talk of the three uses of the Law as curb, mirror, and rule. Malysz's broad and scripturally grounded discussion enriches our understanding of the "third use" of the Law and its organic relationship to the oft-ignored "first use" in light of the restoration of creation in Christ.

Despite the broad scope of these essays and their divergent foci, several shared conclusions can be drawn as the church seeks to understand the relevance of Holy Scripture for its understanding of the Law. First, these essays help us to see the importance of interpreting "law" nomenclature in its immediate scriptural context, as well as the broader "grace" context within the narrative of salvation history. Second, Jesus Christ's fulfillment of the Law is central to our interpretation of the Law, including the *Torah* of the Old Testament. If one separates discussions of the Law from Christ, it is easy to reduce the Law to a model for moralism. Third, these essays reveal the ongoing relevance of the Law in the life of the Christian, both because of its accusatory function for us as sinners and because of its guidance for sanctification as it shows us our true identity as ones who love God and neighbor in Christ.[16] Irenaeus of Lyons wrote with serene succinctness of the living connection between faith and sanctification in the triune God: "To believe in Him is to do His will."[17]

Peter Stuhlmacher concludes his helpful essay "The Law as a Topic in Biblical Theology" with this thesis: "The topic 'law' is an unresolved fundamental problem for a biblical theology that connects the Old and New Testaments. This fundamental problem does not separate the two Testaments from one another but aids in a more precise understanding of their indissoluble connection."[18] I certainly agree. The recognition of this problem and the conviction that probing it will foster greater understanding of biblical theology are the reasons that scholars were asked to write and deliver the essays that follow. I am confident that these essays offer a faithful understanding of the "indissoluble connection" between the two testaments, especially of him who gave the Law, then fulfilled it in Jesus Christ.

---

16. For a brief, helpful discussion, see Paul R. Raabe, "The Law and Christian Sanctification: A Look at Romans," *CJ* 22 (1996): 178–85.

17. *Against Heresies* 4.5.5.

18. Peter Stuhlmacher, *Reconciliation, Law, and Righteousness* (trans. Everett R. Kalin; Philadelphia: Fortress, 1986), 130.

OLD TESTAMENT PERSPECTIVES

THE *TORAH* STORY

IDENTITY OR DUTY
AS THE ESSENCE OF THE LAW

DEAN O. WENTHE

One of the attractive aspects of exegesis is the constant vocation to understand a text fully. It is foundational to confessional Christianity that the texts of Sacred Scripture continually address and define us. Rightly understood, we are to be open to what has been termed a "second naïveté," namely, a fresh and full understanding of a text.[1] This, I hasten to add, is qualitatively different from a scholarly infatuation with novelty or the desire to carve out a scholarly career by proposing the novel. This fresh exegesis, at its best, is also faithful because it further expounds and exposes the richness and depth of Sacred Scripture.

The essays in this volume appropriately focus on one of the classic and foundational components of Sacred Scripture and of any theological construal of reality: the nature, function, and place of the Law. The work of E. P. Sanders, as discussed in other essays in this volume, has especially sparked a vigorous discussion, not only of his proposed "covenantal nomism" but also of the nature and function of the Law in St. Paul.[2] This debate invites anyone who is

---

1. The phrase "second naïveté" is usually credited to Paul Ricoeur; see Ricoeur, *The Conflict of Interpretations: Essays in Hermeneutics* (ed. Don Ihde; Evanston: Northwestern University Press, 1974), and Ricoeur, *Interpretation Theory: Discourse and the Surplus of Meaning* (Ft. Worth: Texas Christian University Press, 1976).

2. See the discussion of Frank Thielman, *Paul and the Law* (Downers Grove: InterVarsity, 1994), 14–47. Noteworthy is his review of responses to Sanders's proposal by the Pauline scholars Heikki Räisänen, J. Christiaan Beker, James D. G. Dunn, and Stephen Westerholm. See also the essays below by Charles A. Gieschen, A. Andrew Das, and Arthur A. Just Jr.

committed to biblical theology as a discipline with its own integrity to bring the Old Testament to the table as well.[3] Therefore, this essay seeks to explore freshly and faithfully the manner in which the Law functions within the larger *Torah* story of the Old Testament. Throughout this exploration, our ecclesial and cultural context will be drawn on to compare and contrast the claims of select texts with the realities of church and cultural life as they are experienced in our day.

A very real question for every Christian generation is the extent to which its faith and life are being defined and shaped by Sacred Scripture. It is all too easy, even within a community that formally subscribes to a high view of biblical authority, to allow a variety of other forces *de facto* to shape and norm the lives of the faithful. Not a few students of Western Christendom suggest that the real life of many churches is a mixture of consumerism, individual enthusiasms, and Western and North American assumptions about the character of religion.[4] Erich Auerbach, a noted scholar of Western literature who is not guided by dogmatic commitments, nonetheless observes:

> The world of Scripture stories is not satisfied with claiming to be a historically true reality—it insists that it is the only real world, and is destined to autocracy . . . . The Scripture stories do not, like Homer's, court our favor, they do not flatter us that they may please us and enchant us—they seek to subject us, and if we refuse to be subjected, we are rebels.[5]

It also is clear that the call of John Bright in his 1967 work *The Authority of the Old Testament* is as appropriate and necessary now as it was then. Bright called for the church to revive its use of the Old Testament as authoritative Scripture and abandon hermeneutical postures that effectively reduce the Old Testament solely to the role of preparing for the Gospel:

> If the Old Testament is accorded only the auxiliary, pedagogical function of preparing men's minds for the reception of the gospel, then the door is thrown open to Marcionism, whether it

---

3. For an overview of the major twentieth-century efforts to describe Old Testament theology, see Ben C. Ollenburger, Elmer A. Martens, and Gerhard F. Hasel, eds., *The Flowering of Old Testament Theology* (Sources for Biblical and Theological Study, Old Testament ser. 1; Winona Lake, Ind.: Eisenbrauns, 1992).

4. Philip D. Kenneson and James L. Street, *Selling Out the Church* (Nashville: Abingdon, 1997).

5. Erich Auerbach, *Mimesis: The Representation of Reality in Western Literature* (trans. Willard R. Trask; Princeton: Princeton University Press, 1953), 14–15.

is intended or not. If that is the only function the Old Testament has, the question will inevitably be raised if it is really needed.[6]

I. THE DIVORCE OF THE LAW FROM ITS NARRATIVE CONTEXT

If we grant for the moment that there is a need to revive the Old Testament as Scripture that actually shapes the thoughts and practice of God's people, the question immediately follows as to what impedes and interrupts such a usage. It is my conviction that too often the laws of the Old Testament have been abstracted and divorced from the narratives in which they are imbedded. Is it not the case that when many in the church reflect on the Old Testament, the entry point is Moses on Mt. Sinai—perhaps pictured as Charleton Heston—and the Ten Commandments?

Unfortunately, these commandments then take on a status of independence with the resulting understanding that God evaluates us against these laws. Hence, the performance of the commandments and the keeping of the Law are construed as a duty that has a certain independence and distance from the narrative framework. This duty, in turn, begins to assume a neutral and universal legitimacy, much like Immanuel Kant's categorical imperative: "Act only on that maxim whereby you can at the same time will that it should become a universal law."[7] Kant's commitment to a consistent universalization is his way to construct an ethic and simultaneously escape appeals to human nature or divine revelation. From Kant's viewpoint, man's reason and his rendering of reality through reason offer sufficient data to ground this categorical imperative. Alasdair MacIntyre, among others, has shown how insufficient such a foundation is:

> But Kant gives us no good reason for holding this position. I can without any inconsistency whatsoever flout it; "Let everyone except me be treated as a means" may be immoral, but it is not inconsistent and there is not even any inconsistency in willing a universe of egotists all of whom live by this maxim. It might be inconvenient for each if everyone lived by this maxim, but it would not be impossible and to invoke considerations of convenience would in any case be to introduce just that prudential ref-

---

6. John Bright, *The Authority of the Old Testament* (Grand Rapids: Baker, 1975), 73.

7. Colin Brown, *Philosophy and the Christian Faith* (Downers Grove: InterVarsity, 1968), 101.

erence to happiness which Kant aspires to eliminate from all considerations of morality.[8]

What is the price paid by those who follow this reading of Old Testament Law? David S. Yeago has captured its impact in a perceptive analysis:

> Where the self is defined in terms of disengagement and power, the will of God comes to be seen as an external factor impinging on the self and limiting it from without. God's authority is reduced to his power to confer reward and impose punishment as we succeed or fail in meeting the exactions he imposes. The commandments of God are redefined as the articulation of these stipulations, and just so enter into an antithetical relationship to human freedom. Freedom easily comes to be defined as freedom precisely from the pressure of such demands, whether imposed by God or anyone else: we are free insofar as we can do what we want, insofar as our power is unchecked, unhindered by expectations or prohibitions imposed from outside ourselves.[9]

As one looks at the collapse of meaningful and evangelical church discipline in large segments of mainline Christianity, it is legitimate to ask whether separating the Law and according it a certain independence from its narrative context has actually impeded the Law's role in the life and practice of many communities of faith. Although having its origin in extremely different soil than Kant or modernity, the Latin phrase *lex semper accusat* ("the Law always accuses") probably captures the spirit in which many Christians think about the Law. When used incorrectly, this formula also suggests that the Law is an entity with its own independent standing apart from an historical and narrative context.

In such an environment, it could be expected that theologians would reach for the most exotic exegetical moves to marginalize and relativize each law by appealing to the culture-bound character of its admonitions. Authors and titles multiply as every scriptural law—particularly the Ten Commandments—is subjected to gleeful deconstruction. David Yeago, again, has his finger on the pulse of what is happening all around us:

---

8. Alasdair MacIntyre, *After Virtue* (South Bend, Ind.: University of Notre Dame Press, 1981), 45.

9. David S. Yeago, "Office of the Keys: On the Disappearance of Discipline in Protestant Modernity," in *Marks of the Body of Christ* (ed. Carl E. Braaten and Robert W. Jenson; Grand Rapids: Eerdmans, 1999), 110.

In light of these changes, the first great gulf separating us from Luther comes fully into view: we no longer readily believe that it could be good news that we have a Lord and King. We cannot easily see how it would be a positive thing to fall under any definite governance with describable goals and substantive purposes, however gracious its operation. Since we no longer believe that human existence has any innate telos or end, except perhaps the purely formal and ungovernably pluralistic end of individual self-realization, the declaration that Christ will unfailingly accomplish the holy will of God in us, that his rule over us will assuredly secure our fulfillment of God's commandments, rings in our ears more like a threat than a promise . . . . Indeed, we identify the graciousness of divine presence precisely with its lack of substantive purpose, its renunciation of dominion, its benign indifference to what we are and how we live. This is the chief historical peculiarity of contemporary mainline Christianity; never before in Christian history has the notion of salvation been so completely divorced from the notion of a hopeful discipline of life.[10]

In this stinging critique, Yeago uses the language of "what we are" and "how we live." I will now explicate the important relationship that exists between these two aspects of reality. It is my conviction that the church would benefit greatly from recovering the scriptural integration of narrative and Law that the *Torah* story so completely displays. The Law, understood in this fashion, is inextricably bound in its proper understanding to the gracious character of the God who is so consistently described in the narrative portions of the Old Testament.

II. LAW WITHIN NARRATIVE FORMS THE IDENTITY OF GOD'S PEOPLE

Examples of the organic unity between law and narrative abound in the Old Testament. When the Ten Commandments are given, they are preceded by the summary statement "I am the LORD your God, who brought you out of Egypt, out of the land of slavery" (Exod 20:2).[11] Entailed in that short formula of self-identification is an entire redemptive history. Likewise, the manner in which Moses provides the Israelites with the historical prologue of Deuteron-

---

10. Yeago, "Office of the Keys," 112–13.
11. Scripture quotations in this essay are from the NIV.

omy 1–4 as background for the presentation of the commandments in Deuteronomy 5 also places these "laws" against the huge canvas of the gracious acts and presence of the Lord, their God. Even a Reformed scholar such as Walter Kaiser recognizes this truth. He writes:

> Accordingly, "the priority and absoluteness of God's grace are constantly reiterated." The law, then, must not be viewed as an abstract imperial tractate that stands overtly over the heads of men and women. It was, first of all, intensely personal . . . . The covenant aims to establish a personal relationship, not a code of conduct in the abstract.[12]

Quite simply, Holy Scripture tells us who God is and who we are through the majestic narratives that unite words and deeds in a seamless portrait that entreats our vocation to act in accord with our being. One of my teachers, Stanley Hauerwas, expresses it in this manner:

> The scripture functions as authority for Christians precisely because by trying to live, think and be faithful to its witness, they find they are more nearly able to live faithful to the truth . . . . The moral use of scripture, therefore, lies precisely in its power to help us remember the stories of God for the continual guidance of our community and of individual lives. To be a community which lives by remembering is a genuine achievement, as too often we assume that we can insure our existence only by freeing ourselves from the past.[13]

To put the point in stark terms: Before laws can be fully understood and appropriately—albeit imperfectly—followed, it is necessary to know the character of the agent (i.e., who we are).

My suggestion, therefore, is that the Law of the Old Testament be viewed not simply as duty but as a portion of a large narrative of indicatives that lead us back to our origin, describe our purpose in and before God, and call us to an obedience that is good, noble, and at the very heart of who God has made us in Christ. It is, to use Kaiser's phraseology, a matter of "personal relationship." Indeed, I would argue that the biblical narratives define the character and

---

12. Walter Kaiser, *Toward Old Testament Ethics* (Grand Rapids: Zondervan, 1983), 77.

13. Stanley Hauerwas, *A Community of Character* (South Bend, Ind.: University of Notre Dame Press, 1981), 66.

nature of that personhood for each of us.[14] In short, the *Torah* story defines our identity.

I am advocating a recovery of what has historically been described within the church as the "third use of the Law," namely, the Law as a wonderful and welcome guide to the man or woman who is in Christ.[15] This use of the Law is supported by the coherence and integration of the indicatives and imperatives in Sacred Scripture. The indicatives describe God's gracious character in creation and his gracious presence with a rebellious people. In episode after episode, in generation after generation, the truth about who God is becomes the truth about who we are because we learn that we have no true being apart from our relationship to him.

Indeed, even the categories of indicative and imperative are too simplistic to describe the manner in which the biblical texts communicate. Thomas W. Mann, in a fascinating study that is subtitled *The Narrative Integrity of the Pentateuch*, makes this point succinctly:

> The integrity of the Pentateuchal narrative, however, derives not only from the form of "story" but also from literary types which are not inherently narrative, especially "law." Law is an essential element in the plot of the Pentateuch, and without that element the story would be incomplete. Indeed, even the discrimination between "story" and "law" however appropriate in terms of distinguishing literary forms, can suggest that narrative

---

14. Alasdair MacIntyre captures the antithesis of such an understanding by referring to Sartre: "The contrast (Sartre) with the narrative view of the self is clear. For the story of my life is always embedded in the story of those communities from which I derive my identity. I am born with a past; and to try to cast myself off from that past in the individualist mode, is to deform my present relationships. The possession of an historical identity and the possession of a social identity coincide. Notice that rebellion against my identity is always one possible mode of expressing it" (MacIntyre, *After Virtue*, 205).

15. The Lutheran Confessions explain the Law in this manner: "The law has been given to men for three reasons: (1) to maintain external discipline against unruly and disobedient men, (2) to lead men to a knowledge of their sin, (3) after they are reborn, and although the flesh still inheres in them, to give them on that account a definite rule according to which they should pattern and regulate their entire life. It is concerning the third function of the law that a controversy has arisen among a few theologians. The question therefore is whether or not the law is to be urged upon reborn Christians. One party said Yes, the other says No. Affirmative Theses. The Correct Christian Teaching in This Controversy. 1. We believe, teach, and confess that although people who genuinely believe and whom God has truly converted are freed through Christ from the curse and the coercion of the law, they are not on that account without the law; on the contrary, they have been redeemed by the Son of God precisely that they should exercise themselves day and night in the law (Ps. 119:1). In the same way our first parents even before the Fall did not live without the law, for the law of God was written into their hearts when they were created in the image of God" (FC Ep. VI, 1–2 [Tappert, 479–80]).

texts "only" recite, whereas legal texts "only" command. To deny an imperative force to "story," however, is to ignore the motivational nature of biblical narrative, that is, its "rhetoric of command." Similarly, to limit the meaning of "law" to its imperative force and its content is to ignore that its meaning and authority are partly dependent on its narrative context. The word torah in its widest sense means "guidance, instruction, discipline," and only in its most narrow sense "law." The Torah is the definitive "guide-book" of ancient Israel, and it guides in the form of both narrative and law so that the two become inseparable and indispensable.[16]

III. THE COMMON CHARACTER
OF LAW AND NARRATIVE: SOME EXAMPLES

The Hebrew word תורה (*Torah*) is a scripturally apt way to capture the inseparable and indispensable character of narrative and law. Here is a word that in repeated instances entails the whole fabric of scriptural revelation for our instruction and guidance.[17] Several Old Testament texts suggest this perspective about *Torah*. Psalm 1:1–2 provides an excellent departure point:

> Blessed is the man
>   who does not walk in the counsel of the wicked
> or stand in the way of sinners
> or sit in the seat of mockers.

> But his delight is in the law of the LORD [בְּתוֹרַת יְהֹוָה],
>   and on his law [וּבְתוֹרָתוֹ] he meditates day and
>   night.

The thought of "delight" in the Law and meditating on it day and night may strike many of us as incipient legalism. An important question attends these two verses: Is the practice of most translations in rendering the word *Torah* with "law" really appropriate and accurate?

Diverse voices challenge this translation. Representative of German critical scholarship, Hans-Joachim Kraus writes:

---

16. Thomas W. Mann, *The Book of the Torah: The Narrative Integrity of the Pentateuch* (Atlanta: John Knox, 1988), 7–8.

17. For a thorough discussion of the semantic range of *Torah*, see Gunnar Ostborn, *Torah in the Old Testament* (Lund: Hakan Ohlssons Koktryckeri, 1945).

Our comprehension of this verse and of the whole psalm now depends on the interpretation of the term Torah (תורה). We must reject the traditional translation "law," which immediately imports all kinds of nomistic prejudices and reflections. תורה is "instruction" in the sense of the "merciful revelation of the will of God."[18]

Wilbert R. Gawrisch, a conservative scholar of the Wisconsin Evangelical Lutheran Synod, also recognizes the broader significance implied with the use of this term:

So, for example, in Psalm 1:2, speaking of the godly man, the Psalmist says, "But his delight is in the law (teaching) of the Lord, and on his law (teaching) he meditates day and night." Since nothing in the context limits the significance of Torah to either the law or the gospel, the Psalmist is saying that the godly man finds delight in God's entire Word, both in the law and the Gospel.[19]

Martin Luther's exposition of Ps 1:2 certainly exhibits this broader understanding of *Torah:*

"And on His Law he meditates day and night." This meditation is not beyond criticism unless the will comes first, for love itself will teach meditation. Truly, as we despair of our own strength, we must through humble faith in Christ pray (as I have said) that the desire be sent down from heaven. Note this well: It is the mode and nature of all who love, to chatter, sing, think, compose and frolic freely about what they love and to enjoy hearing about it. Therefore this lover, this blessed man, has his love, the Law of God always in his mouth, always in his heart and, if possible, always in his ear.[20]

Especially noteworthy here is Luther's emphasis that God's Law (teaching) is the object of love. The Law as the object of love is found in several other *Torah* psalms. Listen to the adoration that *Torah* and its synonyms receive in Psalm 19.[21]

---

18. Hans-Joachim Kraus, *Psalms 1–59* (trans. Hilton C. Oswald; Minneapolis: Augsburg, 1988), 116.

19. Wilbert R. Gawrisch, "The Meaning of the Hebrew Word Torah with Special Reference to Its Use in the Psalms," *Wisconsin Lutheran Quarterly* 89 (1992): 145.

20. LW 14:297–98. This exegesis of Luther is cited by Kraus, *Psalms 1–59*, 117.

21. The versification of the English text (rather than the Hebrew) is used here and in the other quotations from the Psalms.

[7]   The law [*Torah*] of the LORD [תּוֹרַת יְהוָה] is perfect,
        reviving the soul.
    The statutes of the LORD [עֵדוּת יְהוָה] are trustworthy,
        making wise the simple.

[8]   The precepts of the LORD [פִּקּוּדֵי יְהוָה] are right,
        giving joy to the heart.
    The commands of the LORD [מִצְוַת יְהוָה] are radiant,
        giving light to the eyes.

[9b]   The ordinances of the LORD [מִשְׁפְּטֵי־יְהוָה] are sure
        and altogether righteous.

[10]   They are more precious than gold,
        than much pure gold;
    they are sweeter than honey,
        than honey from the comb.

The delight in the *Torah* that can be seen in Psalm 1 is echoed in this extensive characterization of *Torah* and its cognates. Do not these terms entail the narratives of the *Torah* story that in turn display the gracious character of God? Psalm 78 is instructive at this point. Here Asaph invites Israel to give ear to his *Torah* (הַאֲזִינָה עַמִּי תּוֹרָתִי), namely, his instruction. As one observes that instruction unfold, it is nothing less than the narrative of Israel's history. Asaph describes some of the key gracious actions of God in Israel's history:

[5]   He decreed statutes for Jacob
        and established the law [*Torah*, וְתוֹרָה] in Israel,
    which he commanded our forefathers
        to teach their children.

[13]   He divided the sea and led them through;
        he made the water stand firm like a wall.

[24]   he rained down manna for the people to eat,
        he gave them the grain of heaven.

[68]   but he chose the tribe of Judah,
        Mount Zion, which he loved.

[69]   He built his sanctuary like the heights,
        like the earth that he established forever.

[70]   He chose David his servant
        and took him from the sheep pens.

The way in which *Torah* covers both narrative and Law in this psalm surely alerts us to nuances of perceiving the Law that have sometimes been squeezed out for homiletical or theological reasons. As one scholar has written recently:

> It is important to see that tora encompasses not only specific legal or moral instruction, but also a historical review of Israel's past, i.e., the narrative portions of the Pentateuch. In other words, Psalm 78 suggests that the Pentateuch as a whole was seen as tora. The psalmist employs the past events and figures as a means to instruct his readers in what it means (and does not mean) to follow the Lord faithfully. The narrative portions of the Pentateuch have themselves become the content of instruction.[22]

Other texts point in the direction of *Torah* uniting the gracious character of God in the *Torah* narrative with the kind of instruction that the creatures made in his image are to follow. They are not to follow this instruction as those beholden to some external and abstract duty but as those who know their identity as children of Yahweh. For example, Psalm 119 displays a catena of characterizations of *Torah* that challenge any reduction of the Law to alien duty and demand.[23] Note how *Torah* is described in these verses:

[1]   Blessed are those whose ways are blameless,
        who walk according to the law [*Torah*] of the LORD
        [הַהֹלְכִים בְּתוֹרַת יְהוָה].

[18]   Open my eyes that I may see
        wonderful things in your law [*Torah*]
        [וְאַבִּיטָה נִפְלָאוֹת מִתּוֹרָתֶךָ].

[29]   Keep me from deceitful ways;
        be gracious to me through your law [*Torah*]
        [מִמֶּנִּי וְתוֹרָתְךָ חָנֵּנִי].

[55]   In the night I remember your name, O LORD,
        and I will keep your law [*Torah*] [וָאֶשְׁמְרָה תּוֹרָתֶךָ].

[70]   Their hearts are callous and unfeeling,
        but I delight in your law [*Torah*] [אֲנִי תּוֹרָתְךָ שִׁעֲשָׁעְתִּי].

---

22. Peter Enns, "Law of God," *New International Dictionary of Old Testament Theology and Exegesis* (ed. Willem A. VanGemeren; Grand Rapids: Zondervan, 1997), IV:897.

23. See especially these verses: 1, 18, 29, 34, 44, 51, 53, 55, 61, 70, 72, 77, 85, 92, 97, 109, 113, 126, 136, 142, 150, 153, 163, 165, 174.

[72]   The law [*Torah*] from your mouth [טוֹב־לִי תוֹרַת־פִּיךָ]
            is more precious to me
            than thousands of pieces of silver and gold.

[77]   Let your compassion come to me that I may live,
            for your law [*Torah*] is my delight [כִּי־תוֹרָתְךָ שַׁעֲשֻׁעָי].

[92]   If your law [*Torah*] had not been my delight
            [לוּלֵי תוֹרָתְךָ שַׁעֲשֻׁעָי],
            I would have perished in my affliction.

[97]   Oh, how I love your law [*Torah*] [מָה־אָהַבְתִּי תוֹרָתֶךָ]!
            I meditate on it all day long.

[113]   I hate double-minded men,
            but I love your law [*Torah*] [וְתוֹרָתְךָ אָהָבְתִּי].

[142]   Your righteousness is everlasting
            and your law [*Torah*] is true [וְתוֹרָתְךָ אֱמֶת].

[163]   I hate and abhor falsehood
            but I love your law [*Torah*] [תוֹרָתְךָ אָהָבְתִּי].

[174]   I long for your salvation, O LORD,
            and your law [*Torah*] is my delight [וְתוֹרָתְךָ שַׁעֲשֻׁעָי].

Perhaps these descriptions would not seem so new if we would ponder afresh the beauty and integration of the Pentateuch. Listen to Moses' famous summary invitation in Deut 30:11–16, an invitation that presupposes a gracious and good God who has acted consistently in mercy toward his people:

Now what I am commanding you today is not too difficult for you or beyond your reach. It is not up in heaven, so that you have to ask, "Who will ascent into heaven to get it and proclaim it to us so we may obey it?" Nor is it beyond the sea, so that you have to ask, "Who will cross the sea to get it and proclaim it to us so we may obey it?" No, the word is very near you: it is in your mouth and in your heart so you may obey it. See, I set before you today life and prosperity, death and destruction. For I command you today to love the LORD your God, to walk in his ways, and to keep his commands, decrees and laws; then you will live and increase, and the LORD your God will bless you in the land you are entering to possess.

The prophetic literature does not see *Torah* as something that will be displaced in the future but places it at the center of God's eschatological reign. For example, Isa 2:2–3 states:

> In the last days
> the mountain of the LORD's temple will be established
>   as chief among the mountains;
> it will be raised above the hills,
>   and all nations will stream to it.
>
> Many peoples will come and say,
> "Come, let us go up to the mountain of the LORD,
>   to the house of the God of Jacob.
> He will teach us his ways,
>   so that we may walk in his paths."
>
> The law [*Torah*, תּוֹרָה] will go out from Zion,
>   the word of the LORD [וּדְבַר־יְהוָה] from Jerusalem.

Francis Pieper's explanation of this passage affirms that *Torah* should be understood in a broad manner, even as a synonym for divine revelation or the Gospel in many places:

> The term "Law" is used in Holy Writ also in a wider, or general, sense to designate all the divine revelation and, moreover, the divine revelation κατ᾽ ἐξοχήν, the Gospel, as in Is. 2:3: "For out of Zion shall go forth the Law (תּוֹרָה)."[24]

Other prophetic texts carry the same Gospel freight in their use of the word *Torah*. In the great messianic servant passage of Isa 42:1–9, the Messiah is described in this way in vs. 4:

>   he will not falter or be discouraged
> till he establishes justice on earth.
>   In his law [*Torah*] the islands will put their hope
> [וּלְתוֹרָתוֹ אִיִּים יְיַחֵילוּ].

Jeremiah's portrait of the messianic age includes this poignant action concerning *Torah* in Jer 31:33–34:

> "This is the covenant I will make with the house of Israel
>   after that time," declares the LORD.
> "I will put my law [*Torah*] in their minds [נָתַתִּי אֶת־תּוֹרָתִי בְּקִרְבָּם]
>   and write it on their hearts [וְעַל־לִבָּם אֶכְתֲּבֶנָּה]. . . .
> because they will all know me,
>   from the least of them to the greatest,"
>   declares the LORD.

---

24. Francis Pieper, *Christian Dogmatics* (St. Louis: Concordia, 1953), 3:222–23.

IV. CONCLUSION

It is as it was in Eden: life before and in God, or death apart from God. That life before and in God entails love of the Lord who has shown us his gracious character repeatedly in Israel's story and definitively in the face of Christ. Identity, therefore, not duty, is the heart of our calling and understanding of the essence of *Torah*. This identity does display a response.[25] This identity is graciously given in the waters of Baptism, but it then forms and shapes a habit of being that is "in Christ." This habit of being is always imperfect and frequently hidden in our fallen estate, but it is nonetheless real. In Luther's view, as noted by Yeago, such a new pattern of life arises from and reflects the resurrection of our Lord:

> This new way of being present in the bodily world, in obedience to the second table of Moses, is for Luther a kind of beginning of bodily resurrection: "This is the work of the Holy Spirit, who sanctifies and awakens the body also to a new life of this sort, until it is fulfilled in the life to come."[26]

The word *Torah*, therefore, entails a range of meaning from "law" in the narrow sense to "Gospel" in the narrow sense to "revelation" in a broad sense. It has been suggested that this ability to be "matrixed" in a number of ways is not fully understood by appealing to "etymology" (i.e., focusing narrowly on the root ירה "to instruct"); rather, its breadth of scriptural usage witnesses to the seamless fabric of Law and narrative. Like a Flemish tapestry, one cannot remove all the "law" threads and accurately understand the remaining "narrative" nor can one remove all the "narrative" threads and understand "the law" that remains. Instead, for the man or woman who is in Christ, the new identity in the character of God now calls the new person to a created, bodily life that is faithful to God's image. Of course, the desire of Adam and Eve, as well

---

25. Mann describes this dimension of *Torah* in succinct fashion: "The Pentateuchal narrative renders a new world. But as it was 'in the beginning,' so it is now; while that world exists only as a possibility in terms of what Israel will do . . . Just as Adam and Eve could be genuinely human only in responsibility to the divine will, so Israel can be God's holy nation only in responsibility to God's Torah" (*Book of the Torah*, 161).

26. Yeago, "Office of the Keys," 99. In this same context, he also quotes Luther's 1539 "On the Councils and the Church," in which the reformer writes: "For Christ left the Keys as a legacy, to be a public sign and holy thing through which the Holy Spirit (acquired by Christ's death) might sanctify fallen sinners anew, and through which Christians might confess that they are a holy people subject to Christ in this world. Those who do not want to be converted or to be sanctified anew are cast out from this holy people, that is, bound and excluded by the Keys, as happened to the impenitent Antinomians."

as our own desire, "to be like God" is nothing less than the desire to paint our own portrait of the deity and to write a different scriptural narrative. A fallen humanity writes its own evolutionary myths and thereby can kill its own infants. For that Old Adam, both God's story and God's Law accuse and judge. For us who are a new creation in Jesus Christ, however, this story is utter truth and frees us for service to God and delight in his *Torah*.

THE LAW AND FREEDOM
IN THE OLD TESTAMENT

DANIEL L. GARD

Debates among Christians about the nature of the Law in the Old Testament are certainly as old as the church herself (Acts 15). Debates about the Law among Jews are older than the formative postexilic period of Israel's history and have only grown after the destruction of the second temple as Judaism became increasingly defined by its focus on the Law. From ancient times to modern, the extremes of legalism to antinomianism have continued to make their presence felt among both Jews and Christians.

The Lutheran theological tradition addresses the issue of the Law within the context of the Gospel. In this way, the Lutherans of the sixteenth century operated from a distinctly different perspective than did the leaders of the Swiss reformation. For John Calvin, the third use of the Law shone as the brightest of lights, bringing with it the sanctification of Christianity and the establishment of theocratic inter-human relationships. The Lutherans, on the other hand, feared that an overemphasis on the third use of the Law would turn the Gospel itself into a new law.

Karl Barth, the prominent twentieth-century Swiss theologian, particularly challenged the position of Martin Luther and Lutherans concerning the heart of Lutheran theology in an article significantly titled "Gospel and Law."[1] The reversal of the familiar phrase "Law and Gospel" was fully intentional on Barth's part; the Law, according to Barth, does not rival the Gospel but is another form of

---

1. Karl Barth, "Evangelium und Gesetz," in *Community, State, and Church* (Gloucester, Mass.: P. Smith, 1968), 71–100.

it. For Barth, the Law must follow the Gospel. This helps explain
Barth's own involvement in the political world after World War II.
More familiar to American Lutherans is the indirect influence of
Barth in much modern preaching. This influence is seen in the
familiar tripartite sermon outline: Part I contains the second use of
the Law; part II delivers the Gospel; and part III gets to the real
point of the sermon, namely, the third use of the Law. In other
words, the Gospel becomes the empowerment to lead godly lives.

For the Lutheran reformers, the Law served three purposes,
which are known popularly among Lutherans as curb (first use),
mirror (second use), and guide (third use).[2] Each of these is studied
as distinct from the others, though the distinction is not always
clear. They also are, however, collectively and individually distinct
from the Gospel itself. The Lutheran confessors wrote:

> The distinction between law and Gospel is an especially brilliant
> light which serves the purpose that the Word of God may be
> rightly divided and the writings of the holy prophets and apos-
> tles may be explained and understood correctly. We must there-
> fore observe this distinction with particular diligence lest we
> confuse the two doctrines and change the Gospel into law.[3]

This is far removed from the perspective of Calvin and Barth, for
whom Law and Gospel are not all that distinct. This perspective
also is far removed from the perspective of modern preachers whose
three-part sermons culminate in what I prefer to call "the third use
of the Gospel."

Contemporary New Testament scholarship focuses tremendous
attention on the understandings of the Law presented by both Jesus
and Paul.[4] Old Testament scholarship approaches the topic of Law
in the Old Testament in quite a different way, often in isolation
from the broader canon of Scripture[5] and at other times seeking a

---

2. FC SD VI, 1 (Tappert, 563–64).

3. FC SD V, 1 (Tappert, 558).

4. There is a rich bibliography of study of the Law and the New Testament. Among
   other scholars, E. P. Sanders is the major voice to whom others are reacting; see
   Sanders, *Paul and Palestinian Judaism: A Comparison of Patterns of Religion* (Philadelphia:
   Fortress, 1977), and *Paul, the Law, and the Jewish People* (Philadelphia: Fortress, 1983).
   See also Heikki Räisänen, *Paul and the Law* (WUNT 29; Tübingen: J. C. B. Mohr,
   1983), and Francis Watson, *Paul, Judaism, and the Gentiles: A Sociological Approach*
   (SNTSMS 56; Cambridge: Cambridge University Press, 1986).

5. See, for example, F. Crusemann, *The Torah: Theology and Social History of Old Testament
   Law* (trans. Allan W. Mahnke; Minneapolis: Fortress, 1996), and Dale Patrick, *Old Testament Law* (Atlanta: John Knox, 1985).

diachronic reading of the Hebrew canon.[6] I continue to find the work of Brevard Childs to be thought-provoking and valuable, though I fundamentally disagree with his historical-critical methodology. Childs emphasis on the final form of the text in its canonical shape provides a marvelous balance to the splintering of the canon by traditional historical-critical studies.

Childs's magnum opus, *Biblical Theology of the Old and New Testaments: Theological Reflection on the Christian Bible*, provides an important corrective within the discipline of Old Testament theology.[7] He constructs an intriguing analysis of Law and Gospel in both Testaments, including a five-part "theological characterization of Old Testament law."[8] The Law becomes something that is—in Childs's words—the "grounds of Israel's identity as the people of God and remained the sign of her election . . . transforming Israel into the people of God."[9] It appears to me that Childs has understood the Law of the Old Testament from the perspective of a Reformed theologian; that is, he has understood the Law as something external to the nation of Israel. If it is external, then the Law itself is the redeeming act of God in the election and formation of Israel as the people of God. Thus the old Lutheran vs. Reformed debate about the proper role of Law and Gospel is renewed under quite different terminology.

I propose that the Law of the Old Testament is not *external* to Israel as the people of God but actually constitutes their *identity*. It is not the Law that brought about their election nor is it the Law that transforms Israel into the people of God. Rather, the grace of God alone called Israel into being and formed this nation into his people. The Law flows into and from that reality because in, with, and through the Lord's gracious call, the Law becomes essential to the people of Israel. The Law does not transform them *into* the people of God; rather, it transforms them *as* the people of God. It is in this way that the Law of God becomes the means through which true freedom is realized. It does not restrict or coerce the elect; rather, it marks the boundaries of safety and freedom for Israel. To

---

6. J. G. McConville criticizes what he sees as a tendency to read Deuteronomy's laws as only one stage in historical development; see McConville, *Law and Theology in Deuteronomy* (JSOTSup 33; Sheffield: JSOT Press, 1984). As the title indicates, he understands Deuteronomy's laws as theological statements.

7. Brevard S. Childs, *Biblical Theology of the Old and New Testaments: Theological Reflection on the Christian Bible* (Minneapolis: Fortress, 1992).

8. Childs, *Biblical Theology*, 536–37.

9. Childs, *Biblical Theology*, 536.

step outside those boundaries is to enter into idolatry and thus to move outside the essence of their identity. In other words, an identity rooted in God and lived in his character is concomitant with the call of God to be his people.

Childs is frustrated with the disfunctionalism of critical scholarship. I understand that frustration and share it, but I also am frustrated with much of conservative scholarship in which biblical study is confined to morphological, grammatical, and technical analysis in which the meaning of the text is never clearly stated. I do not intend to engage in such safe endeavors in this essay. Nor do I intend simply to cite the positions of various contemporary scholars and position them one against another, as equally safe as that process might be. Rather, this essay is designed to begin a biblical and theological analysis of the function of Old Testament Law within the Christian context with all the risks inherent in such an undertaking. It thus represents an initial probe into a canonical reading of the biblical witness to the function of the Law.

I. THE CHARACTER OF GOD AS A PARADIGM

As Francis Pieper states in his *Christian Dogmatics*, two points must be maintained in any discussion of the attributes and essence of God:

> 1. In God, essence and attributes are not separate, but the divine essence and the divine attributes are absolutely identical, because God is infinite and above space (1 Kings 8:27) and time (Ps. 90:2, 4). . . . 2. Since finite human reason cannot comprehend the infinite and absolute simplex, God condescends to our weakness and in His Word divides Himself, as it were, into a number of attributes which our faith can grasp and to which it can cling.[10]

As it is with God, so it is to be among his people; or, to put it another way, as God is, so his people are to be: "You shall be holy; for I the LORD your God am holy" (Lev 19:2).[11] Holiness is both of the divine essence and of the divine attributes. It is thus also the essence of God's people and is to be identified as an attribute of those who are the elect.

---

10. Francis Pieper, *Christian Dogmatics* (St. Louis: Concordia, 1950), 1:428.

11. Unless otherwise indicated, all Scripture quotations in this essay are taken from the NKJV.

If the people of God are to be holy as he is holy, then the laws of Scripture must relate to the character of the God of Israel. An intriguing paper by the distinguished Old Testament scholar Robert Hubbard of North Park Theological Seminary, entitled "Law Is Grace—At Least Sometimes: Theological Reflections on Old Testament Redemption Laws," approaches this same search for the interrelatedness of divine attributes and Old Testament Law.[12] Hubbard argues from the covenant code concerning the law of the first-born and the kinsman-redeemer (Exodus 21–23) that the character of God can be observed in the Old Testament Law. He states that "as a mirror of God's character, law offers us glimpses of God that deepen our understanding of him."[13]

Hubbard's methodology is helpful, yet I will choose a different path. Rather than argue from the Law to the attributes of God, I will argue from the attributes of God to the Law. To do so is intended to conform this study to the starting point of theology, which is God himself. Our Lutheran theological heritage speaks of God's attributes from several perspectives. In this essay, I will exclude the "negative attributes" of God (unity, simplicity, immutability, infinity, omnipresence, eternity) as described by Pieper because these may be said only of God himself, not of mortals.[14] On the other hand, three positive attributes of the God of Israel will serve as points of theological reflection: the holiness of God, the justice of God, and the power of God.[15]

A. THE HOLINESS OF GOD (*SANCTITAS DEI*)

We begin with the assertion that God is holy. By this we refer both to his supreme majesty and his absolute transcendence, as well as to his ethical purity. In God is found no sin nor can any sinful thing stand before him. He is not a reflection of human culture with its proclivity toward all things impure, a mere theological construction that each generation is free to recreate in its own image. He is the God before whom Isaiah could proclaim only, "Woe is me! For I am lost; for I am a man of unclean lips, and I dwell in the midst of a people of unclean lips" (Isa 6:5 RSV).

---

12. Robert L. Hubbard Jr., "Law Is Grace—At Least Sometimes: Theological Reflections on Old Testament Redemption Laws," http://www.npcts.edu/sem/resources/lawgrace.html.

13. Hubbard, "Law Is Grace—At Least Sometimes."

14. Pieper, *Christian Dogmatics*, 1:437–47.

15. Pieper, *Christian Dogmatics*, 1:456–60.

B. The Justice of God (*Iustitia Dei*)

God is just. It is impossible to charge him with any injustice because he is outside the Law and is himself creator of the Law. In his great song, Moses exulted: "The Rock, his work is perfect; for all his ways are justice. A God of faithfulness and without iniquity, just and right is he" (Deut 32:4 RSV). God's justice is legal, rewarding the good and punishing the evil. Yet it is also evangelical in its unilateral declaration of righteousness for the sinner who fails to conform to God's absolute norm of perfection. The justice of God cannot be viewed apart from his other attributes. Although his justice is perfect, he is still the God of mercy (*misericordia*) and grace (*gratia*). Before him Israel could sing: "If You, LORD, should mark iniquities, O Lord, who could stand? But there is forgiveness with You, that You may be feared" (Ps 130:3–4). He is long-suffering (*longanimitas*) toward the world, waiting 120 years before sending the great flood and sending prophet after prophet before raising the Babylonians against Judah.

C. The Power of God (*Potentia Dei*)

God's absolute power is nowhere more clearly demonstrated than in the opening verse of Scripture, "In the beginning, God created the heavens and the earth" (Gen 1:1). By divine *fiat* all things come into existence; nothing exists apart from his power. Throughout the Old Testament, the God of Israel demonstrates his power. He creates. He destroys through the flood. He delivers the children of Israel from Egypt through mighty signs and miracles. He so orders the course of nations that Israel both takes the land in conquest and later loses it to Babylon.

Although the children of Israel certainly knew God's watchful presence as the Lord of their history, they are often reminded that his power extended beyond them to every nation of the earth. The biblical narrative testifies to the fact that the entire world remains under his eye and power. Although the postdiluvian history quickly passes from the story of the flood (Genesis 6–9) to the calling of Abraham (Genesis 12), there are two intervening chapters with genealogies of the other descendants of Noah (Genesis 10–11). The call of Abraham itself is not in isolation from the concern of God for all his created humanity because it was through Abraham that *all* the families of the earth would be blessed. In the great genealogies of the postexilic period found in 1 Chronicles, the simple beginning "Adam, Seth, Enosh . . ." (1 Chr 1:1) introduces a listing of all the nations of the world. Although the focus is on Israel (1 Chronicles 2–9)—on Judah and the Davidic line in particular—every human being is a creation of God and falls under his power.

II. THE LAW AS REFLECTION OF THE DIVINE CHARACTER

How, then, do these specific characteristics or attributes of God— namely, holiness, justice, and power—relate to the Law of the Old Testament? These characteristics are reflected in the Law. God's very character, therefore, is to be reflected in the life of Israel. God's holiness, justice, and power are to be evident and reflected in his people.

A. ISRAEL IS TO BE HOLY AS THE LORD IS HOLY

If God is holy, the people are to be holy. Herein lies the cultic law of the Old Testament. The nation of Israel was to be a kingdom of priests with the firstborn of every Israelite woman dedicated to the Lord. The law of the firstfruits applied not only to Israel's possessions but also to her sons. However, as the Lord of Israel himself would do in time with his own Son, he provided a substitute: the tribe of Levi (Num 3:11–13).

Sanctified to the Lord, the Levites were to represent all Israel within the sanctity of the cult.[16] Only they were to offer incense and sacrifices on behalf of others and to teach the Law of the Lord to Israel (Deut 33:8–11). Only the Levites were to enter into the presence of God in the Holy of Holies, and then only one of their number on the Day of Atonement. The myriad of laws and regulations pertaining to the cult in Israel all derived from one reality: the character of God. He is above all impurity; the cult must be above all impurity. The temple and its rites did not symbolize the chasm between God and humanity; rather, they demonstrated the desire of God to be present with his people. That presence, however, was to be on his terms, not Israel's.

---

16. There is a long and complicated critical debate about the nature of the Levites and the priesthood. Among the major contributors have been Julius Wellhausen, *Prolegomena to the History of Ancient Israel* (New York: Meridian, 1957), 121–51; Aelred Cody, *A History of Old Testament Priesthood* (Analecta Biblica 35; Rome: Pontifical Biblical Institute, 1969); Menahem Haran, *Temples and Temple-service in Ancient Israel* (Oxford: Clarendon, 1977); and A. H. J. Gunneweg, *Leviten und Priester* (Forschungen zur Religion und Literatur des Alten und Neuen Testaments 89; Göttingen: Vandenhoeck & Ruprecht, 1965).

It is within the cult that the people of God most clearly live out their identity. The cultic law of the Old Testament demands precise representation of the Lord's own holiness. So deeply ingrained in ancient Israelite religion was the holiness of the cult and the identity of the people within that holiness that later Judaism redefined itself according to a cult that no longer existed. Of the numerous sects of Judaism in the first century after Christ's birth, only one could survive the catastrophies of the destruction of the temple in A.D. 70 and the defeat of Bar Kokhba 65 years later. That was the tradition of the Pharisees, whose religious system in the Mishnah transferred the holiness of the temple to the home and village.[17]

The holiness of the people outside the cult did not require a tremendous jump by the Pharisees. Already in Old Testament Law, the external expressions of identification with the holiness of God were ingrained into the lives of the people. It has been said that no Israelite male could forget the covenant because his body bore the mark of circumcision. It has been said also that the most common activities of human beings were regulated so the Israelites could never forget who they were. In particular, complex laws existed in two arenas shared by human beings and animals: reproduction and food. For Israel, these arenas were regulated so the people might never forget that they were unique and different both from the animals and, especially, from other nations. The Law was an inescapable presence.

B. Israel Is to Be Just as the Lord Is Just

Israel's God is not only holy but also just. His people, therefore, are also to be just. The civil laws of the Old Testament, in fact, exhibit the application of this divine justice in the life of Israel. Every person is to be protected and treated with equity. In distinction to the surrounding cultures, women are treated with respect and afforded legal protection from abuse[18] and from betrayal of the marriage covenant.[19] Property rights are protected[20] and inheri-

---

17. See Jacob Neusner, *Judaism, the Evidence of the Mishnah* (Chicago: University of Chicago Press, 1981). Neusner writes: "This still would be what the cult-centered vision had perceived: a holy nation in a holy land living out a holy life and deriving sustenance from the source of life, through sanctification set apart from death and uncleanness" (*Judaism*, 112).

18. For example, see Exod 21:7–11, 20, 26–32; 22:16–17; Deut 21:10–14; 22:13–30; 24:1–5.

19. For example, see Exod 20:14; see also Lev 18:6–23; 20:10–21; Deut 22:13–30.

20. For example, see Exod 20:15; 21:33–36; 22:1–15; 23:4–5; Lev 19:35–36; Deut 22:1–4; 25:13–15.

tances secured.[21] No person is to be exploited or oppressed.[22] Every person is guaranteed a fair trial,[23] and all, including the king, are equally subject to the law.[24]

Many of the civil laws of the Old Testament criminal code appear to be brutal and cruel, leading some to reject the Old Testament altogether, as did the ancient heretic Marcion. Yet these laws were necessary in a brutal and cruel age, especially among a people who were to reflect the sinlessness of their God. In describing the administration of justice in Deuteronomy 17, Moses states that difficult homicide cases, lawsuits, and other legal proceedings are to be referred to the Levitical priests or judges who are in office. Ultimately, their verdict must be obeyed: "So you shall purge the evil from Israel" (Deut 17:12 RSV). It is because Israel is a holy nation that civil laws must remove evil from their midst.

As with divine justice, however, the Law given to Israel was tempered with mercy. The prophet Micah speaks of the offering of sacrifices, even the giving of the firstborn, for rebellious acts, but he contrasts these actions with the more important act of mercy: "He has shown you, O man, what is good; And what does the LORD require of you But to do justly, To love mercy, And to walk humbly with your God" (Mic 6:8). When Jehoshaphat instituted reforms, they began with the merciful teaching of the Law, followed by judicial reforms. Jehoshaphat began as a cultic reformer, then immediately sent out teachers of the book of the Law of the Lord to the cities of Judah (2 Chr 17:1–9). He later implemented judicial reforms (2 Chr 19:4–11), appointing judges and warning them:

> Consider what you do, for you judge not for man but for the LORD; he is with you in giving judgment. Now then, let the fear of the LORD be upon you; take heed what you do, for there is no perversion of justice with the LORD our God, or partiality, or taking bribes. (2 Chr 19:6–7 RSV)

Further, the "Supreme Court" in Jerusalem, according to the Law of the Lord, is told to instruct appellants so they do not incur guilt and wrath. Justice in Israel, as with the Lord himself, must be impartial, merciful, and long-suffering.

---

21. For example, see Leviticus 25; Num 27:5–7; 36:1–9; Deut 25:5–10.

22. For example, see Exod 22:21–27; Lev 19:14, 33–34; 25:35–36; Deut 23:19; 24:6, 12–15, 17–18; 16:18–20; 17:8–13; 19:15–21.

23. For example, see Exod 23:6, 8; Lev 19:15; Deut 1:17; 10:17–18; 16:18–20; 17:8–13; 19:15–21.

24. See Deut 17:18–20.

C. ISRAEL IS TO TRUST IN THE POWER OF GOD

The Old Testament Law also instructs the Israelites about how they are to reflect God's omnipotence in the world. A clear example of this is the law of war in Deuteronomy 20. In this chapter, Israel is instructed about how to fight or, more precisely, to see how the Lord fights for her. The priest is to instruct the Israelites:

> Hear, O Israel: Today you are on the verge of battle with your enemies; do not let your heart faint, do not be afraid, and do not tremble or be terrified because of them; for the LORD your God is he who goes with you, to fight for you against your enemies, to save you. (Deut 20:3–4)

As Israel conquers the land, it is indeed God who exercises his power over her enemies. As Israel fights battle after battle through-out her history, it is God who defeats the enemy in holy war.[25] The same King Jehoshaphat who instituted teaching and judicial reforms also meets a fearsome enemy in battle only to have the Lord destroy the enemy for him. The result was that the "fear of God was on all the kingdoms of those countries when they heard that the LORD had fought against the enemies of Israel" (2 Chr 20:29).

Israel's political viability depended completely on the Lord, the God of Israel. His power was their power because indeed they had none of their own. Alliances with other nations regularly brought disaster when Israel relied on foreign power rather than on the power of their God. Because they are to trust the Lord, they are not to be afraid of any enemy.[26]

III. "I WILL BE YOUR GOD AND YOU WILL BE MY PEOPLE"

God is holy, just, and powerful. Israel, composed of fallen human beings, is to find identity in God and reflect his character. How does such a thing take place? Herein lies, I believe, an often-ignored purpose of the Law of the Old Testament: It allowed the children of Israel to live out who they in fact already were. God had called and redeemed them; they were his elect people. With them he had

---

25. "Holy war" is a term not found in Scripture. The phrase does, however, describe a phenomenon of divine action in Israel's warfare. Although not original with him, it has become a technical term through the work of Gerhard von Rad, *Der Heilige Krieg in alten Israel* (Göttingen: Vandenhoeck & Ruprecht, 1958).

26. The phrase "fear not" is common in the Hebrew Bible and significant in describing reliance on God; see Edgar W. Conrad, *Fear Not Warrior* (Brown Judaic Studies 75; Chico, Calif.: Scholars Press, 1985).

established his everlasting covenant so he could bring all the children of Adam into relationship with their Creator.

To get at the fundamental question of how Israel finds identity in God, one first must ask what it means to be the people of God. The refrain "I will be your God and you shall be my people" (Exod 6:7; Lev 26:12; Ps 95:7; Jer 11:4) reflects a complex and essential relationship between the Lord and his people. Israel was a chosen people, called from the nations of the world to bear a unique and special relationship to God. Deuteronomy provides a clear explication of that identity, which was granted in the calling of the patriarch Abram (Genesis 12):

> For you are a people holy to the LORD your God; the LORD your God has chosen you to be a people for his own possession, out of all the peoples that are on the face of the earth. (Deut 7:6 RSV)

When God called Abram, he did not predicate that call on Abram's holiness. There was nothing remarkable about the man; he simply was one man, chosen by grace, through whom the Creator would bring about the redemption of the creation. From this call flowed the salvific work of God in redeeming Israel from Egyptian bondage:

> You have seen what I did to the Egyptians, and how I bore you on eagles' wings and brought you to myself. Now therefore, if you will obey my voice and keep my covenant, you shall be my own possession among all peoples; for all the earth is mine, and you shall be to me a kingdom of priests and a holy nation. (Exod 19:4–6a RSV)

This people, though not numerous nor powerful, nevertheless bore a unique identity with the Lord who ruled all the earth.

Israel was to find no other identity in the world other than that of people of God. The Lord was always "your God" and Israel was always "his people." The prophet Isaiah, in comforting his people, reminds them that they are the servants of the Lord, chosen in Jacob, descendants of Abraham (Isa 41:8). King Abijah, facing the rebellious northern tribes of Israel in battle, identifies the throne of Judah as "the kingdom of the LORD, which is in the hand of the sons of David" (2 Chr 13:8).

For Israel, there was no other identity than that of the people of the Lord God of Israel. This was not external to her identity; it constituted her identity. Of no other people does God say, "You shall be holy, for I the LORD your God am holy" (Lev 19:2). The character of the Lord of Israel was to be the character of the people of the Lord. The Law of God, therefore, called his people to live according to the very essence of his own being. Through the Law, the Israelites were to live out the "image of God" given to the human race at creation, lost in the fall, and being restored through grace. God's holiness, justice, and power—indeed, all his attributes—are inseparable from his essence. In living out God's laws of holiness, justice, and power, Israel was to share these attributes, and thus God's essence, in the world.

The "moral law" of the Old Testament is given to the entire human race and is explicitly restated in the New Testament, with the exception of the Third Commandment.[27] On the other hand, because of Israel's unique relationship to God, the civil and ceremonial laws given to Israel were unique to that nation. In some cases, this is expressed quite explicitly, as in Deut 14:21:

> You shall not eat anything that dies of itself; you may give it to the alien who is within your gates, that he may eat it, or you may sell it to a foreigner; for you are a holy people to the LORD your God.

Israel is different from the surrounding nations because the Israelites are a people set apart, a nation holy to the Lord.

Freedom for the children of Israel meant understanding that their life was shaped not by the world around them but by their own essence; that is, their life was shaped by who they actually were. When Israel suffered, she did not suffer because she failed to live like other nations. Rather, she suffered precisely because she did live like other nations. The Chronicler, looking back at the rise of Baby-

---

27. The First Commandment (Exod 20:3) is "You shall have no other gods before me" (cf. Matt 4:10; Eph 5:5; 1 John 5:21). The Second Commandment (Exod 20:7) is "You shall not take the name of the LORD your God in vain" (cf. Jas 5:12). The Third Commandment (Exod 20:8) is "Remember the sabbath day to keep it holy" (cf. Col 2:16–17; this text expresses the Christian's freedom from the Sabbath law). The Fourth Commandment (Exod 20:12) is "Honor your father and your mother" (cf. Matt 19:17–19; Eph 6:1–3). The Fifth Commandment (Exod 20:13) is "You shall not kill" (cf. Matt 5:21–22; 19:17–19; Rom 13:9–10). The Sixth Commandment (Exod 20:14) is "You shall not commit adultery" (cf. Matt 5:27–28; 19:17–19). The Seventh Commandment (Exod 20:15) is "You shall not steal" (cf. Matt. 15:19; 19:17–19; Rom 13:9–10). The Eight Commandment (Exod 20:16) is "You shall not bear false witness against your neighbor" (cf. Matt 15:19; 19:17–19). The Ninth and Tenth Commandments (Exod 20:17) are "You shall not covet your neighbor's house[, etc.]" (cf. Luke 12:15; Rom 13:9–10; Gal 5:21).

lon and the destruction and captivity of Judah, noted two reasons why this happened to the Israelites:

> Moreover all the leaders of the priests and the people transgressed more and more, according to all the abominations of the nations, and defiled the house of the LORD which He had consecrated in Jerusalem. And the LORD God of their fathers sent warnings to them by His messengers, rising up early and sending them, because He had compassion on His people and on His dwelling place. But they mocked the messengers of God, despised His words, and scoffed at His prophets; until the wrath of the LORD rose against His people, till there was no remedy. Therefore He brought against them the king of the Chaldeans. (2 Chr 36:14–17a)

The Lord, who called these rebellious people his own and who exercised astounding patience in sending prophet after prophet because of his compassion, finally brought the Chaldeans against Jerusalem to give the people what their actions had brought upon them: captivity. They had refused to live according to God's own attributes, thus they had left the safety of the Law. God's Law was not primarily *Torah* as legal restrictions but as instruction and teaching in the way of life.

IV. THE LAW FULFILLED, NOT DESTROYED

The Law of the Old Testament marked the boundaries of safety and freedom for ancient Israel. But does it have anything to do with the church in the twenty-first century? This is not an unimportant question, just as the events of the exodus were not unimportant for Paul when instructing the Corinthians: "Now these things happened to them as an example, but they were written down for our instruction, on whom the end of the ages has come" (1 Cor 10:11 ESV). In his explanation to the only part of the Decalog set aside in the New Testament, Martin Luther still finds instruction for the Christian:

> Remember the Sabbath day, to keep it holy.

> *What does this mean?* We should fear and love God that we may not despise preaching and His Word, but hold it sacred and gladly hear and learn it.[28]

---

28. *Luther's Small Catechism with Explanation* (St. Louis: Concordia, 1986, 1991), 10.

In other words, the civil and ceremonial laws of the Old Testament, though not applied to the Christian as legal restrictions, still retain their status as *Torah* in teaching and instruction.

A. Avoiding Antinomianism and Legalism

Two extremes are to be avoided in the use of the Law in the church. The first is antinomianism. The third use of the Law is still operative, and Lutherans confess with the Epitome of the Formula of Concord:

> Accordingly we condemn as dangerous and subversive of Christian discipline and true piety the erroneous teaching that the law is not to be urged, in the manner and measure above described, upon Christians and genuine believers, but only upon unbelievers, non-Christians, and the impenitent.[29]

God's Law continues to function in the Christian church despite the influences of modern and postmodern relativism and the resultant desire to be more "open" and "accepting" of alternative morality and ethics.

The second extreme to avoid is legalism. In some cases, as in the so-called Christian Reconstructionist movement, the argument is made that the government of a nation such as the United States should impose the civil law of the Old Testament on the modern, secular state.[30] Rather than a serious or helpful reading of the biblical Law, this movement fundamentally misunderstands the nature of the church, the two kingdoms, and the role of the Old Testament Law. In other cases, the Old Testament Law and compliance to its provisions are demanded within religious communities, such as within Seventh Day Adventism and some fundamentalist sects.[31]

B. Embracing the Law as Freedom

In the Epitome of the Formula of Concord, the Lutheran confessors rightly understood the Law as related to the freedom to be who we are in Christ:

> We believe, teach, and confess that although people who genuinely believe and whom God has truly converted are freed

---

29. FC Ep. VI, 8 (Tappert, 481).

30. For example, see Andrew Sandlin, *A Christian Reconstructionist Primer* (Vallecito, Calif.: Ross House Books, 2001).

31. For a discussion of Seventh Day Adventism and its adherence to particular Old Testament laws, see F. E. Mayer, *The Religious Bodies of America* (St. Louis: Concordia, 1961), 439–50.

through Christ from the curse and the coercion of the law, they are not on that account without the law: on the contrary, they have been redeemed by the Son of God precisely that they should exercise themselves day and night in the law (Ps. 119:1).[32]

According to the Lutheran Confessions, this exercising ourselves in the Law does not occur because we are extorted and coerced by punishment and God's wrath; such good works would be merely works of the Law.[33] Rather, the Epitome stresses:

> Fruits of the Spirit, however, are those works which the Spirit of God, who dwells in the believers, works through the regenerated, and which the regenerated perform in so far as they are reborn and do them spontaneously as if they knew of no command, threat, or reward. In this sense the children of God live in the law and walk according to the law of God. In his epistles St. Paul calls it the law of Christ and the law of the mind. Thus God's children are "not under the law, but under grace" (Rom. 7:23; 8:1, 14).[34]

To be one redeemed by Christ from the power of the Law is to live a paradox: both freed from the Law and subject to the Law.

What is at issue, it seems to me, is not the application of the moral law, at least among those who take seriously the Bible as the Word of God. Instead, at issue is the role of civil and ceremonial law and these as *Torah* (namely, teaching and instruction). This is precisely where Luther and his explanation to the Third Commandment are so helpful. Although the keeping of the Sabbath is no longer required of the new Israel (the church) as it was of the old Israel, nevertheless Luther finds important principles in the commandment that have continuing significance.

It is with this perspective from Luther that the Old Testament Law marks the depth and breadth and height of the freedom won through Christ. That which defined the identity of the old Israel as the people of God also defines the new Israel. The church has no other identity. Nor is that identity any different than it was for the old Israel; it is essential and not external. The life of the elect is the life of God. His attributes are to be the attributes of his people. His

---

32. FC Ep. VI, 2 (Tappert, 480).
33. FC Ep. VI, 5 (Tappert, 480).
34. FC Ep. VI, 6 (Tappert, 480–81).

character is to be their character as a called and holy people. To live in freedom is to live within the life that is his.

B. THE CHURCH IS TO BE HOLY AS THE LORD IS HOLY

Thus as God is holy and Israel was to be holy, so the church is to be holy. Her holiness, like Israel's, is not of and from herself. It is a holiness derived from the Lord of the church. It is an election by grace, a separation from the peoples of the earth to be a holy nation and a kingdom of priests for the Lord.

Within the holy church are found those who are to represent the community to the Lord and the Lord to the community. Although qualitatively different from the Old Testament priesthood, the New Testament ministry bears resemblance to those who served before: Ministers are to preside in the cult and are to teach the *Torah* of the Lord. It was never the people of Israel or their priests who sanctified the cult of the Old Testament. It was always the presence of the Lord within the cult. So it is that his presence in the sacraments, his presence in the proclaimed Word, and his presence in the divine absolution forgives and sanctifies the people of God.

It is God's cult, not ours. Thus the cult of the church is to reflect God's essence; that is to say, the church is to reflect God's holiness. Israel was not to worship like the other nations of the world. Nor can the church dare to adopt aspects of the culture of death that surrounds her, reducing the liturgy of the church to heathen ceremonies with a few religious words thrown in. The presence of God in the Divine Service is the essence of the church because through it God's essence—his holiness—is communicated to humanity.

C. THE CHURCH IS TO BE JUST AS THE LORD IS JUST

The Lord is just. Israel, therefore, was to be just. The church also is to be just. A major difference is, of course, the distinction between ancient Israel as both people of God and political entity and the church as people of God without political identity. It is to the "kingdom of the left" rather than to the "kingdom of the right" that the administration of civil and criminal law is now committed.[35]

Within the church and among her people, however, there is to be justice because God himself is just. The value and dignity of individual human beings is to be maintained. Women and children are to be protected. Marriage is to be honored and upheld. The

---

35. Luther articulated this distinction at some length; see Gustaf Wingren, *Luther on Vocation* (trans. Carl C. Rasmussen; Philadelphia: Muhlenberg, 1957), 1–36, 107–23.

church's voice is to be raised in defense of those who suffer and those who are oppressed, whose lives, born or unborn, are at risk.

Yet justice always is to be tempered with mercy. The repentant sinner is to be received as the merciful God receives the repentant. As the Lord, for Christ's sake, cannot but pour out his absolution even before it is requested, so, too, the church cannot but say to the sinner that his sins already are forgiven. Once given, the justice of God is complete and the sin is remembered no more. The culture of death around us never forgets the sins of others but plots revenge and calls it "justice."

When the church and her members live like the world, they surrender freedom for chains. When the church fails to do justice, love mercy, and walk humbly with her God, she enters the way of death. She and her members bind themselves to the greatest captivity of all: the bonds of not being who she in fact is. The people of Israel suffered not because they did not live like the culture surrounding them; they suffered precisely because they *did* live like those nations. In the same way, the church suffers bondage precisely because she fails to live according to her essence.

D. THE CHURCH IS TO TRUST IN THE POWER OF GOD

Finally, the power of the Lord is the power of the church. In her more lucid moments, Israel realized that her continued existence was not dependent on herself or on the alliances she made with other nations. Her trust in God inevitably brought victory; reliance on others brought defeat. Israel's identity was to be so intensely that of the people of God that she relied solely on him and his power.

Therefore, the people of God, the church, cannot but live in his power. It is not by alliances with others that the church finds security. Adopting the management models of corporate America and replacing the vocabulary and language of the church with more contemporary expressions in harmony with the culture of the world may appear to give security to the church, but in fact such actions do the opposite. They vivify the church with a life that is not her own and, thus, not the life of the Lord of the church. Such actions lead to bondage, not freedom.

IV. CONCLUSION

The Law of the Old Testament tells us about God's will for his people, but it does more. The Old Testament Law is derived from God's own attributes and essence; thus it defines the character and essence of God's elect people. The Law is more than directions on how to live and what to do; it is about who we are.

In this way the Law functions as a marker of freedom and life for both ancient Israel and the church. Inside the Law, we live in freedom because we live as who we in fact are in Christ. The church continues to need the preaching of the second use of the Law because the old Adam continues to cling to us, and the people of God share with all the fallen children of Adam the weaknesses of the flesh. But we are called to a life of repentance and restoration.

The people of God also need the proclamation of the third use of the Law. This is not, however, a use of the Law that threatens and coerces. It is a use that gives definition to life in God. It is teaching and instruction that have meaning only for the baptized because in Baptism everything changed. There we died. There we were buried. There we rose again in Christ's own resurrection. There we were united to him and to his holy people and called to a life that is no longer our own. There we became the people of the Lord, a people who know the freedom of bearing the image of God, an image once lost in Eden but now being restored in us through Christ.

DELIGHTING IN THE GOOD LAW OF YAHWEH

PAUL R. RAABE

In the liturgy, Lutherans pray: "Forgive us, renew us, and lead us, so that we may delight in your will and walk in your ways to the glory of your holy name."[1] This prayer reflects good Old Testament theology. The Psalms are replete with similar prayers. They express the prayer of faith, the godly desire to love what Yahweh loves, to delight in God's good commandments, and to walk in God's upright ways. Only faith in Yahweh, the God of Israel, can talk that way. Followers of Baal or Chemosh or the other gods and goddesses of the nations do not talk that way because they desire to walk in other paths. The psalmists want to be taught the true paths by the true God and to walk in those godly ways. Why? Because those paths taught by Yahweh are true, good, righteous, upright, holy, salutary, praiseworthy, and perfect. Those who fear, love, and trust in Yahweh above all things love his ways. The ways of Yahweh deserve to be taught and extolled, not the ways of the nations nor the ways of the wicked. As the Large Catechism puts it: "From all of this we see once again how highly these Ten Commandments are to be exalted and extolled above all orders, commands, and works that are taught and practiced apart from them."[2]

I. THE *TORAH* PSALMS

The Hebrew word *Torah* means, simply, "instruction." The word is a *tau*-prefixed noun formation from the root *yarah*, "to instruct." It

---

1. *Lutheran Worship* (St. Louis: Concordia, 1982), 158, 178.
2. LC, "Ten Commandments," 333 (K-W, 431).

is important to remember this basic meaning of the word *Torah* when reading the Old Testament's laws because they are first and foremost instruction and teaching from Yahweh. Unlike the law books of today, which are written in a cold, impersonal, and objective style, the laws recorded in the Old Testament display a strong didactic character. They often take the form of direct address with second person verbs. In Deuteronomy, the laws comprise part of Moses' sermons to the people; they are preached laws, filled with exhortations and motivational clauses.

The "instruction," or *Torah*, of Yahweh is extolled in many places throughout the Old Testament. Here I draw your attention to the Psalms. Many of the Psalms praise the *Torah*. A common petition is that Yahweh "teach me" (*hip'il* of ירה; *pi'el* of למד; *hip'il* of ידע). The psalmists desire to be taught by God and to be taught the instructions of God. They do not want to follow the advice of the wicked and the godless. They want the God of truth to teach them, and they want to follow God's way wholeheartedly: "Teach me, O Yahweh, your way; I will walk in your truth; unite my heart to fear your name" (Ps 86:11).[3] God "teaches" his people the ways to go, and his people respond by praising God and his ways.

Let us consider some examples. Psalm 32, a well-known penitential psalm, begins by proclaiming how blessed is the one "whose transgression is forgiven" (32:1). The psalmist confessed his sin and God forgave him (32:5). Then, later in the psalm, God speaks:

> "I will make you wise and I will instruct you in the way in which you should walk; I will counsel you with my eye upon you. Do not be as the horse or as the mule which have no understanding." (32:8–9)[4]

God teaches his people and urges that they be teachable. Notice how both the emphasis on God's forgiveness and the emphasis on God's instruction in the way to go belong together. Clearly, we should not think of a works-righteous legalism here.

Psalm 143 provides a good example of the close connection between faith in God's steadfast love and the desire to walk in God's way. The psalmist prays: "And do not enter into judgment with

---

3. Unless otherwise indicated, all Scripture quotations in this essay are the author's own translation.

4. It remains unclear where the quotation of the divine speech ends—either at the end of v. 8 or v. 9. In any case, v. 8 should be taken as a divine speech set within the psalm. The clause "I will counsel you with my eye upon you" points toward this interpretation. The phrase "my eye upon you" refers to divine protection.

your servant, for no one living is righteous before you" (143:2). The psalmist does not claim to be without sin; he implores God's undeserved mercy and steadfast love. Despite his sin and in light of God's mercy, the psalmist also yearns to walk in God's ways. The psalmist seeks God's steadfast love, God's teaching, and God's leading. He prays:

> Let me hear your steadfast love in the morning, for in you I trust; make me know the way in which I should walk; for to you I lift up my soul. (Ps 143:8)

> Teach me to do your will, for you are my God; let your good Spirit lead me on level ground. (Ps 143:10)

This desire to be taught and led by God also strikes a dominant note in the prayer within Psalm 25:

> Your ways, O Yahweh, make me know; your paths teach me. Lead me in your truth and teach me, for you are the God of my salvation; for you I wait all the day. (25:4–5)

> Good and upright is Yahweh; therefore he instructs sinners in the way. He leads the humble in justice, and he teaches the humble his way. (25:8–9)

> Who is the man who fears Yahweh? He [Yahweh] will instruct him in the way he should choose. (25:12)

The God to whom the prayer is addressed is Yahweh, "the God of my salvation." Because Yahweh is "good and upright," he is the God who can be trusted to teach and lead in good ways. To be taught and led by Yahweh is a great gift and much to be desired. Once again, closely associated with the petition for instruction is the petition for forgiveness:

> The sins of my youth and my acts of rebellion do not remember. (25:7)

> For your name's sake, O Yahweh, forgive my iniquity, for it is great. (25:11)

> Forgive all my sins. (25:18)

Any legalistic works-righteous interpretation of these psalms would greatly distort their meaning.

Psalms 1, 19, and 119 are so dominated by praise of the *Torah* that they are labeled "Torah Psalms."[5] Psalm 1 declares blessed the one who refuses the counsel of the wicked but meditates on Yahweh's *Torah*. Like a tree planted by water, he bears much fruit. The *Torah* is likened to water that nourishes and fructifies a tree. The psalm goes on to contrast the wicked: "Not so the wicked but like the chaff which the wind blows away" (1:4). The wicked vanish so quickly that they do not even get a verb. They have no roots and no water source. The message is clear: Do not be chaff; be a tree by the water.[6]

Psalm 19:7–9 extols the *Torah* with six sentences, each of which uses a nominal clause followed by a participial phrase, as seen in parallel columns below (except for the last colon, which breaks the pattern by using a finite verb).

The *Torah* of Yahweh is perfect,	restoring the soul.
The testimony of Yahweh is sure,	making the simple wise.
The precepts of Yahweh are upright,	making the heart glad.
The commandment of Yahweh is pure,	enlightening the eyes.
The fear of Yahweh is clean,	standing forever.
The judgments of Yahweh are true;	they are altogether righteous.

The instruction of Yahweh gladdens the soul and heart, enlightens the eyes, and makes one wise. Those who love Yahweh find his *Torah* more desirable than gold and sweeter than honey (Ps 19:10).[7]

The most famous Torah Psalm is Psalm 119. It is structured around eight key words that function as near-synonyms for the Law of Yahweh: "saying" (אִמְרָה), "word" (דָּבָר), "statute" (חֹק), "commandment" (מִצְוָה), "judgment" (מִשְׁפָּט), "testimonies" (עֵדוֹת), "precept" (פִּקּוּד), and "Torah" (תּוֹרָה). These key words occur 177 times in 176 verses, basically one *Torah*-word per verse. Four verses omit a key word and four verses compensate by using two key words; the psalm throws in an additional occurrence for extra measure so as to overflow with *Torah*-words.[8]

---

5. For stimulating comments on the significance of these psalms within the Psalter, see James Luther Mays, "The Place of the Torah-Psalms in the Psalter," *Journal of Biblical Literature* 106 (1987): 3–12.

6. See also Jer 17:5–8.

7. For a good treatment of Psalm 19 that shows how the whole psalm makes coherent sense, see Peter C. Craigie, *Psalms 1–50* (WBC 19; Waco: Word Books, 1983).

8. On the complex patterns of Psalm 119, see David Noel Freedman, *Psalm 119: The Exaltation of Torah* (Biblical and Judaic Studies from UCSD 6; Winona Lake, Ind.: Eisenbrauns, 1999).

Psalm 119 exalts Yahweh's instruction. Repeatedly throughout the psalm, one finds expressions of delight in the *Torah*, petitions to be taught by Yahweh, and declarations of the wish to keep the commandments. Because Yahweh is good and righteous, his statutes are good and righteous: "You are good and you do good; teach me your statutes" (119:68); "You are righteous, O Yahweh, and upright are your judgments" (119:137). Love of Yahweh and love of his Law go together. As the psalmist loves the ways of Yahweh, so he hates the ways of the wicked:

> Incline my heart to your testimonies and not to false gain; make my eyes turn away from looking at vanity; in your ways revive me. (119:36–37)

> Hot indignation seizes me because of the wicked, those who forsake your *Torah*. (119:53)

> From your precepts I gain understanding; therefore I hate every false path. (119:104)

> The double-minded I hate, but your *Torah* I love. (119:113)

> Therefore all your precepts concerning everything I consider right; every false path I hate. (119:128)

> Falsehood I hate and I abhor; your *Torah* I love. (119:163)

Who is your teacher, and what do you desire? Either the wicked teach you or the God of Israel teaches you. Either you learn the ways of the wicked or you learn the ways of God. Either you delight in and meditate on the instruction of falsehood or you delight in and meditate on the instruction of truth. Those are the two radically different roads, and this psalm and others like it encourage hearers to set their hearts on God's road. That is the framework necessary for understanding these psalms.[9] They do not intend to promote legalistic works-righteousness or pharisaical pride but to shape our loves and our hates, what we admire and what we despise. They are designed to form and inform God-pleasing prayer and praise.

---

9. The Torah Psalms exhibit a "Newtonian" perspective, as it were (i.e., a perspective based on our experience), that views reality as we perceive it, rather than an "Einsteinian" view that looks at things from God's eternal perspective; see James W. Voelz, "Reading Scripture as Lutherans in the Post-Modern Era," *Lutheran Quarterly* 14 (2000): 309–34.

II. THE NARRATIVE FRAMEWORK FOR ISRAEL'S LAWS

The laws given to ancient Israel appear in three major places: Exodus 20–23; Leviticus; and Deuteronomy 5 and 12–26. It is important to understand these laws within their narrative context. The biblical narrative begins with creation, the fall, the first promise, and the spread of sin and death throughout the world. Then the narrative narrows down to Abraham and his descendents. The maker of the heavens and earth calls Abraham and promises him offspring, the land of Canaan, blessing, and that through him and his seed all the families of the earth will be blessed.

Now fast-forward in the biblical narrative 400-plus years. Abraham does have many descendents, but they do not live in the land of Canaan. Instead, they find themselves in bondage in Egypt. It is not merely an economic or political bondage, but it is also a theological bondage. Israel is not free to serve and worship Yahweh, at least not openly and publicly; they are forced to serve Pharaoh. They do not deliver themselves and they cannot deliver themselves; they are helplessly and hopelessly stuck in bondage. Nevertheless, their God looks on them in his abounding steadfast love; he remembers his covenant with Abraham and "comes down" to deliver them (Exod 3:8). Yahweh defeats Pharaoh with a strong hand and an outstretched arm and brings Israel out of Egypt. Only God and God alone redeemed Israel from bondage.

Yahweh does not only deliver Israel *from* bondage to Pharaoh. He also delivers Israel *for* a different future and a different life. The creator of the heavens and earth brings the people of Israel to himself at Sinai and makes himself their God and makes them his own people.[10] Yahweh renews the covenant he previously made with Abraham, but now he makes it with Israel as a whole nation.[11] Moreover, Yahweh promises to bring Israel into the land of Canaan, just as he promised Abraham. The narrative is nicely summarized by God's speech to Moses in Exod 6:2–8:

> "I am Yahweh. And I appeared to Abraham, to Isaac, and to Jacob, as El Shadday, but with respect to my name Yahweh, I did

---

10. On the covenant formula, "I will be their God and they will be my people," see Rolf Rendtorff, *The Covenant Formula: An Exegetical and Theological Investigation* (trans. Margaret Kohl; Old Testament Studies; Edinburgh: T&T Clark, 1998 [original 1995]).

11. For good theological treatments of the relationship between the Abrahamic covenant and the Sinaitic covenant, see John P. Milton, *God's Covenant of Blessing* (Rock Island, Ill.: Augustana Press, 1961), and Walter R. Roehrs, "Divine Covenants: Their Structure and Function," *CJ* 14 (1988): 7–27.

not make myself known to them. And I also established my covenant with them, to give to them the land of Canaan, the land of their sojourning-places in which they sojourned. And moreover I have heard the groaning of the Israelites whom the Egyptians are enslaving, and I have remembered my covenant. Therefore, say to the Israelites, 'I am Yahweh, and I will bring you out from under the burdens of the Egyptians, and I will deliver you from their bondage. And I will redeem you with an outstretched arm and with great acts of judgment. And I will take you to myself for a people, and I will be your God; and you will know that I am Yahweh your God, who brought you out from under the burdens of the Egyptians. And I will bring you to the land which I swore to give to Abraham, to Isaac, and to Jacob, and I will give it to you for a possession. I am Yahweh.' "[12]

Israel has been redeemed from bondage and has been brought to God and made God's own special possession. It was all by God's undeserved grace and mercy and his abundant steadfast love. They have been delivered from one way of life, called "bondage," and delivered for a different way of life marked by service to Yahweh. The Israelites were purchased and won from death, as it were, so they may be God's own and "live under him in his kingdom, and serve him in everlasting righteousness, innocence, and blessedness."[13] Now, at Sinai, Yahweh reveals to the nation of Israel the new way of life they are to follow in the land of Canaan. God did not free them from bondage only to put them back under bondage again. God freed them from bondage for a life of freedom in service to him. That life of freedom in service to God has a definite, describable shape to it, and that shape is given in the pentateuchal laws.

III. THE WAYS OF YAHWEH
OR THE WAYS OF THE NATIONS

In Deut 4:6–8, Moses says to the people:

> "Keep and do [the statutes and judgments], for that is your wisdom and your understanding in the eyes of the peoples who will hear all these statutes and say, 'Surely this great nation is a wise and understanding people.' For what great nation is there that

---

12. On the passage and its significance for biblical theology, see Elmer A. Martens, *God's Design: A Focus on Old Testament Theology* (Grand Rapids: Baker, 1981).

13. Cf. Small Catechism, "The Creed," 4 (K-W, 355).

has a god as near to it as is Yahweh our God whenever we call to him? And what great nation is there that has statutes and judgments as righteous as all this Torah which I am placing before you today?"

The logic of this kind of passage and others like it can be unpacked in this way. The nations grope in the darkness as they follow the dictates of their own confused minds. They do not know which way is up. Israel is to live among the nations, but Israel is not to emulate the nations. Israel is to keep Yahweh's statutes and thereby gain the respect of the nations and even attract the nations to Yahweh and to Yahweh's *Torah* (cf. Deut 26:19).

The laws given by Yahweh describe the shape of Israel's future life in the Promised Land. These laws envision Israel living in the land of Canaan, yet they call Israel to a life quite unlike that of the Canaanites. Throughout the Pentateuch, the reader frequently comes upon warnings for Israel to avoid imitating the other nations. For example, Lev 18:3–4 states:

"According to the deeds of the land of Egypt, where you used to dwell, you shall not do, and according to the deeds of the land of Canaan, to which I am bringing you, you shall not do, and in their statutes you shall not walk. My judgments you shall do, and my statutes you shall keep by walking in them. I am Yahweh your God."

Yahweh's command, in essence, is this: "Don't walk in *their* benighted statutes; walk in *my* enlightened statutes."

The conduct of Israel in the land is to be distinctly different from that of the surrounding nations in several ways. Israel is not to worship the gods of the surrounding nations or to follow their practices (Exod 23:23–24). Israel is prohibited from worshiping Yahweh by following the worship practices of the other nations (Deut 12:2–4, 29–31). According to Deut 18:9–14, Israel should not follow the abominable practices of the nations by engaging in child sacrifice or by attempting to communicate with the supernatural world through divination, soothsaying, augury, sorcery, casting spells, and necromancy.[14] Leviticus 18 prohibits Israel from emulating the

---

14. On these practices among the Canaanites, see Jeffrey H. Tigay, *Deuteronomy* (JPS Torah Commentary; Philadelphia: Jewish Publication Society, 1996), 172–75.

nations in terms of incest, adultery, human sacrifice to Molech, homosexuality, and bestiality.[15]

Israel is commanded to annihilate the Hittites, Amorites, Canaanites, Perizzites, Hivites, and Jebusites precisely "in order that they may not teach you to do according to all their abhorrent things which they do for their gods, and you sin against Yahweh your God" (Deut 20:18; cf. Exod 23:33). Yahweh is to be the teacher of the Israelites, not the idolatrous nations. What will happen if Israel does imitate the nations? Then Israel will experience the same judgment as the nations. Just as God drives the nations out of the land because of their great wickedness, so he will drive a *goy*-like Israel out of the land as well (Deut 8:20; 9:4–5; Lev 18:24–30; 20:22–23).

A few general observations from specific laws will illustrate how they functioned to share Israel's life. The laws are addressed to each individual Israelite and to Israel as a whole. Ancient Israel was a theocracy, both a nation and a worshiping community at the same time. Therefore, the laws address a wide array of concerns, from worship to warfare, from parents to property, from disputes to disease. The traditional threefold division of the laws into moral, ceremonial, and civil soon breaks down when one studies the laws. Ceremonial considerations inform some "moral" laws, moral considerations inform some "ceremonial" laws, and so on. Although the laws address a host of issues, they should not be understood as a random or irrational jumble of commands. Certain theological, social, and economic considerations inform them. The laws make sense when studied contextually.

The First Commandment is always first and foremost. Deuteronomy repeatedly accents that the commandments are to be kept with joy from a wholehearted "fear" and "love" of God. The commandments do not call for action done to merit God's favor or for slavish and reluctant action but for glad-hearted action that flows from faith. The God whom one is to fear and love is always the specific God named Yahweh, the God who mercifully brought the Israelites out of bondage and made them his own people. It is of paramount significance for understanding the laws to see them in

---

15. On these practices among the nations, see Gordon J. Wenham, *The Book of Leviticus* (New International Commentary on the Old Testament 3; Grand Rapids: Eerdmans, 1979), 251–60. On Molech, see George C. Heider, *The Cult of Molek: A Reassessment* (JSOTSup 43; Sheffield: JSOT Press, 1985), and John Day, *Molech: A God of Human Sacrifice in the Old Testament* (Cambridge: Cambridge University Press, 1989). Leviticus 18 also prohibits sexual relations with a woman during menstrual impurity (18:19), a prohibition that is part of Israel's unique system of ritual purity.

connection with the opening statement: "I am Yahweh your God who brought you out of the land of Egypt, out of the house of slavery" (Exod 20:2; Deut 5:6). The identity of the one giving the laws is not some malevolent deity or some abstract philosopher's god; instead, he is the revealed God who not only created but also redeemed Israel, who showed himself to be "gracious and compassionate and abounding in steadfast love."[16] To disobey this God is to disobey the loving Savior. There are also frequent warnings that disobedience eventually provokes God to wrath.[17] God takes his commandments seriously and punishes the transgressors. We should not, however, think of the God giving the laws as angry, malicious, and desiring to punish. The legal material repeatedly reminds Israel that the one who is speaking is the same one who saved them.

IV. THE LAW ALWAYS ACCUSES SINNERS

Those who trust in Yahweh and in his steadfast love extol his Law and commandments. They desire to walk in God's ways. But if we look at the picture from a different angle and ask if sinners measure up to God's commandments, then the Old Testament uniformly answers with a strong "No!" Sinners transgress God's good Law. The Law always accuses sinners. This is what happens when the good, holy, and righteous Law of God meets transgressors and lawbreakers. The accusing and condemning function of God's Law manifests itself throughout the Old Testament. Already with the giving of the Law at Sinai, provision was made for atonement and forgiveness of sins through the sacrificial system. The entire sacrificial system presupposes that the Israelites would disobey and break commandments. Why else would they need atonement and forgiveness?

God's Law accused and condemned both individual Israelites and Israel as a whole. The main reason given for the exile of the Israelites is that they continually broke the First Commandment. Because of their continual idolatry and apostasy, they provoked Yahweh to anger and brought down on themselves the curses of the

---

16. This frequently recurring phrase is virtually a creedal statement in the Old Testament (e.g., Ps 103:8).

17. On the wrath of God in the Old Testament, see Bruce E. Baloian, *Anger in the Old Testament* (American University Studies Series 7, Theology and Religion 99; New York: Peter Lang, 1992), and H. G. L. Peels, *The Vengeance of God: The Meaning of the Root NQM and the Function of the NQM-texts in the Context of Divine Revelation in the Old Testament* (Oudtestamentische Studiën 31; Leiden: Brill, 1995).

Mosaic covenant. This is how the biblical historians and prophets explain the destruction of Samaria and Jerusalem and the exiles of the north and the south. The Old Testament historians narrate the history of Israel as one of continual rebellion against Yahweh on the part of Israel, to which Yahweh responded with acts of judgment. There is only one exception to this narrative of sin and judgment: the time of Joshua, when, according to Judges 2, the people faithfully served Yahweh. After that generation died, every succeeding generation rebelled until the axe of judgment came down and Israel as an independent nation ceased to exist. According to the usual chronology, the North was exiled ca. 732 B.C., Samaria was destroyed in 722 B.C., much of Judah was exiled already in 701 B.C., and Jerusalem was destroyed in 587/586 B.C.

V. A New and Different Future

Throughout the entire Old Testament, one reads of Yahweh desiring an obedient Israel. Although the history of Israel turned out to be marked by disobedience, God still desired an obedient people. It is not as if God gave up on that idea and turned to a backup plan. On the contrary, God announced through the prophets that in the future there would be an obedient Israel. God himself would see to it. The prophets repeatedly announce a future for Israel and the nations that would be radically different from the sorry past.

According to the prophets, the status quo was completely unacceptable, characterized as it was by lack of faith in Yahweh, by going after other gods, by injustice and wicked behavior, by the total inability to do what is right, and by the constant inclination to do what is wrong. So the prophets announced the coming judgment against Israel and all the nations. But that would not be the end of the story. Out of the ashes God would create a new and different reality. The prophets promise the messianic King who will rule in perfect righteousness, unlike the kings of the past. Isaiah's servant songs announce an obedient servant, the servant of Yahweh who suffers not for his own sins but for the sins of others. The prophets also declare that God will build a new Israel out of the remnant, and this new Israel will be different.

Jeremiah's well-known prophecy of a new covenant sets forth these promises: Yahweh will write his *Torah* on Israel's heart; Yahweh will be their God and they will be Yahweh's people; and all Israel will perfectly know Yahweh. This new reality will be grounded on the gift of divine forgiveness: "[F]or I will forgive their iniquity, and their sin I will remember no more" (Jer 31:31–34). Ezekiel has a similar promise: "I will give to you a new heart and a new spirit I will put within you; and I will remove the heart of stone from your flesh and I will give to you a heart of flesh. And my Spirit I will put within you and I will cause you to walk in my statutes, and my judgments you will keep and you will do" (Ezek 36:26–27). The people were supposed to make for themselves a new heart and a new spirit (Ezek 18:31), but because they failed, now God promises that he himself will give them a new heart and a new spirit and that his own Spirit will enable them to be his obedient Israel.

The prophets depict the future not as a mere repetition of the past but as something radically different. Part of that difference is a different Israel. In place of the old faithless and disobedient Israel there will be a new Israel, a faithful and obedient Israel enabled by the Spirit to walk in Yahweh's ways. The future will be different, not only for Israel but also for the nations. Isaiah announces the future time when the nations will stream to the exalted Zion:

> And many peoples will come and say,
> "Come, let us go up to the mountain of Yahweh,
> to the house of the God of Jacob,
> so that he may teach us from his ways,
> and so that we may walk in his paths."
> For from Zion will go forth the *Torah*,
> and the word of Yahweh from Jerusalem. (2:3)

Instead of teaching themselves their own constructed and false ideas, instead of walking in their own wicked ways, the nations will be taught by Yahweh and will walk in Yahweh's ways. The future life and conduct of the Gentiles will be different, and that difference is characterized as walking in the ways of the *Torah* given by the God of Jacob. According to the prophets, one of the gifts that Yahweh will give Israel and the nations is a new and different life, a life with Yahweh and a life of walking in Yahweh's ways. That is the way the Old Testament ends, with the promise of a future marked by obedience.

VI. Reflections in the Light of the New Testament

To this point, Old Testament theology of the Law has been described from within the Old Testament itself. To hear the Old

Testament witness from within the Old Testament itself is a legitimate and necessary task, an essential part of the exercise of doing biblical theology. Limiting oneself to the Old Testament, however, is not the entire theological task from a Christian point of view. Therefore, the scope of this study includes the New Testament and offers some brief reflections on the significance of the Old Testament material for Christian theology and life.

The Old Testament's prophetic hope of a new and different future, a future marked by obedience, has great significance for Christology. The church confesses that Jesus of Nazareth is the fulfillment of the Old Testament. He is the righteous and faithful Messiah, the innocent Suffering Servant. This also means that Jesus of Nazareth is the promised Israel, "Israel condensed into one,"[18] the obedient and faithful Israel. Matthew provides a good illustration of this point through his emphasis that Jesus is to be seen as Israel.[19] Jesus recapitulates and fulfills Israel's history; for example, he is called out of Egypt and tested for a period of forty days in the wilderness. He fulfills the promises given by God to ancient Israel. Therefore, it is not surprising that Matthew also stresses the obedience of Jesus toward God his Father. God desires an obedient Israel, and Jesus Christ is first and foremost that obedient Israel. Only on the basis of Christ's perfect obedience are those baptized into Christ reckoned before God as his obedient Israel.

The rich Old Testament theology of the Law of God also has great significance for understanding the Christian life.[20] One of the gifts from God is a new way of life. Just as the *Torah* depicting Israel's alternative life was a gift and was received by the faithful with joy, so also the alternative life God gives Christians is a gift. Not only "justification" but also "sanctification," the new obedience, the new way of godliness and holiness, is to be received with thankfulness. The Holy Spirit has converted the baptized, regenerated them, liberated their will, and given them new impulses and a new orientation. The Spirit so transforms them that now it can be said of them that they "fulfill the law" by serving the neighbor in

---

18. I borrowed this phrase from my colleagues Horace Hummel and James Voelz.

19. For a good treatment of Jesus as Israel in Matthew, see David E. Holwerda, *Jesus and Israel: One Covenant or Two?* (Grand Rapids: Eerdmans, 1995), 27–58.

20. For a classic treatment of the Christian life of new obedience, see Adolf Köberle, *The Quest for Holiness* (1936; repr., Evansville, Ind.: Ballast Press, 1997).

love, though it must also be said of them that they keep the Law imperfectly because of sin (Rom 13:8–10; cf. Gal 5:13–14; 6:2).[21] As St. Paul states in 1 Cor 9:20–21, the Christian is neither "under the law" (ὑπὸ νόμον) nor "without the law" (ἄνομος) but "in the law of Christ" (ἔννομος Χριστοῦ). "In the law of Christ" is the third alternative to legalistic bondage under the Law on the one hand and antinomian libertinism on the other hand.

What should receive more stress in catechesis, sermons, and Bible classes, in my opinion, are both the goodness of the Law and the joy of obedience. The Law of God should not be demonized.[22] It is not sin, as St. Paul reminds the Romans (Rom 7:7). Just as God is good, so his Law is good. "The law is holy, and the commandment is holy and righteous and good" (Rom 7:12), and even "of the Spirit" (Rom 7:14). That is why one must say more than only "Christ frees from the law." Because the Law is God's Law and therefore good, righteous, holy, and of the Spirit, Christians delight in it. Furthermore, "obedience" is not a dirty word. Sinners do not have all the fun. Actually, sin is quite boring and tiresome. Fun, excitement, and real action are in the daily adventure of obedience and service to Christ. To live under the end-time rule of God inaugurated by Christ is to live in an alternative universe in which what is "right" is good and delightful and what is "wrong" is bad and boring.

---

21. Werner Elert asserts that the "law" throughout the Scriptures is always the law of retribution; see *Das christliche Ethos* (Tübingen: Furche-Verlag, 1949), 90. This assertion is patently false. When Paul states in Rom 13:8–10, for example, that Christians "fulfill the law," he does not mean that they fulfill the law of retribution or the law that threatens with the wrath of God. By the word *law* (νόμος) in this passage, Paul means simply the content of God's will for human conduct as expressed in the Ten Commandments. We must reckon with the polysemy of the word *law*, even in Pauline usage; see Paul R. Raabe, "The Law and Christian Sanctification: A Look at Romans," *CJ* 22 (1996): 178–85. This view also is reflected in Lutheran theology, as can be demonstrated by numerous texts in the Lutheran Confessions. Ap. IV, 136 maintains that "the keeping of the law must begin in us and then increase more and more" (K-W, 142). Ap. XII, 82 states in the German version that the regenerate receive the Holy Spirit and "therefore they begin to become friendly to the law and to obey the same" (*"Darum fangen sie an, dem Gesetz hold zu werden und demselbigen zu gehorchen"*). The Large Catechism introduces the creed by stating that the Apostles' Creed "is given in order to help us do what the Ten Commandments require of us" (LC, "The Creed," 2 [K-W, 431]). Furthermore, the Large Catechism introduces the Lord's Prayer by saying that "nothing is so necessary as to call upon God incessantly and to drum into his ears our prayer that he may give, preserve, and increase in us faith and the fulfillment of the Ten Commandments and remove all that stands in our way and hinders us in this regard" (LC, "The Lord's Prayer," 2 [K-W, 440–41]).

22. Sometimes, at least in some Lutheran circles, the Law is spoken of only in negative terms. For a discussion of twentieth-century debates over the role of the Law, see Scott Murray, *Law, Life, and the Living God: The Third Use of the Law in Modern American Lutheranism* (St. Louis: Concordia, 2002).

The theological structure is the same for both Testaments. Just as God freed ancient Israel from bondage for a new and different life of service to God, so also—but in a far greater way because of eschatological fulfillment—the Good News of Jesus Christ frees all sinners from their old ways to a new and different way. The New Testament often presents a contrast between the old pre-baptismal way of life and the new baptismal way of life, a theology of "before and after," one might say. Consider, for example, 1 Pet 1:14–19 in which the appeal is made to the readers to leave behind their former lives and dedicate themselves to a different life of holiness:

> As obedient children, do not be conformed to the passions of your former ignorance, but as he who called you is holy, be holy yourselves in all your conduct; since it is written, "You shall be holy, for I am holy." . . . You know that you were ransomed from the futile ways inherited from your fathers, not with perishable things such as silver or gold, but with the precious blood of Christ, like that of a lamb without blemish or spot. (RSV)

In this text, the contrast between "before" and "after" is evident. The readers are exhorted to live by the will of God because they have spent enough time acting like the Gentiles. As the readers live by the will of God, they receive abuse from the Gentiles, who "are surprised that you do not run with them into the same excess of dissipation, and they blaspheme" (1 Pet 4:3–4). Because the readers no longer join the "Gentile" crowd, their former pagan friends are surprised and upset by this change of behavior, so upset, in fact, that they "blaspheme" (βλασφημέω).[23]

The apostle Paul picks up on the same theme in Ephesians 2 by setting forth two pairs of contrast: First, whereas the readers used to be "dead" in their sins, now God made them "alive" with Christ; second, whereas they formerly *"walked* according to the age of this world" (2:2), now God created them in Christ "for good works, which God prepared beforehand that in them we should *walk*" (2:10). What do these "good works" and this alternative way of life look like? Paul goes on in Ephesians 4–6 to specify this life with significant description and instruction. For example, Eph 4:28 urges: "Let him who steals steal no longer; but rather let him labor, performing with his own hands what is good, in order that he may have something to share with him who has need" (NASB). Notice the

---

23. The verb can denote "to malign, defame" the readers, but in this context it more likely means "to blaspheme" God; see Paul J. Achtemeier, *1 Peter* (Hermeneia; ed. Eldon Jay Epp; Minneapolis: Fortress, 1996), 284.

contrast being stressed between the one *ethos* and the other *ethos*: "Stop robbing people and instead get an honest job so you may give generously to the poor."

VII. CONCLUSION

It seems to me that today, more than ever, the baptized need to be taught how radically different the ways of the Lord are from the ways of the world. Ancient Israel was called to live *among* the nations but *unlike* the nations. In the language of the Gospel of John, the church is to live *in* the world but not *of* the world (17:14–16). Lest the ideologies of the day become the pattern for the church to follow with the result that she uncritically and unwittingly marches to the imperatives of the cultural *Zeitgeist*, the church needs to be taught the distinction between the patterns of life advocated by the world and the very different pattern of life set forth by God.

I am not encouraging legalism. The Law always accuses sinners, and Christians continue to be sinners. Our justification is always "apart from works," even after Baptism and even at the final judgment. Christ remains the mediator after one's Baptism. What I am stressing is the simple observation that both Testaments devote a great deal of space to describing the life and conduct of God's people. Not only external actions matter but also internal movements of the heart. Conversely, not only internal movements of the heart matter but also external actions. This is true for individuals and also for the church. What does the church look like, how does she conduct herself, and how does her behavior differ from that of other groups? These questions deserve serious attention, lest the church actually behave as if she were just another religious organization among a smorgasbord of religious organizations, trying to sell her religious commodities to religious consumers.

Finally, the Old Testament's promise of an obedient Israel relates to eschatology. The Christian life of new obedience remains inchoate and imperfect because we continue to be sinners. We still live in a "not yet" condition as we wait for the day when the Old Testament promise of an obedient Israel reaches its eschatological consummation. Only at the Parousia will we have no original sin. Only then will our thoughts, words, and deeds become perfectly holy and pure, perfectly obedient to the will of our Creator. Only then will Jeremiah's promise reach its consummation, when it can be said of us that we "know the Lord" perfectly without the need of a teacher and that we live as God's people with the *Torah* written on our hearts in perfect obedience. That is a day to long for with eager anticipation because with the psalmists of old we delight in God's good Law and we desire to walk in his good ways to the glory of his holy name.

NEW TESTAMENT PERSPECTIVES

JESUS AND THE *TORAH*

DALE C. ALLISON JR.

Let me begin not with Jesus but with the early church. Shortly after Easter, Christians found themselves at odds over the Mosaic Law. Some, compelling Gentiles to live like Jews, required circumcision. Others, such as Paul, promoted a gospel of the uncircumcision. In addition, there were moderates between the extremes. The so-called Apostolic Decree, known from the Book of Acts, did not impose circumcision, but, echoing Levitical rules for resident aliens, it did outlaw certain foods and ban intercourse with near kin.

How do we move from the quarrels in the early church back to Jesus? If Jesus taught that not one letter or its stroke will pass from the Law until heaven and earth dissolve (Matt 5:17–20), then the radicalism of the Hellenists and Paul appears to be a secondary development, without precedent in the pre-Easter period. But if Jesus was a radical who pronounced all foods clean (Mark 7:19), then there was, in the matter of *Torah*, profound discontinuity between his thought and the conservativism of James and like-minded Jewish Christians. Put a bit differently, if Jesus abolished the Law, as Mark seems to say, then how do we explain Paul's opponents in Galatia and the impositions of the Apostolic Decree? And if, as Matthew has it, Jesus clearly upheld the Law, then how do we account for the Law-free apostle to the Gentiles?

I recognize, of course, that it can be difficult to define the connection between what Jesus taught about the Law and what some of his followers believed. It would be folly to ascribe everything various early Christians believed or did to their founder. We cannot blame him for all that went wrong. Jesus' followers sometimes reaped where he did not sow. In the present case, however, this observation does not end the discussion. The early traditions about Jesus contain, as we shall see, a striking antinomy. There are sayings that strongly sanction the *Torah*. Likewise, there are sayings that seem to undermine it. So the post-Easter debates are mirrored in traditions that purport to derive from Jesus himself.

One explanation for this circumstance is that participants in the post-Easter disputes renovated the tradition to suit their own theological tastes. Is not Matthew making Jesus as observant as possible? Is not Mark making Jesus as liberal as possible? Yet our story is more complex than this. It does not suffice to say that radicals made the tradition more radical or that conservatives made it more conservative or even that both things happened. The original tradition was not a blank slate waiting for ecclesiastical scrawl. Jesus himself taught memorable things about the *Torah*, and because these things were memorable, they were not forgotten. Indeed, Jesus contributed to the later confusion because sometimes he sounded like a faithful disciple of Moses while at other times he sounded not so faithful. Early Christians had trouble sorting out the Law because Jesus left them with a lot of sorting to do. That this was the case, and how it could be so is the subject of this essay.[1]

The topic is a large one. To make it more manageable, I will pay special attention initially to Jesus' attitude toward the Decalogue as the Synoptics depict it. This is altogether appropriate because Jewish tradition had long regarded the ten words written by God's finger as standing for the Law in its entirety. The Decalogue was the foundation of Israel's legislation, a list of the broad principles or "categorical law" behind the detailed "case law." The Pentateuch puts the ten words at the front of its corpus of ordinances as a sort of introduction, and they are repeated a second time in Deuteronomy. Later, Philo called the ten words "heads summarizing the particular laws,"[2] and he claimed that the Ten Commandments "are summaries of the laws which are recorded in the sacred books and run through the whole of the legislation."[3] From a later time, *Targum Pseudo-Jonathan* on Exod 24:12 has God declare: "I will give to you [Moses] the tablets of stone upon which are hinted the rest of the Law and the six hundred and thirteen commandments." Given the representative status of the Ten Commandments, I suggest that

---

1. For a recent survey of the entire subject, see William R. G. Loader, *Jesus' Attitude towards the Law* (WUNT II.97; Tübingen: Mohr Siebeck, 1997).

2. Philo, *De decalogo* 19–20.

3. Philo, *De decalogo* 154; cf. *De specialibus legibus* 1.1.

if we can form some account of what Jesus taught about the commandments, then we can begin to fathom his interpretation of the Law in its entirety.

I. THE CONSERVATIVE JESUS

Let us begin with Jesus in Mark. In Mark 7, Jesus rebuts some Pharisees and scribes with this observation:

> You have a fine way of rejecting the commandment of God in order to keep your tradition! For Moses said, "Honor your father and mother"; and, "Whoever speaks evil of father or mother must surely die." But you say that if anyone tells father or mother, "Whatever support you might have had from me is Corban" (that is, an offering to God)—then you no longer permit doing anything for a father or mother, thus making void the word of God through your tradition that you have handed on. (7:9–13)[4]

Here Jesus' opponents are castigated precisely because their tradition has led them to neglect one of the Ten Commandments.

Just a few verses later in Mark, Jesus takes his disciples aside and says to them: "[I]t is from within, from the human heart, that evil intentions come: fornication, theft, murder, adultery, avarice, wickedness, deceit, licentiousness, envy, slander, pride, folly. All these evil things come from within, and they defile a person" (7:21–23). The second, third, and fourth items in this list—theft, murder, adultery—also occur together in the Decalogue: "You shall not murder. You shall not commit adultery. You shall not steal" (Exod 20:13–15). Within the space of only a few verses (Mark 7:9–13, 22–23), Jesus has taught the validity of four of the Ten Commandments.[5]

Something similar occurs in Mark 10. When a rich man asks Jesus what he must do to inherit eternal life, Jesus responds: "You know the commandments: 'You shall not murder; You shall not steal; You shall not bear false witness; You shall not defraud; Honor your father and mother'" (10:19). Of these five imperatives, four are from the Ten Commandments. When we put them beside the list of sins in Mark 7, Jesus upholds fully half of the Decalogue. He

---

4. Unless otherwise indicated, all the Scripture quotations in this essay are taken from the NRSV.

5. He also condemns covetousness, which the Decalogue likewise prohibits. But Mark's word is the noun πλεονεξία, whereas LXX Exod 20:17 and Deut 5:21 have the verb ἐπιθυμέω.

enjoins the honoring of parents and repudiates murder, adultery, theft, and false witness.

The next Markan passage to consider is 12:28–31. Here a scribe asks Jesus, "Which commandment is the first of all?" Jesus responds by citing Scripture: "The first is, 'Hear, O Israel: the Lord our God, the Lord is one; you shall love the Lord your God with all your heart, and with all your soul, and with all your mind, and with all your strength.' The second is this, 'You shall love your neighbor as yourself.' There is no other commandment greater than these." What would ancient hearers have made of this combination of two famous texts—Deut 6:4–5 and Lev 18:17?

We know what at least one Jew would have thought. If Philo, as already observed, believed that the Decalogue is a précis of the entire Mosaic legislation, he also thought that the Decalogue can be summarized by reducing the ten words to two. As have so many since, our philosophical exegete divided the Ten Commandments into "two sets of five, which he [God] engraved on two tables."[6] The first set of five, each one of which names YHWH, contains the prohibition of other gods, the ban on graven images, the interdiction against taking the Lord's name in vain, the injunction to keep the Sabbath, and the commandment to honor one's father and mother. The second set of five, none of which mentions God's name, consists of the prohibitions of adultery, murder, theft, false witness, and covetousness.[7] Philo's twofold division, also attested to in Josephus, is more than formal. The partitioning is also thematic. The first set of injunctions are "more concerned with the divine."[8] The "second" set has to do with "the duties of individual to individual."[9] This twofold explanation, with its focus on duty to God and to humanity, brings us near Mark 12:28–31.

There is, however, more that can be learned from Philo. He summarily characterizes the two chief duties in terms of love.[10] Those who observe the first five words are "lovers of God" (φιλο-θέοι). Those who observe the last five words are "lovers of people" (φιλανθρώποι). This interpretation, which is offered as though well-known and obvious, makes plain that the summary of *Torah*, the Decalogue, may itself be summarized by two demands: the demand

---

6. Philo, *De decalogo* 50; cf. *De decalogo* 106.
7. Cf. Philo, *De decalogo* 51.
8. Philo, *De decalogo* 121.
9. Philo, *De decalogo* 106.
10. See Philo, *De decalogo* 108–10.

to love God and the demand to love neighbor. The parallel to Mark 12:28–31 is all the closer because, for Philo, the commandments concerning love of God are the "first [προτέρας] set" and those concerning love of humanity are the "second [δευτέρᾳ] set,"[11] while Deut 6:4 ("and you shall love the Lord your God") is the "first [πρώτη]" commandment in Mark and Lev 19:18 ("you shall love your neighbor as yourself") is the "second [δευτέρα]." Philo, then, would almost certainly have construed the commandments to love God and neighbor as a synopsis of the Decalogue, a resume of the two tables given to Moses.

It is beyond our purpose to review all the reasons why others beside Philo also would have understood Mark 12:28–34 in this manner. I can observe, however, that the second half of the Decalogue often was associated with Lev 19:18. Romans 13:9 reads: "The commandments, 'You shall not commit adultery, You shall not murder; You shall not steal; You shall not covet'; and any other commandment, are summed up in this word, 'Love your neighbor as yourself.' " Here Lev 19:18 sums up the Decalogue's second table. In similar fashion, Matt 19:18–19 cites the same commandments as does Paul, then adds the imperative to love father and mother. Finally, the evangelist cites Lev 19:18 as the general rule that contains the preceding particulars. Again, Jas 2:8–13 refers to Lev 19:18 as "the royal law," then cites the prohibitions of adultery and murder as instances of that law. Obviously, there were early Christians who regarded the commandment to love one's neighbor as a summary of the second half of the Decalogue.

But what about the commandment to love God? It comes from Deut 6:4–5, the *Shema*, a liturgical text for ancient as well as for modern Jews. Already in the Old Testament, the *Shema* closely trails Deuteronomy's version of the ten words (cf. Deuteronomy 5). Many have observed the link between the *Shema*'s imperative to love the Lord (Deut 6:4–5) and the Decalogue's mention of those "who love me and keep my commandments," which ends the word about idolatry in the first set of five commandments (Exod 20:6; Deut 5:10). That some around the turn of the era closely associated the Decalogue and the *Shema* is evidenced by the Nash Papyrus (first or second century B.C.E., from Egypt, in Hebrew). On a single sheet (perhaps used for lectionary purposes), this text combines the Decalogue and the *Shema*. No less important, rabbinic sources inform us, and in this particular case there is no reason to disbelieve them,

---

11. Philo, *De decalogo* 106.

that recitation of the *Shema* followed the recitation of the Decalogue in the Second Temple period.[12]

My conviction is that when Jesus condensed the divine demand into Deut 6:5 and Lev 19:18, he was not doing anything new except probably enunciating a common digest of the Decalogue. Certainly an impressive cloud of witnesses within our tradition has regularly taken these two Old Testament texts to sum up the purport of the Ten Commandments. The 1928 *Book of Common Prayer* (in its catechism), John Gill, Matthew Henry, Jonathan Edwards, the Heidelberg Catechism, the Westminster Confession, John Calvin, Thomas Aquinas, the *Apostolic Constitutions* (2.5.36), and Irenaeus (*Adversus haereses* 4.16.3), for example, all regard the commandment to love God and the commandment to love neighbor as the basic content of the Decalogue.[13] They have, I believe, rightly understood Mark 12:28–34.

But what, then, about the Sabbath in Mark? How do Jesus' Sabbath activities accord with an endorsement of the Decalogue? What about Mark 1:21–28, which recounts how Jesus performed an exorcism on a Sabbath? Or Mark 1:29–31, which describes how Jesus healed Peter's mother-in-law on a Sabbath? Or Mark 2:23–28, which relates that Jesus plucks grain on a Sabbath? Or Mark 3:1–6, which records that Jesus healed a man with a withered hand on the Sabbath? Here things become a bit murky, and, though we will not examine these episodes in any detail, we do need to consider briefly the two stories in which Jesus finds himself in trouble.

The episode in Mark 2, in which Jesus' disciples pluck grain on the Sabbath, is an occasion for Jesus' enemies to object, and understandably so.[14] Many, if not most, learned Jews would have under-

---

12. See *m. Tamid* 5.1 and *b. Ber.* 12a. See also the prohibition of reciting the Decalogue with the *Shema* in *Sipre Deut.* § 34 (on Deut 6:5–6).

13. For evidence, see John Gill, *A Body of Divinity* 4.6; Matthew Henry, *Exposition of the Old and New Testaments ad* Matt 22:34–40; Jonathan Edwards, *Charity and Its Fruits* I.2.ii; *Heidelberg Catechism* 3, 14–16 (questions 93–112); *Westminster Confession* § 21; John Calvin, *Inst.* 2.8.11; and Thomas Aquinas, *De decem parae.* 4 and 11 (the first three commandments concern love of God, the last seven love of neighbor).

14. Some critics reckon it unlikely that, if it really happened, Jesus and his disciples were, on the occasion of Mark 2:23–28, truly famished; see D. M. Cohn-Sherbok, "An Analysis of Jesus' Arguments Concerning the Plucking of Grain on the Sabbath," *JSNT* 2 (1978): 5. I do not share this skepticism. Not only does the text presuppose genuine need but, according to the synoptic instructions for missionaries, Jesus also sends out itinerants without food or money. In Matthew and Luke, Jesus exhorts followers not to keep worrying about what they are to eat or what they are to drink (Matt 6:25–34; Luke 12:22–32). Why should he do this unless the disciples are anxious about eating or drinking? Similarly, would the brevity of the Lord's Prayer permit a petition for daily bread if daily bread were never a problem? It is entirely plausible that, at times, Jesus and his disciples, who relied on the hospitality of others, went hungry.

stood plucking to be reaping, which the Old Testament was thought to prohibit on the Sabbath (Exod 34:21; Philo, *De vita Mosis* 2.22). How does Jesus respond? He does not say, as did some later Christians, that the Sabbath has been abolished. Nor does he say, as did some later heretics, that the true God did not institute the Sabbath. Jesus does not attack the Sabbath; instead, he appeals to David and the hunger of his men as described in 1 Samuel 21. Jesus seems to be saying that one imperative can trump another imperative, that human need can, in some cases, overrule Sabbath keeping, which (it is assumed) remains intact. We are not told how effective Jesus' audience took his riposte to be, whether or not they accepted the force of the analogy between Jesus' disciples plucking corn out of hunger on the Sabbath and David's hungry company breaking the *Torah* by eating the bread of the presence, which only the priests, by law, could eat. But Jewish law in its wisdom certainly knew that Sabbath observance might be the lesser of two goods. This principle allowed the Maccabeans to fight on the Sabbath, and it allowed the Mishnah to rule that a physician could attend a patient if that patient's life is in danger.[15]

What then of Mark 3:1–6? Here Jesus heals a man with only a few words: "Stretch out your hand." That some would have regarded this as work is implicit in what follows. The Mishnah certainly equates practicing medicine with work.[16] How then does Jesus address the issue? He again makes no general declaration encouraging Sabbath breaking. Rather, he appeals to compassion as an exception to the rule of Sabbath law: "Is it lawful to do good or to do harm on the sabbath, to save life or to kill?" (Mark 3:4). Many would have dissented, as do the Pharisees and Herodians in Mark 3. After all, the man with the lame hand is not near death. Surely Jesus could, one supposes, wait another day (cf. Luke 13:14)? As already stated, however, the idea that humanitarian concern can interfere with Sabbath observance was accepted in Judaism. Few, if any, would have disputed the principle, though maybe its applicability to the present case. Furthermore, Jesus does not glory in his shame and say, "Well, you're right after all; I guess I do want to obliterate the Sabbath." Instead, Jesus implies that what he does is ἔξεστιν (i.e., permitted and lawful). He does not assail Sabbath observance but cites a circumstance that, in his view, qualifies such observance.

---

15. See *m. Yoma* 8.6.
16. See *m. Sabb.* 14.3–4; cf. CD 11.10; *t. Sabb.* 12.8–14.

We have now looked, albeit briefly, at some of the relevant texts in Mark. We cannot spend as much time with Matthew, Luke, or John. Three observations must suffice. First, the Lord's Prayer may be linked to the Third Commandment: "You shall not make wrongful use of the Lord's name." In both its Matthean and Lukan versions, the first petition of the Lord's Prayer is "Hallowed be your name." Christian commentators through the ages have regularly read this as a general or vague call to honor God, as though it meant simply "May we honor you." In a first-century Jewish context, however, God's name had a specific meaning. God's name was YHWH, the Tetragrammaton, the sacred name that, according to later legend, was pronounced only once a year by the high priest in the Holy of Holies on the Day of Atonement. In Jesus' world, the hallowing of the divine name involved all sorts of superstitions. Some did not pronounce it. Some did not write it. Some used it in magical incantations. Although the Lord's Prayer does not spell out what hallowing the holy name should mean, this petition does put Jesus firmly on the side of those who conscientiously observed the Third Commandment.

Second, Matthew has Jesus explicitly affirm the validity of the *Torah*: "Do not think that I have come to abolish the law or the prophets; I have come not to abolish but to fulfill. For truly I tell you, until heaven and earth pass away, not one letter, not one stroke of a letter, will pass from the law until all is accomplished" (Matt 5:17–18). Indeed, Matthew's Jesus, in the idiom of the rabbis, builds a fence around part of the Decalogue. In the Sermon on the Mount, Jesus prohibits anger and lust (Matt 5:21–30), and, as Augustine observed, "The one who does not commit adultery in the heart much more easily guards against committing adultery in actual fact. So he who gave the later precept confirmed the earlier; for he came not to destroy the law, but to fulfil it."[17] The same holds true for anger and murder.

Third, Luke's Jesus makes a similar statement: "But it is easier for heaven and earth to pass away, than for one stroke of a letter in the law to be dropped" (16:17). This saying, which is clearly related to Matt 5:17–18, assumes the same sort of blameless, Law-observant Jesus as does the Sermon on the Mount.

So far we have seen one side of things: Jesus commending the Decalogue and, when accused of lawless behavior, repudiating the

---

17. Augustine, *De sermone domini in monte* 1.12.33.

accusation. This, however, is not the only portrait of Jesus' relationship to the Law that we find in the Synoptic Gospels. It is time to move beyond examining the conservative Jesus to look at the radical Jesus.

III. THE RADICAL JESUS

If Jesus accuses others of not honoring parents in Mark 7, the accusation seems to rebound against him in Mark 3. Here Jesus returns home, and his family (οἱ παρ' αὐτοῦ) comes to restrain him because it is going around that he is out of his mind (Mark 3:21). When Jesus learns that his mother and siblings are outside, he asks scornfully, "Who are my mother and my brothers?" (Mark 3:33). He answers himself: "Here are my mother and my brothers! Whoever does the will of God is my brother and sister and mother" (Mark 3:34b–35). This is hardly honoring one's mother. We are light-years from *b. Qidd.* 31b, according to which Rabbi Joseph, when he heard the footsteps of his mother, exclaimed, "I rise up before the Shekinah which is approaching."

Even more troublesome is the little call story in Matt 8:21–22, which is also found in Luke 9:59–60. A would-be disciple makes what appears to be a wholly reasonable request: "Lord, first let me go and bury my father." Jesus harshly responds: "Follow me, and let the dead bury their own dead." These disquieting words have long scandalized commentators, who have freely exercised their imaginations to revise their meaning. Maybe the Aramaic has been mistranslated. Maybe the Greek is corrupt. Maybe the man's father is sick and not yet dead, thus the inquirer will not be free to follow Jesus for days or even weeks. Or maybe the father is hale and hearty and his son is saying that he has to stay home to take care of his parents in their old age. But the offense cannot be erased so readily. Martin Hengel has remarked that "Let the dead bury their own dead" could easily be taken as "an attack on the respect for parents that is demanded in the fourth commandment."[18] E. P. Sanders concurs and renders this verdict: "At least once Jesus was willing to say that following him superseded the requirements of piety and of the

---

18. Martin Hengel, *The Charismatic Leader and His Followers* (New York: Crossroad, 1981), 8.

Torah. This may show that Jesus was prepared, if necessary, to challenge the adequacy of the Mosaic dispensation."[19]

Things become even more interesting in Luke 14:26: "[H]ate [your] father and mother." Commentators old and new have consistently wrestled with the tension between this verse and the famous commandment to "[H]onor your father and your mother" (Exod 20:12; Deut 5:16). Chrysostom asked:

> What then? Are not these things contrary to the Old Testament? . . . It is a sacred duty to render them [parents] all other honors; but when they demand more than is due, one ought not to obey . . . . [Jesus is] not commanding simply to hate them, since this were quite contrary to the law, but rather "When one desires to be loved more than I am, hate him in this respect."[20]

Ulrich Luz, in summarizing the history of the interpretation of our verse in its Matthean guise, remarks that, in ecclesiastical tradition, there is an order of those to be loved: God, father, mother, children. Luz states:

> [O]nly in cases of necessity should one transgress the commandment to love parents. As a matter of principle the first table of the Ten Commandments comes before the second, at the beginning of which stands the commandment to love parents. Only then, when parents hinder us from doing the will of God may the fourth commandment be rescinded.[21]

Given that this statement has, over the centuries, incessantly put commentators in mind of the Decalogue, one cannot help but wonder whether it was intended to do so; that is, that it was provocatively formulated in deliberate contrast to the commandment to honor father and mother. This would seem to be the case because not only does the content make the scripturally literate ponder the relationship to Exod 20:12 and Deut 5:16 but also the sentence's structure moves us to do this, as can be seen from the Greek texts:

---

19. E. P. Sanders, *Jesus and Judaism* (Philadelphia: Fortress, 1985), 255. See further Menahem Kister, " 'Leave the Dead to Bury Their Own Dead,' " in *Studies in Ancient Midrash* (ed. James L. Kugel; Cambridge: Harvard University Press, 2001), 43–56. Although Kister finds parallels to Matt 8:21–22 and Luke 9:59–60 in traditions about Abraham leaving his father, the tension with the Decalogue remains, especially in view of Jesus' challenging formulation.

20. Chrysostom, *Homiliae in Matthaeum* 35:3 (PG 57.406).

21. Ulrich Luz, *Das Evangelium nach Matthäus (Mt 8–17)* (Evangelisch-katholischer Kommentar zum Neuen Testament 1/2; Zürich: Benziger, 1990), 141.

Luke 14:26	μισεῖ τὸν πατέρα	ἑαυτοῦ καὶ τὴν μητέρα
LXX Exod 20:12	τίμα τὸν πατέρα	σου καὶ τὴν μητέρα
LXX Deut 5:16	τίμα τὸν πατέρα	σου καὶ τὴν μητέρα σου

Both lines consist of a verb + τὸν πατέρα + personal pronoun ending in σου + καὶ + τὴν μητέρα. This construction occurs in the Greek Bible in the Decalogue (LXX Exod 20:12; LXX Deut 5:16), in quotations of that line (Mark 7:10; 10:19; Luke 18:20), in Luke 14:26, and, to judge by my vain *TLG* search, nowhere else. So Luke 14:26 rewrites Exod 20:16 by substituting "hate" for "honor." What is one to make of this curious fact? Is it possible that the Jesus of Mark, who twice commends honoring parents, can also be the Jesus of Luke 14:26 who demands hatred of parents? Can Sanders be right when he interprets "Let the dead bury their own dead" as "a one-time only requirement"?[22] Was it only once that Jesus said or did anything that would make one wonder what he thought about the commandment to honor parents? What then of Luke 14:26?

We shall return to this question, but first I wish to return to the Sabbath. I argued above that Jesus' words about the Sabbath in Mark do not make him an antinomian. He did not come to abolish the Sabbath.[23] But this is not the whole story. In Mark 2:23–28, when grain is plucked on the Sabbath, Jesus does not deny that he is transgressing a divinely sanctioned custom. Instead, he appeals to David's precedent and argues that he is justified in temporarily disregarding such custom in these circumstances. In Luke 13:10–17, when the leader of the synagogue objects that healing on the Sabbath is doing work on the Sabbath, Jesus does not deny the equation. Instead, he appeals to his audience's experience: "Does not each of you on the sabbath untie his ox or his donkey [cf. Deut 5:14] from the manger, and lead it away to give it water? And ought not this woman, a daughter of Abraham whom Satan bound for eighteen long years, be set free from this bondage on the sabbath day?" (Luke 13:15–16).

In both of these episodes, Jesus puts one commandment before another. He is not rejecting a rule; he is acknowledging exceptions to a rule, even as his Pharisaic opponents do in Mark 7 when they put Corban before honoring parents. In other words, Jesus recognizes that two commandments may sometimes conflict with each

---

22. E. P. Sanders, *Jewish Law from Jesus to the Mishnah: Five Studies* (London: SCM, 1990), 4.

23. This is why some of Jesus' female followers attend to his tomb only after the Sabbath; they are still Sabbath observant.

other, in which case one must choose between them. This, in and of itself, implicitly concedes that the Law is not perfect, or at least not perfectly applicable. Moreover, one gets the sense from the Gospels, in their recording of several Sabbath conflicts, that Jesus liked to go out of his way to make this point. After all, he presumably could have waited to heal on a Monday or a Tuesday. But maybe we should not too quickly dismiss the possibility that sometimes Jesus was in one place for one day only, and if that happened to be a Sabbath, then that was his only time to heal the sick in that place.

One also senses the Law's inadequacy in Matt 5:21–26, 27–30, where Jesus passes from murder to anger and from adultery to lust. As already noted, the *Torah* is certainly not broken here. Indeed, the one who observes Jesus will necessarily observe Moses all the more. But when Jesus formulates his imperative as a contrast with Moses, he clearly is signaling that Moses does not suffice. God demands more than the *Torah* demands, which is why Jesus demands more than Moses.

Even this, however, is not as far-reaching as what we find in other places. Jesus prohibits divorce in Matt 5:31–32 (cf. 19:3–9; Mark 10:2–12; Luke 16:18), which Moses permits (Deut 24:1–4). Incidentally, the formulation in each instance identifies remarriage as the sin of adultery, thus the Decalogue is in place. Then there is Matt 5:33–37, which prohibits swearing (cf. Jas 5:12) and does so by paraphrasing Moses, who does not forbid it (cf. Exod 20:7; Lev 19:12; Num 30:3–15; Ps 50:14). To say that oaths are not needed seems a plain rejection of Scripture. Both the commandment not to make wrongful use of the name of the Lord and the commandment not to bear false witness assume the validity of taking oaths. Furthermore, God and the saints swear in the Bible. In Gen 14:22–23, Abraham declares: "I have sworn to the LORD, God Most High, maker of heaven and earth, that I would not take a thread or a sandal-thong or anything that is yours . . ." In Gen 22:16, the angel of the Lord appears to Abraham and says: "By myself I have sworn, says the LORD: Because you have done this, and have not withheld your son, your only son, I will indeed bless you . . ." (cf. Exod 6:8; Isa 45:23). One understands why Theophylact decided that, at the time of Moses, "it was not evil to swear. But after Christ, it is evil."[24]

---

24. Theophylact, *Comm. on Mt.* ad 5:33–37.

IV. RHETORIC AND CONFLICT

There is a paradox here. On the one hand, the Gospels portray a Law-observant Jesus. He teaches the Decalogue and upholds the *Torah* in its entirety. On the other hand, this same Jesus plays fast and lose with the commandment to honor one's parents, he finds multiple occasions on which to depart from Sabbath law, he uses a formula that starkly contrasts his own words with those of Moses, and he disallows oath-taking and divorce, which the Old Testament allows. What are we to think?

Complex problems do not have simple answers, and this is a complex problem. The easy way out would be to shove the traditions of one or both sorts into the post-Easter period and attribute them to early Christian communities. This option, however, is unavailable to me because I find, in looking over my own publications, that I have considered various "conservative" and "radical" traditions about the Law to be authentic Jesus tradition.[25] Therefore, I cannot equate the real Jesus with the conservative Jesus alone (though at one time I tried to do this) or with the radical Jesus alone. I also see no good reason to imagine that Jesus was once friendly to the *Torah* and later changed his mind or that, alternatively, he became friendlier to the *Torah* as time passed. How else can we do justice to the evidence?

One possibility is that we should think less about theology and more about rhetoric. Some of us are wont to think of ancient Jews, at least the pious ones, as though they were modern fundamentalists; therefore, they would never have sounded as revolutionary as Jesus sometimes does. But this perception is misperception. Some Jews not only felt free to rewrite Scripture—consider, for example, such Pseudepigrapha as *Jubilees* and the *Life of Adam and Eve*, both of which freely transform Genesis. Some were further able, in the words of Michael Fishbane, to use "authoritative Torah-teaching as a didactic foil."[26] Indeed, "the Jewish device of twisting Scripture, of subjecting the earlier canon to radical reinterpretation by means of subtle reformulations, is now recognized as central to the Bible as a whole."[27] When Job gripes, "What are human beings, that you

---

25. See, for example, W. D. Davies and Dale C. Allison Jr., *A Critical and Exegetical Commentary on the Gospel according to Saint Matthew*, 3 vols. (ICC; Edinburgh: T&T Clark, 1988–1997).

26. Michael Fishbane, "Torah and Tradition," in *Tradition and Theology in the Old Testament* (ed. Douglas A. Knight; Philadelphia: Fortress, 1977), 277.

27. David G. Roskies, *Against the Apocalypse: Responses to Catastrophe in Modern Jewish Culture* (Cambridge: Harvard University Press, 1984), 19.

make so much of them, that you set your mind on them . . . ?" (7:17), is he not recalling the famous Psalm 8—"What are human beings that you are mindful of them, mortals that you care for them?" (v. 4)—and thereby inverting and mocking a psalm? Or consider Joel 3:9–10 ("Prepare war . . . . Beat your plowshares into swords, and your pruning hooks into spears"), which prophesies war in the language of a famous prophecy of peace (Isa 2:4; Mic 4:3: "They shall beat their swords into plowshares, and their spears into pruning hooks . . . neither shall they learn war any more"). In a similar sense, Isa 40:28 declares that God needs no rest, while Isa 45:7 states that God creates darkness; both are about-faces from the primeval history.

Examples of reversing or subverting sacred tradition also appear outside the Bible. *Ascen. Isa.* 3:8–9 makes this observation: "Moses said, 'There is no one who can see the Lord and live.' But Isaiah has said, 'I have seen the Lord, and behold I am alive.' " According to Rabbi Jeremiah, in *b. B. Mes.* 59b, it is written in the *Torah*, "After the majority one must incline," whereas Exod 23:2 in fact states "After the majority you will not incline." The Targumim sometimes engage in what has been called "converse translation," making the Bible say the opposite of what it says. In *Targum Onqelos* on Gen 4:14, for example, Cain's remark that he will be hidden from God's face becomes "It is impossible to hide from before you." As an example from early Christian literature, recall Matt 2:6 in which οὐδαμῶς ("not at all") is inserted into its quotation of Mic 5:2 so despite Micah's remarks about Bethlehem's insignificance, Matthew denies such a perspective.

Returning to Jesus, I suggest, in light of the texts just reviewed and in light of a multitude of similar texts, that some of his radical utterances belong to a rhetorical tradition within Judaism. Religious Jews were quite capable of saying surprising things, of turning Scripture upside down and inside out, of unraveling sacred texts and reweaving the threads. They did this to startle, to drive home a point, and to find permanent lodging in memory. Is this not what Jesus is doing when he transforms the pious "Honor your father and your mother" into the provocative "Hate your father and mother" or when he puts his teaching into the form "You have heard that it was said to those of old . . . but I say to you?" This is not irresponsible lawlessness but loud and daring rhetoric. While "I say such and such" may be interesting, "I say such and such even though

Moses said something else" is arresting. If you are sleeping, it is going to wake you up.

There is more to Jesus, however, than rhetoric. Something more is going on in the Sabbath controversies and in the demand that a man not bury his father but let the dead bury their own dead. Jesus was, I submit, keenly interested in the problem of competing moral imperatives. We moderns often speak of choosing between the lesser of two evils. Do I bear false witness when it will save a life? Do I abet a murder by telling the would-be assassin that his intended victim is hiding in my closet? Unless I am Augustine or Kant, I choose the smaller sin and bear false witness. Lying is wrong, but I lie if it saves an innocent life. I prefer the lesser transgression.

So it is with Jesus. Jesus nowhere extols breaking the Sabbath, but he breaks it if doing so restores a human body to wholeness or feeds the hungry. Parents should be honored, as the Decalogue enjoins and as Jesus repeats in Mark 7 and 10, but if showing such honor hinders hearkening to the call to discipleship, then it must slide. Compassion prevails over the Sabbath; discipleship outweighs filial obligation.

I would like to emphasize that Judaism knew all too well that commandments can conflict with each other; therefore, to break the *Torah* was not to abolish it. The Hasidim did not abolish the Sabbath when they went to war on Saturday nor were their actions intended in any way to nullify the authority of the *Torah* or to lessen the sanctity of the Sabbath. Rather, they faced a moral dilemma: Do we sin by breaking the Sabbath or do we sin by letting the nation perish? They chose the lesser of two evils—breaking the Sabbath— to obtain the greater of two goods, the life of the nation. This was not lawlessness but the subordination of one imperative to another imperative. In a less anxious setting, the rabbis debated at leisure the tensions between the various commandments and which have priority of obedience over others. What do you do, for example, when your father implores you to do something that desecrates the Sabbath? Do you dishonor your father or do you dishonor the Sabbath?[28] Do you circumcise a male infant on the eighth day if that day is the Sabbath? Which commandment should you break?[29] Sometimes imperatives cannot be harmonized, and the rabbis knew this fact.

---

28. See *b. Yeb.* 5b.

29. See *m. Sabb.* 18:3; 19:1–3.

The discussions in the Mishnah and in the Talmud concern clashes that arise in the normal course of Jewish life and ritual. This is not the case in the Gospels. The rabbis discussed which of two competing commandments comes first when circumstances force a reluctant choice. But when Jesus compels people to choose between imperatives, it is because he has deliberately created a conflict that requires decision. As I see it, he heals on the Sabbath precisely to press the issue of compassion vs. observance. Similarly, he crafts the conditions of discipleship so they necessarily interfere with honoring parents. When he prohibits divorce, he compels hearers to choose between himself and Deuteronomy.

Why does Jesus create these conflicts? Why make problems for yourself and others? Why read the Bible in such a way that the primeval will of God revealed in Genesis 2–3 is not in accord with the later legislation in Deuteronomy 24?

IV. THE ESCHATOLOGICAL CONTEXT

I already have observed that Judaism knew about competing imperatives. I need now to add that it also knew about discrepant accounts of God's will. In contrast with Gen 1:29 ("I have given you every plant yielding seed that is upon the face of all the earth, and every tree with seed in its fruit; you shall have them for food"), Gen 9:3 grants permission for the post-Edenic world to eat meat. These texts reflect two different directives on food: one directive for Eden, one for after Eden. Similarly, Deuteronomy promulgates divine precepts for the king, yet other portions of Scripture regard kingship as God's reluctant concession to Israel's frailty.[30] Thus the *Torah* can be—and has been—viewed as containing divine concessions to, or compromises for, human sin and, therefore, as promoting less than the ideal human behavior.[31]

Old Jewish texts do not declare in any place that such concessions have come and gone, whereas this is what Jesus says. He does so, I submit, largely because of his eschatological worldview.[32] Jesus' treatment of the Law cannot be isolated from the coming of the kingdom of God. If the kingdom is at hand, then the renewal of the

---

30. Cf. Judg 8:22–23; 1 Sam 8:4–22.

31. David Daube, "Concessions to Sinfulness in Jewish Law," *JJS* 10 (1959): 1–13.

32. It makes no difference to this discussion how one understands Jesus' eschatology. One can follow Albert Schweitzer and think of a near end or concur with C. H. Dodd and his realized eschatology or applaud N. T. Wright and his metaphorical eschatology. What matters is that Jesus understood himself as the fulfillment of Jewish prophetic expectations.

world is nigh. Furthermore, if the renewal of the world is nigh, then paradise is about to be restored. Finally, if paradise is about to be restored, then concessions to sin should no longer be needed. This is certainly the implicit logic of Mark 10:1–12. As the *Epistle of Barnabas* 6:13 states: "The last things [will be] like the first." For Jesus, because the last things have come, then so have the first. Therefore, Jesus requires a prelapsarian ethic: "[F]rom the beginning it was not so" (Matt 19:8). Insofar as the Law contains concessions to the fall of man, it requires repair.

This illuminates Matt 5:33–37, where Jesus prohibits oaths. The presupposition of the oath is the lie because if everyone always told the truth, why would anybody need to take an oath? Oath-taking assumes that there are two types of statements: one that demands commitment (the oath) and one that need not (the statement without an oath). But in a sin-free world, a world like Eden or like paradise regained, human beings invariably would be committed to every statement. If they were so committed, then the superstition of the oath would be redundant. The saints will not be swearing in heaven, will they? The point is recognized in the earliest extra-canonical reference to Jesus' saying. Justin Martyr takes Jesus' prohibition of swearing to mean that we should "always [be] speaking the truth."[33] In short, Jesus' prohibition of swearing is akin to his prohibition of divorce. Both set forth a prelapsarian standard that mends a temporal limitation in the *Torah*.

That, for Jesus, the coming of the kingdom indeed impinges on the Law appears from a line that is usually attributed by scholars to the Sayings Source. Matthew 11:12–13 reads: "From the days of John the Baptist until now the kingdom of heaven has suffered violence, and the violent take it by force. For all the prophets and the law prophesied until John came." Luke 16:16 has this: "The law and the prophets were in effect until John came; since then the good news of the kingdom of God is proclaimed, and everyone tries to enter it by force." These two closely related lines clearly go back to an original that distinguished between the time of the law and the prophets and the time of the kingdom. This means that, in some sense, the time of the Law has been superceded. Things are not now as they always have been.

Consistent with this, Jesus can declare that no one born of a woman has arisen who is greater than John the Baptist (Matt 11:11; Luke 7:28). This is, to understate the matter, a remarkable state-

---

33. Justin, *Apologia i* 16:5.

ment, even an outrageous one. Can John really be greater than Abraham, who is judged by some Jews to have been perfect or pure from sin?[34] Can John be greater than the Lawgiver, who is called θεός in some sense by Philo (*De vita Mosis* 1.158; *De mutatione nominum* 129, etc.), who is nearly omniscient in rabbinic literature, and who sits on God's throne, holds the divine scepter, and numbers the stars in Ezekiel the Tragedian?[35] Second Temple Judaism defined itself in terms of the past, in terms of its great heroes, such as Moses and David, and in terms of stupendous miracles, such as the parting of the Red Sea and the giving of the Law on Sinai. In the Gospels, however, the new outshines the glorious past. The new wine cannot be put in old wineskins without bursting them (Mark 2:22). The center of gravity is moved from the past, where Moses was, to the present, where Jesus is. How can the Law remain unaffected?

Jesus may well have interpreted his teaching in light of the Jewish expectation that the Messiah or some other eschatological figure would bring eschatological instruction. Isaiah 42:1–4 says that the servant will bring *Torah*. This is a passage that Matthew, at least, thought fitting for Jesus because he cites it (see Matt 12:18–21). 4Q175 implies that the Qumran community expected an eschatological prophet like Moses, of whom God said: "I will put my words into his mouth and he shall tell them all that I command them" (Deut 18:15, 18). 11QMelch 2.15–21 prophesies the coming of "an anointed one, a prince" (cf. Dan 9:25) who will instruct those who mourn in Zion (cf. Isa 61:2–3). In *1 Enoch* 51.3, we see the Elect One, the Son of man, sitting on God's throne, and we are told that "from the conscience of his mouth shall come out all the secrets of wisdom" (cf. 46.3; 49.3–4). *Psalms of Solomon* 17.43 foretells that the Messiah's "words will be purer than the finest gold, the best. He will judge the peoples in the assemblies, the tribes of the sanctified. His words will be as the words of the holy ones, among sanctified peoples."

None of these passages, I concede, openly declares that the eschatological future will add to or change the *Torah*. There are, however, rabbinic texts that are much more explicit about future changes to the *Torah*. For example, these texts state that certain sac-

---

34. See *Jubilees* 23:10, *Prayer of Manasseh* 8, and *Testament of Abraham* (long recension) 10:13–4.

35. See Eusebius, *Praeparatio evangelica* 9.29.

rifices and festivals will cease,[36] that the laws covering things clean and unclean will be revised,[37] or even that there will be a new *Torah*.[38] Some later Jewish teachers certainly did entertain thoughts about eschatological alterations of the *Torah*. If they did so, maybe Jesus anticipated them. I believe that he did. Not only is Jesus an eschatological prophet who modifies the *Torah* (as when he disallows oath-taking and divorce), but Jesus also is particularly interested in the interiority of the *Torah*. In Joseph Klausner's words, Jesus overemphasizes this idea.[39] Jesus seeks to shift attention from murder to anger, from adultery to lust. He wants us to reflect on the light within, or the lack thereof (Matt 6:22–23; Luke 11:34–35), because what is inside defiles (Mark 7:15).

How does all this relate to eschatology? Jeremiah 31:31–34 famously prophesies the interiorization of the Law:

> "The days are surely coming, says the LORD, when I will make a new covenant with the house of Israel and the house of Judah. It will not be like the covenant that I made with their ancestors when I took them by the hand to bring them out of the land of Egypt—a covenant that they broke, though I was their husband, says the LORD. But this is the covenant that I will make with the house of Israel after those days, says the LORD: I will put my law within them, and I will write it on their hearts; and I will be their God, and they shall be my people.

According to Jeremiah, a new covenant will someday be established, and the *Torah* will then be engraved internally (cf. the related idea in Ezek 36:26–27). According to Jesus, the kingdom of God has come, and the Law must be effective even within one's heart. It should not surprise us that the author of Hebrews, as well as Justin Martyr, claimed the fulfillment of Jer 31:31–34 in what Jesus wrought[40] nor should we be surprised that the tradition of the Lord's Supper common to Luke and Paul alludes to Jeremiah's "new covenant" (Luke 22:20; 1 Cor 11:25).

So far I have urged that Jesus' attitude toward the Law should be correlated with his eschatological outlook. The coming of the kingdom explains the return to Edenic standards, the prohibitions of

---

36. *Yal.* on Prov 9:2; *Lev. Rab.* 9.7.

37. *Midr. Ps.* on Ps 146:7; *Lev. Rab.* 13.3.

38. *Lev. Rab.* 13.3; *Tg.* on Isa 12:3; *Tg.* on *Cant.* 5:10; *Midr. Qoh.* 2.1; *Yal.* on Isa 26:2.

39. Joseph Klausner, *Jesus of Nazareth: His Life, Times, and Teaching* (London: Macmillan, 1925), 393.

40. See Heb 8:8–12; 10:16–17; Justin, *Dialogus cum Tryphone* 11.3.

divorce and oath-taking, and the other imperatives so often reckoned to be impractical. Eschatology also clarifies Jesus' focus on intention, in explicit contrast with Moses, because the internalization of the *Torah* is an eschatological expectation of Jeremiah. But there is also a third way in which eschatology and *Torah* are linked. The kingdom of God, as the pearl and the hidden treasure illustrate, matters far more than anything else (Matt 13:44–46). To find it means to find everything, and to lose it means to lose everything. Because the kingdom matters more than anything else, the call to obtain it and to assist others in obtaining it must outweigh all other demands. This is why Jesus can hyperbolically demand hatred of parents and why he can call a man to neglect his father's burial: The prophet is here today and may not be here tomorrow; now may be the only chance to follow him. When obligation to parents might interfere with the missionary task or with conversion to the kingdom, then such obligation must lapse. Zebedee must be left in the boat. Eschatological demands get the better of filial responsibility.

The Talmud contains the following: "Come and hear: Him you will listen to (Deut 18:15), even if he tells you, 'Transgress any of all the commandments of the Torah' as in the case for instance of Elijah on Mount Carmel [in 1 Kings 18 Elijah sacrifices outside the temple], obey him in every respect in accordance with the needs of the hour."[41] In this startling passage, the Talmud teaches that, in a time of crisis, the messianic prophet, like Moses, may have to go against Moses by doing what the *Torah* does not want to be done. There can be no greater crisis than the coming of the kingdom, the arrival of the eschatological world. So the explicit logic of the Talmud is analogous to the implicit logic of Jesus. Whatever interferes with preparing for and hastening the new world must, even if it stands in opposition to the Decalogue, defer to the greater that has come.

V. CONCLUSION

We have covered a lot of ground. Unfortunately, we have had to run rapidly over most of it when it would have been safer to stroll leisurely and inspect everything along the way. But we have seen enough to learn that Jesus sometimes sounded like a radical and sometimes like a conservative. His eschatological convictions turned

---

41. *b. Yeb.* 90b.

him into an occasional liberal because the demands of the kingdom sometimes created tension with demands in the Pentateuch. But Jesus was also a conservative, a fact that needs no comment other than that he was a pious Jew, and how could a pious Jew not admire Moses? How could a Jew calling Jews to repentance, a Jew "for whom the ethical ideal was everything,"[42] not direct listeners to the *Torah*?

Finally, let me return to the beginning and again ask: What of the debates in the early church? Those who felt at home in the Law would not have been rebuked by Jesus because he exhorted his hearers to keep the commandments. On the several occasions when he broke the *Torah*, he did so without abolishing it. Instead, it was a question of deciding between two legitimate imperatives, not between a good commandment and a bad commandment. Furthermore, in the few instances in which eschatology requires revision of the *Torah*, the one who obeys Jesus will not disobey Moses. What law do you break if you do not divorce your wife or refuse to take an oath? These things are not commanded anywhere. So Jesus is no antinomian. In fact, he demands more, not less.

At the same time, those Christians who promoted a Law-free mission may have looked to Jesus' teaching for legitimacy. They would have learned that Jesus was an imaginative interpreter of the *Torah*, that he on occasion relaxed this or that commandment, that he replaced a couple Mosaic imperatives with Edenic imperatives, and that his demands exceeded the *Torah*, thereby implying that Moses is not enough. All this is, admittedly, a long way from the Law-free Gentile gospel, which the Gospels do not directly address. Yet we may believe that the traditions underlining the limitations of *Torah* and the memory of Jesus' liberalism with *Torah* played some role in the church's own liberalism with *Torah*. This means that Jesus' subordination of the Law to eschatology may have been one factor in the church's eventual recognition that the Gentile followers of God need not live like *Torah*-observant Jews.

---

42. Klausner, *Jesus of Nazareth*, 389.

Luke, Jesus, and the Law

Peter J. Scaer

The evangelist Luke can hardly be accused of encouraging moral laxity. With the coming of Christ, new and greater demands are made of God's people. Followers of Christ are called to bear crosses (Luke 9:23; 14:27).[1] Disciples are urged to sell their possessions and leave everything for the sake of the kingdom (Luke 5:11, 28; 18:22, 28). They must be willing to put aside family obligations (Luke 18:29; 9:59–62), even to the point of hating their own family members (Luke 14:26–27). The rich are summoned to invite the blind, the lame, and the poor to their dinner parties and to lend money to those unable to pay them back (Luke 6:34–35; 14:12–14), thereby mounting a frontal assault on the Greco-Roman social order.[2] Divorce is strictly forbidden (Luke 16:18). Such radical dominical demands make the burden of the Mosaic Law appear light by comparison.[3] No wonder Luke thought that Christianity would turn the world upside down (Acts 17:6).

In his presentation of the Mosaic Law, however, Luke appears remarkably traditional. Unlike Paul, Luke launches no direct critique of the Old Testament Law (cf. Rom 5:20). Unlike Matthew, Luke does not portray Jesus as a new Moses standing high on the Mount, offering a better and higher Law (cf. Matthew 5–7). Nor does Luke directly challenge the Jewish Law, at least in his Gospel,

---

1. Unless otherwise indicated, all Scripture quotations in this essay are taken from the NIV.

2. See Jerome Neyrey, "Ceremonies in Luke-Acts," in *The Social World of Luke-Acts* (Peabody, Mass.: Hendrickson, 1991), esp. 385–86. See also David A. deSilva, *Honor, Patronage, Kinship and Purity: Unlocking New Testament Culture* (Downers Grove: Inter-Varsity, 2000), 95–119.

3. Interestingly, Luke does not record the words of Jesus found in Matt 11:30: "For my yoke is easy and my burden is light."

in the manner of Mark (cf. Mark 7:15). From the beginning of his Gospel to the end of Acts, Luke depicts God's people as pious and Law-observant. Luke's consistent praise for a distinctly Jewish piety has led Jacob Jervell to the conclusion that, in reference to the Law, "Luke has the most conservative outlook within the New Testament."[4]

I will argue, however, that Luke's position *vis á vis* the Law is not as conservative as it first appears. He narrates a change that is both theologically adept and strategically diplomatic. Within Luke-Acts the ceremonial law begins to lose its binding force. More specifically, the nature of *Torah* observance changes from divine mandate to pious custom. With the advent of Christ, the Law retains a place of honor, but it becomes merely one vehicle by which God's people can demonstrate their allegiance to the one true God. To borrow a phrase from Eric Franklin, the Law, for Luke "is not belittled, but it is downgraded."[5] The Mosaic Law has become part of the past: happily observed by some but not entirely necessary for the future.

Let us begin with a little bookkeeping. The word νόμος appears nine times in Luke's Gospel and seventeen times in Acts. Luke can speak of "the Law of the Lord" (Luke 2:23), "the Law of Moses" (Luke 2:22), "the custom of the Law" (Luke 2:27), "the [L]aw of our fathers" (Acts 22:3), or, simply, "the Law" (Acts 16:17).[6] Frequently the name "Moses" is used as its synonym (Luke 5:14; 16:29, 31; 24:27). In many of these cases the Law is prescriptive, informing and mandating certain actions (see Luke 1:6, 28, 64; 2:4, 25, 36, 41).[7] Because the Law involves performing certain customary duties, it serves also as an identity marker by which God's people are set apart and known. As such, the Law does not simply govern, it *defines* a distinct people with a distinct way of life. Sacrifices, rituals, and feasts shape the culture of God's people. Furthermore, the Law can also have a predictive, Christological sense, especially when the word is coupled with "the prophets." We think of the watershed moment on the road to Emmaus when Jesus reveals himself to the two disciples and explains to them that everything "in the Law of

---

4. See Jacob Jervell, "The Law in Luke-Acts," in *Luke and the People of God* (Minneapolis: Augsburg, 1972), 141.

5. Eric Franklin, *Luke: Interpreter of Paul, Critic of Matthew* (JSNTSup 92; Sheffield: JSOT Press, 1994), 199.

6. For a more thorough summary of Luke's use of the word νόμος, see S. G. Wilson, *Luke and the Law* (SNTSMS 50; Cambridge: Cambridge University Press, 1983), 1–11.

7. For a discussion of the normative use of the Law in Luke, see Joseph Fitzmyer, *Luke the Theologian: Aspects of His Teaching* (New York: Paulist, 1989), 176–81.

Moses and the Prophets" in fact pointed toward him (Luke 24:27, 44). Likewise, the conclusion of the Book of Acts presents Paul drawing on the Mosaic Law and the Prophets to preach Christ crucified and risen to those in Rome (28:23). In this sense, the Law of Moses is, for Luke, pure Gospel.

I. MOSAIC LAW AND THE INFANCY NARRATIVE

We are still left to ask how the Jewish ceremonial laws functioned in the life of Jesus and that of his followers. In what sense was the ceremonial law normative for Jesus, and in what sense did it remain so for the early church?

It is noteworthy that within Luke's Gospel the word νόμος occurs most frequently in the infancy narrative (Luke 1–2). As William Loader observes, "The Lukan infancy narratives of John and Jesus are strong in Jewish coloring."[8] The word *coloring* is well chosen because it captures the artistic essence of the infancy narrative. Luke paints for us a picture of Jewish piety at its best. All the main characters within the first two chapters appear righteous and *Torah* observant. Concerning Jesus' immediate family, Luke informs us that Mary and Joseph brought Jesus to the temple "according to the Law of Moses" (Luke 2:22), where they presented Jesus "as it is written in the Law of the Lord" (Luke 2:23). Again, Mary and Joseph sacrificed "in keeping with what is said in the Law of the Lord" (Luke 2:24). Yet again, Luke tells us that they "brought in the child Jesus to do for him what the custom of the Law required" (Luke 2:27). Finally, we are told that the holy family left Jerusalem only after they had "done everything required by the Law of the Lord" (Luke 2:39).

Now, we may interpret these passages as Christ's active obedience, whereby, even as a child, he fulfills all the duties of the Law.[9] Or we might see in Jesus' circumcision his first shedding of blood for the sin of the world. Surely, we are meant to marvel as the infant Lord enters his Father's house (cf. Mal 3:1). I would contend, however, that Luke's repeated mention of the Law tells us even more about the essential goodness and honor of Christ's Jewish heritage. Borrowing from the Old Testament palette of colors in his portrait of history, Luke paints an idyllic picture of Jesus' earthly family.

---

8. William R. G. Loader, *Jesus' Attitude towards the Law* (WUNT II.97; Tübingen: Mohr Siebeck, 1997), 300.

9. For a helpful description of how the infant Jesus fulfills the Old Testament Law, see Arthur A. Just Jr., *Luke 1:1–9:50* (St. Louis: Concordia, 1996), 117–19.

The holy family, nevertheless, is not the *only* holy family in the infancy narratives. John's parents, for example, are portrayed as "upright in the sight of God, observing all the Lord's commandments and regulations blamelessly" (Luke 1:6). We meet Zechariah as he performs his priestly duties in the temple (Luke 1:5–23). Although he initially doubts the angel Gabriel's message, he soon becomes an Old Testament prophet (Luke 1:67–79). Elizabeth, introduced as a member of the priestly family of Aaron, likewise appears as the consummate Old Testament mother, a "Sarah" who gives birth in old age (Luke 1:25). As he waits for "the consolation of Israel," Simeon is portrayed as "righteous and devout" (Luke 2:25). Anna, an 84-year-old widow, likewise is pictured as a temple-dwelling prophetess who worships night and day, fasting and praying (Luke 2:36–38). Each of these characters represents a recognizable Old Testament type whose piety is formed and informed by the Mosaic Law.

It should also be noted that the language of the infancy narrative, littered as it is with Semitisms, is decidedly Septuagintal.[10] After opening his Gospel with an elegant literary preface (Luke 1:1–4), Luke shifts into a stylized, archaic writing style meant to jar the reader. That is to say, Luke writes in an Old Testament Greek style to capture the texture and feel of Old Testament life.[11] Through a type of literary time machine, Luke transports his reader from the modern-day Greco-Roman world back into the world of Old Testament Jerusalem. "Once upon a time" might serve as a dynamic equivalent of "And it came to pass in those days." Luke's literary style leads us to conclude that Jesus' family tree is Jewish down to its roots. Furthermore, the archaizing style may also lead us to wonder whether Jesus was born into an older world that no longer exists, a world that he himself had transformed and turned upside down.

By filling the infancy narrative with winsome, pious characters painted in Old Testament colors, Luke creates an impressionist portrait of Old Testament life, a picture that is, ironically, rarely to be found within the Old Testament itself. Contrast Luke with Matthew, whose genealogy exposes the sins of the past and high-

---

10. For a discussion of the language of Luke 1–2, see Gregory Sterling, *Historiography and Self-Definition: Josephus, Luke-Acts, and Apologetic Historiography* (NovTSup 64; Leiden: Brill, 1992), 352–63.

11. This was common literary practice. Lucian, for example, spoke of the need for historians to make the language suitable to their material; see *Quomodo Historia Conscribenda sit*, 45.

lights the inability of Jewish heroes to keep the Law.[12] Imagine that Paul had written the third Gospel. Simeon, Mary, and Anna would surely have declared themselves to be wretched sinners, unable to fulfill the Law's demands. By contrast, the subjects in Luke's painting are happy to serve the Lord, and they do it blamelessly (Luke 1:6). Luke describes Jewish piety as a way of life that is beautiful, yet a way of life that has become part of the past. What is happening, I propose, is that Luke has come to see the ceremonial law less as a universally binding force and more as a series of customs; he sees it as noble and ancient customs, but customs nevertheless.

II. *ETHOS, ETHNOS,* AND THE LAW

In a number of places, Luke actually uses the words νόμος ("Law") and ἔθος ("custom") interchangeably.[13] In this Luke is unique among New Testament writers. For example, within the infancy narrative itself, we are told that Zechariah was chosen to serve in the temple "according to the custom of the priesthood" (Luke 1:9). Again, when Jesus was 12 years old, we are told that he and his parents went to Jerusalem "according to the custom" (Luke 2:42). The word ἔθος comes to be associated with Moses, especially in Acts. In Acts, Luke frequently refers to "the customs which Moses delivered to us" (Acts 6:14; 15:1; 21:21; 28:17). The word ἔθος is a term of the ethnographer, the type of word one might use to describe the particular religious customs of an ethnic group. As such, Luke would have written good copy for *National Geographic.* Josephus and Philo, Luke's near contemporaries in the Hellenistic-Jewish world, both speak of the Law in this same way. Philo, for example, makes it clear that every nation has its own customs and that these customs are at times noble and at other times superstitious.[14] The Jews, Philo contends, have their own customs, such as Sabbath observance and circumcision, which compare favorably to those of other nations.[15] By labeling the Sabbath and circumcision as "customs," Philo does not deny that they have the force of Law for the Jews. The word, however, describes the way people live. Religious custom equals Law minus divine mandate. Likewise, Josephus can speak of the attendance at annual festivals, Sabbath observance, circumcisions,

---

12. See, for example, Matt 1:6 in which the reader is reminded of David's infidelity.

13. For a fine discussion of Luke's use of ἔθος, see Wilson, *Luke and the Law,* esp. 4–11.

14. Philo, *De somniis* 2.56; *De specialibus legibus* 3.13. See also Wilson, *Luke and the Law,* 5–7.

15. See, for example, Philo, *De specialibus legibus* 1.3; 2.148.

and the like as Jewish "customs."[16] As did Philo, Josephus uses the word *custom* especially when comparing Jewish Law with the practices of other religions. The term is being used apologetically, as S. G. Wilson explains: "He uses it to locate the religious observances of Judaism within the broader context of national customs and at the same time to appeal for tolerance."[17]

How is it that Luke has come to label the ceremonial law of Moses as a type of custom? Perhaps it has to do with Luke's own apologetic interest. He was keen to paint a favorable portrait of Christianity. To God-fearers, Luke was intent on demonstrating that Christianity, through Judaism, had a long and revered tradition; it had, in essence, roots and antiquity. Luke demonstrates that Christianity has much continuity with Judaism and that the customs of the Jews should be respected. At the same time, Luke would have his Gentile readers know that the observance of ceremonial aspects of the Law is not necessary. Thus within the infancy narrative Luke is less concerned with furthering the reader's understanding concerning the place of the Law in the Christian life than he is with portraying the Jewish faith as a pious and honorable way of life. As such the Jewish people and their customs provide noble stock from which the Savior would arise.

III. SALVATION HISTORY:
THE LAW IN THE PERIOD OF JESUS

Luke, we should note, was not only an artist but also a theologian. His understanding of the Law is intertwined with his vision of salvation history. Hans Conzelmann is known for his proposal that Lukan salvation history can be divided into three periods: (1) the Period of Israel, (2) the Period of Jesus, and (3) the Period of the Church.[18] Such a labeling of history is problematic for those of us who see every age as the age of Christ. This division, however, has merit. Jesus himself asserts that he is ushering in a new age in which people drink new wine (Luke 5:39) under a new covenant (Luke 22:20). This new age is consummated at Pentecost, when the apostles' Spirit-filled prophecy makes some think they have had too much wine (Acts 2:13).

---

16. See Josephus, *Jewish War* 1.26; *Jewish Antiquities* 12.324; 1.214.
17. Wilson, *Luke and the Law*, 9.
18. Hans Conzelmann, *The Theology of St. Luke* (trans. Geoffrey Buswell; New York: Harper & Row, 1960).

In the first period, the Period of Israel, the Law was binding and normative. Rather than being assessed critically, the Law is taken for granted, a theological "given." Rituals involving purification, circumcision, and the like constituted the God-given way of life. Law served as both custom and divine mandate. This is the age that Luke depicts within the infancy narrative. In Christ's ministry, a transition begins to occur, and the Law finds its fulfillment in his very person. Throughout his earthly ministry, Jesus lives as a Law-observant Jew. Jesus challenges the Law, even appears to bend the Law, but he never breaks it. At the same time he prepares the church for a time when the Old Testament ceremonial law will no longer hold sway. Through his teaching, Jesus begins to offer theological reasons for the end of the Law, all the while recognizing that he must first fulfill the Law perfectly before he sets it aside.

Consider the question of the Sabbath. Luke would have us know that Jesus was, in fact, a Law-observant Jew. Thus we are told that when he went to Nazareth, he went to the synagogue, "as was his custom" (Luke 4:16; also 4:31; 13:10). Yet the Sabbath issue is also one in which Jesus is challenged and in which he issues his own challenge (Luke 6:1–5; 13:10–17; 14:1–6). In Luke 6:1–5, some of the Pharisees accuse Jesus' disciples of breaking the Sabbath command by picking grain. Did Jesus' disciples, and by association Jesus, break the Law? According to Deut 23:25, plucking grain from a neighbor's field is, in fact, permitted.[19] Moreover, while plowing was prohibited, plucking was not (Exod 34:21). Technically, Jesus' disciples are innocent, and so is he. Jesus, however, does not argue on technical grounds.

To the Pharisees' challenge Jesus offers a threefold riposte. First, he appeals to precedence. Had not the great King David eaten priestly bread (Luke 6:3)? Perhaps here there is a claim to Messiahship. Second, Jesus appeals to the idea that mercy must take precedence over rules and regulations. David took the priestly bread to feed hungry companions. In this the Law is made for man, not man for the Law. Third, and most important, Jesus claims to be the Lord of the Sabbath and therefore not subject to its requirements (Luke 6:5). As such the Law becomes somehow less relevant, subservient to the one who first gave it. Thus Jesus wins the argument and theologically paves the way for the abrogation of the Sabbath law by means of teaching. As time goes on, Jesus takes the offensive, tweaking his opponents by healing on the Sabbath not only for the

---

19. See Fitzmyer, *Luke the Theologian*, 184–85.

sake of the one who is ill but also as a teaching device (see the healing of the man with dropsy in Luke 14:1–6). Before putting the
ceremonial law to the side, Jesus must first fulfill it. His final fulfillment of the Sabbath-day law comes by his own Sabbath-day rest in
the tomb.[20] With the death and resurrection of Jesus, everything is
in place for the Period of the Church, during which the Sabbath
changes from law to custom. But until all is fulfilled, Jesus remains
Law-observant.

Consider also Jesus' approach to the Old Testament Law concerning purity. As we have seen in the infancy narrative, Jesus was
born into a family in which the purity laws were piously observed
(Luke 2:22). Throughout his ministry, Jesus remains kosher and
urges others to do the same. Consider the man with leprosy in Luke
5:12–16. The leper cries out to Jesus, "Lord, if you are willing, you
can make me clean" (Luke 5:12). Having expressed his willingness,
Jesus declares, "Be clean!" (Luke 5:13). That is not, however, the
end of the story. After cleansing the leper, Jesus commands him to
show himself to the priests according to the Levitical mandate,
adding: "[O]ffer the sacrifices that Moses commanded for your
cleansing, as a testimony to them" (Luke 5:14; see Lev 13:2–3;
14:2–32).

Once again Jesus remains Law-observant and encourages others
to do likewise, but he also paves the way for a new age, one in which
Levitical purity will be superceded. By sending the lepers to the
temple, Jesus sends a message: He is the one who makes men clean.
By cleansing the lepers, by healing those with hemorrhages, and by
his practice of inclusion, Jesus lays the theological foundation for
setting aside the purity laws. Finally, by his death as the spotless
lamb, Jesus tears open the temple's veil, thereby purifying all peoples, places, and things. God is impartial (Acts 15:9) because all
people are called to be holy. Christ's presence, not geography,
makes space sacred. All has been redeemed and sanctified.

Finally, consider briefly the Passover. Jesus celebrated the
Passover regularly, according to the custom of the Law (Luke
2:41–42; 22:8). Yet through his new covenant, he assumes the place
of the Passover lamb (Luke 22:7), thus fulfilling and completing
the Law within himself. Soon the Passover is replaced with a new
and better meal. As Arthur Just puts it, Jesus "followed the OT
Law and often commanded others to do the same (e.g., 5:14; 17:14).

---

20. See Just, *Luke 1:1–9:50*, esp. 957–60.

However, Jesus also began to lay aside the OT Law after completing it (e.g. 6:1–11; 13:10–17; 14:1–6)."[21]

Luke addresses the topic of the place of the Law most directly, if
not most clearly, in chapter 16. Here Luke offers us a picture of salvation history:

> The Law and the Prophets [were] until John. Since that time,
> the good news of the kingdom of God is being preached, and
> everyone is forcing his way into it. It is easier for heaven and
> earth to disappear than for the least stroke of a pen to drop out
> of the Law. Anyone who divorces his wife and marries another
> woman commits adultery, and the man who marries a divorced
> woman commits adultery. (Luke 16:16–18)

Fitzmyer and others have interpreted this to mean that, with the
coming of the kingdom, "the Law remains valid."[22] Admittedly, the
passage is enigmatic. Luke appears to relegate the Law to the past:
"The Law and the Prophets [were] until John" (Luke 16:16). Yet
Jesus seemingly reasserts its permanence: "It is easier for heaven and
earth to disappear than for the least stroke of a pen to drop out of
the Law" (Luke 16:17). By comparing the end of the Law to the
passing away of heaven and earth, does Jesus claim that the Law will
remain in effect forever? Perhaps we find a parallel in Luke's statement concerning the possibility of a rich man entering heaven:
"Indeed, it is easier for a camel to go through the eye of a needle
than for a rich man to enter the kingdom of God" (Luke 18:25). Yet
rich men do enter heaven because with God all things are possible
(Luke 18:27). Likewise, the Law is not easily fulfilled. Through the
cross, however, Jesus accomplishes what had appeared to be impossible. And with the life and death of Jesus, the Law is fulfilled.

Does such a reading make Jesus an antinomian? By no means.
After he announced the dawning of a new age, Jesus reasserts the
law against divorce, only this time he closes the Mosaic loopholes
(Luke 16:18). The Mosaic Law, even in its moral application, gives
way to the moral law on which the Mosaic Law is based. The Decalogue should be seen as a summary of the moral law, perhaps the
best summary, yet it is not the final word. Because Christ indeed
inaugurates a time of salvation, it is incumbent on Christians to act
accordingly. Luke testifies to ethics that recognize the arrival of the
kingdom. Family obligations are clearly understood in the com-

---

21. Just, *Luke 1:1–9:50*, 377.
22. Fitzmyer, *Luke the Theologian*, 180.

mandment to honor one's parents. When a would-be follower expresses his wish to bury his father before joining the Lord, however, he is admonished to "let the dead bury their own dead" (Luke 9:60). The Lord tells others that discipleship involves the hating of one's own family, that it means to count nothing in comparison with him (Luke 14:26; 18:28). Again, the *Torah* informs us that we should not steal. Jesus, the radical kingdom preacher, encourages would-be disciples to go further: to give up everything they own for the sake of the kingdom (Luke 19:22). As the kingdom of God arrives, the moral law remains intact; however, it is not completely contiguous with the Mosaic Law. The ceremonial concerns are laid aside and often the moral bar is raised.

IV. SALVATION HISTORY:
THE LAW IN THE PERIOD OF THE CHURCH

Given Jesus' teaching and his fulfillment of the Law, we might have expected that the early Christians would quickly put aside the Mosaic Law, especially in its ceremonial aspects. No less a leader than Peter calls the Law "a yoke that neither we nor our fathers have been able to bear" (Acts 15:10). The early Christians, however, remain largely *Torah* observant. Christ's disciples continue to make the temple central to their piety (e.g., Acts 3:1) and to observe the Jewish hours of prayer (Acts 2:46; 3:1; 5:42). They continue to practice circumcision (Acts 16:3) and regularly attend synagogue on the Sabbath (e.g., Acts 17:2). Jewish converts in Jerusalem are explicitly praised by James as being "zealous for the law" (Acts 21:20). Even the Gentiles are called on to keep parts of the Law, abstaining from "the meat of strangled animals and from blood" (Acts 15:20; cf. Lev 17:10–12). The "*Torah*-faithfulness" of Jewish Christians in the Book of Acts has led William Loader to assert that even in the early church "the Law remains in force."[23] Joseph Fitzmyer concurs: "As for the Period of the Church the normative character of the law of Moses is further recognized."[24]

I would agree that the ceremonial law continues to play a significant role in the Book of Acts, but it begins to take on the character of pious religious custom. Circumcision, Sabbath observance, attendance at the temple, the keeping of purity laws, and the like remain

---

23. Loader, *Jesus' Attitude towards the Law*, 378.
24. Fitzmyer, *Luke the Theologian*, 185. Similarly, Jervell writes: "For Luke it is impossible that the law should be abrogated, replaced, or conceived as an epoch" (*Luke and the People of God*, 145).

viable means to express Christian piety. They are, however, no longer the *only* means nor are they *necessary* means. Decisions on keeping the Law begin to have more to do with tradition, diplomacy, and strategy.

Early Christian beliefs and observance of the Law change slowly, if at all. Why? First, the Law served as an identity marker. Think, for example, of Peter's vision in which he is commanded to eat nonkosher food. Peter replies, "Surely not, Lord! . . . I have never eaten anything impure or unclean" (Acts 10:14). Peter's response is that of one who has been startled. Surely, he had sinned. In fact, he had denied his Lord three times. Never, though, had he eaten anything unclean. To do so would amount to a radical change in life or at least in lifestyle. It would shake the foundations of who Peter was or whom he thought himself to be. Peter's experience may be analogous, on a smaller scale, to the Philippine missionary who, for the first time, is served dog for dinner. It may not be forbidden, but it is simply not done. Such social taboos govern our self-identity and have a stronger hold on us than even the moral law. Not surprisingly, at the Council of Jerusalem, food laws remained in place for the Jews. Furthermore, Gentiles were called on to abstain from blood and the meat of strangled animals.[25]

The second reason for the ceremonial law's persistence is this: Although it was no longer considered necessary for salvation, ceremonial law remained a strong and often beneficial ἔθος. Custom may not carry the weight of divine mandate, but it is important. Through custom, Christians learn to worship in specific ways that link them to the past and unite them as a people. Through various customs, Jewish Christians expressed themselves in praise to God. Consider the practice of keeping the Sabbath. The Sabbath day may no longer have the force of Law, but who would deny that, practiced as a custom, it provides certain benefits? The Sabbath allows time for prayer, worship, and rest. Thus we should not be surprised that when the Jews of Jerusalem came to believe in Christ, they honored God in the way they knew: They became "zealous for the law" (Acts 21:20). Nevertheless, given Jesus' own claim to be Lord of the Sabbath and the impact of Jesus' resurrection, neither should we be surprised that Sunday, the day of the Lord, would

---

25. Jervell, Loader, and others interpret Peter's vision to have a purely symbolic meaning, namely, that the Gentiles are not to be considered unclean; see Jervell, *Luke and the People of God*, 149, and Loader, *Jesus' Attitude towards the Law*, 370. Such a view, however, does not take into account the totality of Jesus' work of purification: Peoples, times, places, and foods have all been sanctified by Christ's work.

eventually trump the Sabbath tradition. It fit the theology of the age of the church, in which Christ had completed his creation on the eighth day, and it also served as a new identity marker by which Christians would define themselves. Thus the day of the Lord gradually replaced the Sabbath without duplicating it. But this took time.

Things change slowly for a third reason: The church has to engage in theological dialogue through which it considers the ramifications of Christ's life, death, and resurrection. Theology does not happen overnight. For the Council of Jerusalem to issue its decree, a number of things had to happen. The missionary activity of Paul turned the question of circumcision into a practical issue that urgently needed an answer. Peter's own experiences offered a needed apostolic sanction. Finally, the presence of James, the bishop of Jewish Christendom, provided the necessary imprimatur from the Jerusalem church.

There is, surely, a fourth reason why Christians remained Law observant throughout the Book of Acts: for the sake of unity. As the Christian message was received by the Gentiles, two things happened. The Jerusalem church had to concede that such things as circumcision were no longer necessary for salvation (Acts 15:1) or for citizenship in God's kingdom, and a little diplomacy had to be exercised. Those promoting the Gentile mission had to demonstrate a certain sensitivity toward God's covenant people and their long-held, divinely given customs. Otherwise, the Jerusalem church, offended by Paul's missionary work, might have rejected him.[26] Another possible negative outcome could have been that the Gentile church might have gone off on its own, abandoning its Jewish roots and turning into the type of church that would make Marcion proud.

V. PAUL AND THE LAW

Nowhere is Luke's stance toward the Law in the church more nuanced and interesting than in his presentation of Paul. In fact, the Lukan Paul appears so different from the Paul of the Epistles that many scholars have concluded that Luke either misrepresented or misunderstood Paul, or perhaps that he did not know Paul at all.[27]

---

26. Here Jervell is correct when he sees Luke's picture of Paul as a defense for his Gentile ministry; see *Luke and the People of God*, 185–207.

27. See P. Vielhauer, "On the 'Paulinismus' of Acts," in *Studies in the Book of Acts* (ed. L. E. Keck and J. L. Martyn; Philadelphia: Fortress, 1980 [1966]), 33–55.

In his Epistle to the Galatians, Paul asserts: "All who rely on observing the law are under a curse" (Gal 3:10). To the church at Rome Paul boldly claims that the Law, rather than diminishing sin, actually causes sin to increase (Rom 5:20). Perhaps because of such teaching, a report went out that Paul was teaching the Jews "to turn away from Moses, telling them not to circumcise their children or live according to [their] customs" (Acts 21:21). In response to such charges, Luke was keen to demonstrate that Paul was not an antinomian and that though his teaching appeared radical it had the sanction of the Jerusalem church.

Consider, then, how Luke portrays Paul's attitude toward the Law. Luke would have us know that Paul customarily attends synagogue, where he preaches on the Sabbath (Acts 14:1; 17:2; 17:10; 17:17; 18:4; 18:19). He honors Jerusalem, even as he is received warmly by the leaders in Jerusalem (21:17). In fact, Paul still practices circumcision. After the Jerusalem council, at which it was decided that circumcision was not necessary, Paul had Timothy circumcised. Paul even cuts off his hair as part of a Nazarite vow (Acts 18:18).[28] Further, Paul undergoes purification rites and pays the expenses for four men so they also might be purified (Acts 21:23–24). Paul further claims to be thoroughly trained in the ancestral law (Acts 22:3). Before Governor Felix, Paul proclaims to believe "everything that agrees with the Law" (Acts 24:14). Paul speaks of purifying himself before entering the temple (Acts 24:18). Before Festus, Paul proudly claims, "I have done nothing wrong against the law of the Jews or against the temple or against Caesar" (Acts 25:8). In fact, Paul appears the consummate Jew and a faithful adherent of *Torah*. Thus in many respects nothing had changed. Even Paul, the great apostle to the Gentiles, remains a pious Jew.

Things, however, had indeed changed. Paul's Law observance is not like that of Mary and Joseph in the infancy narrative. Paul adheres to the Law for different reasons: the first, apologetic, and the second, diplomatic. Admittedly, these reasons overlap.

Many of Paul's claims to be *Torah*-observant come during trials at which he is accused of being a "ringleader of the Nazarene sect," a "troublemaker," one who "[stirs] up riots among the Jews," and

---

28. Samson and John the Baptist are the best known of those who have taken such a vow. For them it was a lifelong commitment; however, one could take the vow temporarily, as did Paul. For the duration of the vow, one was prohibited from cutting one's hair or from taking strong drink. At the end of the vow, one made a sacrifice to God. For further discussion, see John B. Polhill, *Acts* (New American Commentary 26; Nashville: Broadman, 1992), 390.

one who "tried to desecrate the temple" (Acts 24:5–6). Thus before Felix, Paul defends himself by saying that he was "ceremonially clean" when he entered the temple (Acts 24:18). And when faced with the same charges before Festus, Paul claims, "I have done nothing wrong against the law of the Jews or against the temple or against Caesar" (Acts 25:8). Was Paul telling the truth or was he merely saying what needed to be said to secure his release? There are two answers to the question. On one level, Luke would have us know that Paul indeed remained a faithful Jew and followed the customs of purification and the like. Paul's teaching was meant to be provocative, not offensive. As such, much of the Book of Acts is an apology for Paul's ministry to the Gentiles. Luke was sending a message to the Jerusalem church and also to the God-fearers that Paul was not as radical as he might appear.

On another level, when Paul claimed allegiance to the Law, he was claiming allegiance to the Law properly interpreted: the Law that had been fulfilled in Christ. Before Agrippa, Paul sums it up this way: "I am saying nothing beyond what the prophets and Moses said would happen—that the Christ would suffer and, as the first to rise from the dead, would proclaim light to his own people and to the Gentiles" (Acts 26:22–23). In so doing, Paul defends himself against the charge that he has broken the Mosaic Law. Furthermore, he points to the fulfillment of what the Lawgiver had foretold: the death and resurrection of Christ, which would bring salvation to all peoples. Thus as the Book of Acts comes to an end, we find Paul preaching from "the Law of Moses and from the Prophets" (Acts 28:23).

What can we say of Paul and his cutting of his hair as part of a Nazarite vow (Acts 18:18)? No reason for the vow is given. At best we can conclude that Luke aims to demonstrate that Paul continued to live as a Jew. The underlying message is clear enough: Paul and his mission to the Gentiles should not be feared but embraced. Paul is no radical.

As we have noted, at times in the Book of Acts Paul appears to be the most Law-observant of Jews, performing Nazarite vows and other works of supererogation. When he makes a point to follow conspicuously the Jewish Law, however, it is not a question of divining the letter of the Law as much as it is acting in a spirit of reconciliation with the church at Jerusalem. The pattern of Paul's *Torah* observance is largely modeled on that of the Council of Jerusalem, which might be seen as a decree of reconciliation. Gentiles were told to avoid blood and the meat of strangled animals. Concerning these stipulations, Thomas Schreiner writes: "They [these requirements] were suggested as a means of facilitating fellowship between Jews and Gentiles. Gentiles did not have to observe the decree to be saved, but their acceptance of the decree would make relationships between Jews and Gentiles smoother."[29]

As Gentiles were asked to make concessions for the sake of the Jews, so also Paul acted in a manner that would keep peace with the church at Jerusalem. In Gospel freedom, Paul submitted himself to the yoke of Jewish Law. For example, when Timothy joined the apostle to the Gentiles on his missionary journey, Paul had him circumcised. Is this the same Paul who claimed that circumcision is a matter of the heart (Rom 2:29)? Is this the same Paul who admonished the Galatians: "[I]f you let yourselves be circumcised, Christ will be of no value to you at all" (Gal 5:2)? Considering Paul's teaching in the Epistles, some scholars have dismissed the story of Timothy's circumcision as "sheer fantasy"; others think it is misplaced, occurring before the Council at Jerusalem.[30] Such criticism misses the point. Paul circumcises Timothy not because the rule of the Law required it but "because of the Jews who lived in that area, for they all knew that his father was a Greek" (Acts 16:3). The Jews have not challenged Timothy's salvation, they are only made uncomfortable by his way of life. Therefore, Paul fulfills the Law, not because he is under it but for the sake of Christian unity. Even as he was known as a "Gentile for the Gentiles," Paul proves himself a "Jew for the Jews." Gospel freedom includes freely submitting to the customs of others for the sake of others, though the custom is no longer divine command. As Paul states in the fourteenth chapter of Romans: "Let us therefore make every effort to do what leads to peace and to mutual edification" (Rom 14:19).

This motivation for fulfilling the Jewish Law may be seen in Acts 21, where Paul is accused of turning Jews away from Moses and telling them not to circumcise their children (Acts 21:21). James asks:

> What shall we do? They [the Jews of Jerusalem] will certainly hear that you have come, so do what we tell you. There are four men with us who have made a vow. Take these men, join in their

---

29. Thomas R. Schreiner, *The Law and Its Fulfillment: A Pauline Theology of Law* (Grand Rapids: Baker, 1993), 231.

30. See Wilson, *Luke and the Law*, 64–65.

purification rites and pay for their expenses, so that they can have their heads shaved. (Acts 21:22–24).

On the surface, we could see this as yet another example of Paul, the Law-observant Jew. When looked at more closely, however, Paul's motivation is twofold. First, he submits to James and, therefore, to the church. Second, he wishes to show no offense to the Jerusalem church. Once again, Paul fulfills the Law not because he is under it but for the sake of peace and unity.

VI. CONCLUSION

From the evidence presented, we see that Luke has articulated a practical and Christological theology of the Law. When he writes about the Jewish ceremonial law in the infancy narratives, he does so as an historian or ethnographer, describing the customs of a foreign, historic people. He recognizes that with the coming of Christ a new age has dawned. The ceremonial law makes no direct demands on the Christian. Luke also recognizes, however, that the ceremonial law is still a precious custom for the Jewish people; thus he encourages Gentile Christians to act in such a way as not to damage the faith of the Jews. Paul, in particular, is depicted as one who is free from the ceremonial law's demands, yet he fulfills them, at times, for the sake of the consciences of Jewish Christians. Although he is free from the demands of the Jewish laws, Paul is also free to keep them for the sake of his neighbor. This reminds us that we as Christians do well to respect the ways and customs of others, even when they are not binding on us as Christians.

Luke further demonstrates that the Law, at least in its moral aspect, remains intact. However, this moral law is not to be completely equated with the Mosaic Law. Surely the Mosaic Law is the best summary of the moral law, but the moral law predated Moses. Now, in the age of the church, the moral law makes new and greater demands on Christ's followers. As we live in the age of Christ, we are called to redouble our efforts and to live and serve our neighbor as if our lives depended on it.

Finally, Luke would have us know that the most important truth of Moses and of the Law is that Jesus is its fulfillment. Jesus has fulfilled all the demands of the Law, even as the *Torah* points to him as the Messiah and Savior.

PAUL AND THE LAW

WAS LUTHER RIGHT?

CHARLES A. GIESCHEN

There is little doubt that the exegesis of Martin Luther has impacted the interpretation of the apostle Paul's understanding of the Law more than that of any other interpreter during the last five centuries.[1] Luther's magisterial *1535 Lectures on Galatians* offers abundant examples of the reformer's interpretation of Paul and the Law, such as this statement:

> The truth of the Gospel is this, that our righteousness comes by faith alone, without the works of the Law. The falsification or corruption of the Gospel is this, that we are justified by faith but not without the works of the Law. The false apostles [at Galatia] preached the Gospel, but they do so with this condition attached to it. The scholastics do the same thing in our day. They say that we must believe in Christ and that faith is the foundation of salvation, but they say that this faith does not justify unless it is "formed in love" [i.e., shows itself in particular works]. This is not the truth of the Gospel; it is falsehood and pretense.[2]

Luther saw parallels between Paul's struggle with Jewish attitudes toward righteousness through obedience to the Law and his own struggle in the Roman Church concerning how one becomes

---

1. See Stephen Westerholm, *Israel's Law and the Church's Faith: Paul and His Recent Interpreters* (Grand Rapids: Eerdmans, 1988), 3–12. This volume has been updated and expanded; see Westerholm, *Perspectives Old and New on Paul: The "Lutheran" Paul and His Critics* (Grand Rapids: Eerdmans, 104), esp. 22–41.
2. LW 26:88.

and remains righteous before God.[3] In contrast to the Roman Church's view of infused grace producing a moral change that is part of one's righteous status before God, Luther emphasized that Paul taught that one is justified before God solely by grace through faith in Christ's atoning work, apart from any human work (Rom 3:28). This teaching became one of the central banners of the Reformation and the material principle of the Lutheran Church.[4]

The latter half of the twentieth century, however, has witnessed an immense shift among many New Testament scholars away from the understanding of Paul and the Law set forth by Luther. One can drown in the overwhelming sea of secondary literature recently published on this topic. This essay will introduce some of the key players and their contributions to the current debate concerning Paul's position on the Law, including several who "plea for the abandonment of Lutheran presuppositions in interpreting Paul."[5] It is widely acknowledged that some of Luther's characterizations of Judaism were flawed and that his treatment of Paul's teaching of the Law does not consistently do justice to its complexities. This study, however, will argue that the voice of Luther continues to ring clearly concerning Paul's teaching about man's condition, the primary function of the Law, the centrality of justification in Paul's theology, and that man's righteous status before God is both established and maintained by grace through faith alone. If this vital teaching of Paul is no longer recognized and espoused by New Testament scholars, it also will ebb among pastors influenced by such scholarship. Eventually it will not reach the flocks such teaching was intended to feed.

I. THE "NEW PERSPECTIVE" ON PAUL AND THE LAW

Several Jewish and Christian scholars in the first half of the twentieth century sought to overcome the widespread understanding that first-century Judaism was a legalistic works-righteous religion.[6]

---

3. For Luther's description of the discovery of this teaching when he was meditating on Rom 1:16–17, see LW 34:336–37.

4. See especially AC IV (K-W, 39–40) and Ap. IV (K-W, 120ff.).

5. Francis Watson, *Paul, Judaism, and the Gentiles: A Sociological Approach* (SNTSMS 56; Cambridge: Cambridge University Press, 1986), 179.

6. See the history presented in Frank Thielman, *From Plight to Solution: A Jewish Framework to Understanding Paul's View of the Law in Galatians and Romans* (NovTSup 61; Leiden: Brill, 1989), 1–27. Theilman highlights especially the work of George Foot Moore, and those whom he influenced, in laying the groundwork for E. P. Sanders's position.

Even as the understanding of Judaism at the time of Paul began to improve through the vigorous study of Jewish literature, many New Testament scholars continued "to consider Luther's soteriological intensification and theological evaluation of Paul's doctrine of justification to be correct and trailblazing."[7] Luther's interpretation of Paul, however, came under direct attack by Krister Stendahl in a number of essays written between 1963 and 1976.[8] Stendahl, a bishop of the Lutheran Church of Sweden, argued that Luther's conscience-stricken approach to reading Paul was inappropriate because Paul suffered no pangs of conscience concerning his ability to keep the Law. Stendahl was able to go around Romans 7, a key text that legitimated Luther's approach to Paul, by following W. G. Kümmel's exegesis, which argued that this chapter was a defense of the Law, not an autobiographical reflection of Paul's struggle to obey the Law as a Christian.[9] The defining issue driving Paul's teaching about the Law, according to Stendahl, is the Gentile mission. Stendahl sees much continuity with first-century Judaism in Paul, to the extent that he speaks of Paul's "calling" on the road to Damascus rather than his "conversion."[10]

E. P. Sanders is widely heralded as turning the tide among New Testament scholars by bringing about a "New Perspective" on Paul and the Law in the years following 1977 through his book *Paul and Palestinian Judaism*.[11] Much of this volume is devoted to describing Judaism in the centuries after the birth of Christianity through an impressive array of Jewish literature, most of which is early rabbinic

---

7. Peter Stuhlmacher, *Revisiting Paul's Doctrine of Justification: A Challenge to the New Perspective: With an Essay by Donald A. Hagner* (Downers Grove: InterVarsity, 2001), 36.

8. See Krister Stendahl's collected essays in *Paul among Jews and Gentiles* (Philadelphia: Fortress, 1976). The first of Stendahl's essays was "The Apostle Paul and the Introspective Conscience of the West," originally published in *Harvard Theological Review* 56 (1963): 199–215. Donald A. Hagner notes the relationship between this research and the post-Holocaust context; see "Paul and Judaism: Testing the New Perspective," in Peter Stuhlmacher, *Revisiting Paul's Doctrine of Justification: A Challenge to the New Perspective: With an Essay by Donald A. Hagner* (Downers Grove: InterVarsity, 2001), 79.

9. W. G. Kümmel, *Römer 7 und die Bekehrung des Paulus* (Untersuchungen zum Neuen Testament 17; Leipzig: J. C. Hinrichs, 1929). For an extensive history of exegesis of this chapter, see Michael Paul Middendorf, *The "I" in the Storm: A Study of Romans 7* (St. Louis: Concordia Academic Press, 1997), 15–51.

10. For a more balanced and contrasting perspective, see Alan F. Segal, *Paul the Convert: The Apostolate and Apostasy of Saul the Pharisee* (New Haven: Yale University Press, 1990).

11. See the brief history in E. P. Sanders, *Paul and Palestinian Judaism: A Comparison of Patterns of Religion* (Philadelphia: Fortress, 1977), 1–12. The "New Perspective" label is from James D. G. Dunn, "The New Perspective on Paul," *Bulletin of the John Rylands University Library of Manchester* 65 (1983): 95–122.

literature, namely, the Mishnah and its related writings from the second to the sixth century. Sanders focused on the broader "pattern" of Jewish religion, especially "how getting in and staying in are understood."[12] Sanders argues that the vast amount of Jewish literature about the commands of God must be examined in light of Israel's election and covenant.[13] He emphasizes that obedience to the Law was not viewed as the condition of salvation but as the result of being members of the covenant through God's gracious election:

> We saw that the Rabbis were of the opinion that Israel stands in a special relationship to God as a result of God's election of them. God acted on their behalf, and they accepted his rule. It pleased God to give his people commandments, and the fulfilling of them is the characteristic religious act of the Israelite: it is his way of responding to the God who chose and redeemed him. In attempting to give a rationale for the election, the Rabbis appealed to the free grace of God and sometimes to the concept of merit.[14]

Sanders observed that the obedience required of Jews once in the covenant was not perfect obedience but the intent to obey: "God was merciful towards those who basically intended to obey."[15] Therefore, Sanders emphasizes that grace and the covenant are the basis for "getting into" salvation, while obedience to the Law was viewed by Jews as the way one maintained one's position in the covenant or "stayed in" salvation. He titles this pattern "covenantal nomism" and explains it in the following manner:

> Briefly put, covenantal nomism is the view that one's place in God's plan is established on the basis of the covenant and that the covenant requires as the proper response of man his obedience to its commandments, while providing means of atonement for transgression.[16]

This description of Judaism is the foundation for Sanders's discussion of Paul, both in *Paul and Palestinian Judaism* and in his sub-

---

12. Sanders, *Paul and Palestinian Judaism*, 17.
13. Sanders, *Paul and Palestinian Judaism*, 84–107.
14. Sanders, *Paul and Palestinian Judaism*, 106.
15. Sanders, *Paul and Palestinian Judaism*, 125.
16. Sanders, *Paul and Palestinian Judaism*, 75.

sequent volume *Paul, the Law, and the Jewish People*.[17] Sanders highlights two primary convictions that determined Paul's approach to
the Law: Jesus is Lord, and he (Paul) has been called to be an apostle to the Gentiles.[18] Conversely, Sanders does not see the righteousness of God and justification as the center of Paul's theology.[19]
He emphasizes that Paul began with the solution, Christ, then later
developed particular convictions about the plight of humanity,
including the Jews.[20] In Sanders's view, therefore, what drives Paul's
discussion about the Law is not that there is something inherently
wrong in Judaism's focus on getting in and staying in the covenant,
but that Christ and the Gentiles are not part of the Jewish system.
Sanders bluntly states: "In short, *this is what Paul finds wrong in
Judaism: it is not Christianity*."[21]

According to Sanders, Paul's teaching that obedience to the Law
was not an entrance requirement is in conformity with Palestinian
Judaism. The difference between the Jewish and Christian understandings of entrance to the covenant is that Jews understood election to the covenant as the entrance while Christians entered
through participation in Christ by faith.[22] Although Sanders
acknowledges that Paul attempts to emphasize that the true function of the Law is to bring sin to light, he argues that Paul continues
the Jewish focus on obedience to the Law as an expectation of those
"staying in" Christ. Sanders further argues that Paul was not systematic in his expectation of what "Law" Christians were to obey
because circumcision, Sabbath, and food laws were no longer
required.

N. T. Wright was quick to build on Sanders's work, molding it
with his own modifications.[23] With Sanders, Wright emphasizes
that Judaism taught a gracious election to the covenant people
("getting in" by grace) and critiques the projection of the Lutheran
struggle with legalism at the time of the Reformation back to first-
century Judaism. His major modification of Sanders is that "works
of the Law" in Paul reflect Jewish national boundary markers that

---

17. Sanders, *Paul and Palestinian Judaism*, 431–556; and E. P. Sanders, *Paul, the Law, and
the Jewish People* (Philadelphia: Fortress, 1983).
18. Sanders, *Paul and Palestinian Judaism*, 442.
19. Sanders, *Paul and Palestinian Judaism*, 439.
20. Sanders, *Paul and Palestinian Judaism*, 442.
21. Sanders, *Paul and Palestinian Judaism*, 552 (*Sanders's emphasis*).
22. Sanders, *Paul, the Law, and the Jewish People*, 17–64.
23. This is visible already in a lecture given during his doctoral studies; see N. T. Wright,
"The Paul of History and the Apostle of Faith," *Tyndale Bulletin* 29 (1978): 61–88.

define those who are in the covenant. "Works of the Law" should not be understood as moral deeds done by Jews to maintain their status in the covenant.[24] These "works of the Law," Wright asserts, are to be understood primarily as Sabbath observance, dietary restrictions, and circumcision.

Heikki Räisänen follows Sanders's basic position by arguing that the Judaism that Paul faced was not legalistic. Räisänen, however, goes beyond Sanders by contending that Paul gives "a distorted picture of Judaism."[25] Räisänen emphasizes at least four major inconsistencies in Paul's theology of the Law.[26] First, Paul does not use the word *law* (νόμος) consistently, which leads to confusion. Second, Räisänen argues that in some texts Paul claims that the Law is abolished and Christians are free from it, while in other texts he urges Christians to obey and fulfill the Law. Third, Räisänen states that Paul says that no one can obey the Law perfectly, yet the apostle maintains elsewhere that even non-Christian Gentiles can obey the Law. Fourth, Räisänen thinks Paul struggles to explain the origin of the Law and its function: Does the Law make sin known, define sin, or cause sin? Räisänen's approach to the complexities of the Law in Paul has not been as warmly embraced by scholars as has Sanders's work. John Drane and Hans Hübner, whose books came out about the same time as those of Sanders and Räisänen, also recognized these so-called inconsistencies in Paul. Drane and Hübner attribute these inconsistencies to a development in Paul whereby he jettisoned the Law in his Epistle to the Galatians but had a more balanced view by the time he penned Romans.[27]

The prolific James Dunn also expresses great appreciation for Sanders's work in overturning the Reformation perspective on Jewish legalism and follows his "covenantal nomism" understanding of

---

24. See several essays in N. T. Wright, *The Climax of the Covenant: Christ and the Law in Pauline Theology* (Minneapolis: Fortress, 1992), esp. 240–42.

25. Heikki Räisänen, *Paul and the Law* (WUNT 29; Tübingen: J. C. B. Mohr, 1983), 187; see further Heikki Räisänen, *Jesus, Paul and Torah: Collected Essays* (trans. David E. Orton; JSNTSup 43; Sheffield: JSOT Press, 1992).

26. See the critique in Thomas R. Schreiner, *The Law and Its Fulfillment: A Pauline Theology of Law* (Grand Rapids: Baker, 1993), 21–23.

27. John W. Drane, *Paul, Libertine or Legalist? A Study in the Theology of the Major Pauline Epistles* (London: SPCK, 1975); and Hans Hübner, *Law in Paul's Thought* (ed. John Riches; trans. James C. G. Greig; Edinburgh: T&T Clark, 1984). Such a view is especially problematic if one accepts a later date for Galatians, such as A.D. 55, with Romans following less than three years later in early A.D. 58; see Bo Reicke, *Re-examining Paul's Letters: The History of the Pauline Correspondence* (ed. David P. Moessner and Ingalisa Reicke; Harrisburg, Penn.: Trinity Press International, 2001), 45–48.

Judaism.[28] Dunn, however, argues that Sanders and Räisänen have replaced the "Lutheran Paul" with an "idiosyncratic Paul" because they have not recognized the important flaw in Judaism that Paul addresses: nationalism.[29] Dunn argues that Paul's conversion experience and call to be the apostle to the Gentiles sensitized him to the exclusiveness of Judaism that is visible in its requirements of particular nationalistic practices. Paul's reference to the "works of the Law," according to Dunn, refers to nationalistic practices such as circumcision, dietary restrictions, and Sabbath laws, not to all the Mosaic Law. In this Dunn is quite close to the position of N. T. Wright. Furthermore, Dunn understands the curse of the Law that Jesus overcame through his death to be specifically this attitude that confines the covenant to Jews.[30]

Francis Watson also has critiqued Lutheran understandings of Paul.[31] His approach attempts to explain Paul's argumentation in Galatians, Philippians, and Romans in terms of the sociological situation of Jewish and Gentile members of these Christian churches. He states that his sociological approach bears this fruit:

> Attention to the social context and function of Paul's arguments produces an interpretation of Paul in some respects very different from that which stems from the Lutheran tradition. For example, the fundamental antithesis between faith and works is not to be understood as a primarily theological contrast between receiving salvation as a free gift and earning it by one's own efforts, but as a sociological contrast between two different ways of life: "faith," the way of life practised in the Pauline congregations, marked by the abandonment of certain of the norms and beliefs of the surrounding society; and 'works', the ways of life of the Jewish community, which sought to live in conformity with the law of Moses.[32]

Similar to Sanders's emphasis on "staying in" the convenant by works, Watson argues that, for Paul, "human obedience as a response to divine grace is a necessary condition of salvation."[33]

---

28. Dunn, "New Perspective on Paul," 95–122.

29. Dunn, "New Perspective on Paul," 100–101; see also James D. G. Dunn, *Jesus, Paul, and the Law: Studies in Mark and Galatians* (Louisville: Westminster/John Knox, 1990), 188.

30. Dunn, *Jesus, Paul, and the Law*, 229.

31. Watson, *Paul, Judaism, and the Gentiles*, 1–22.

32. Watson, *Paul, Judaism, and the Gentiles*, 178–79.

33. Watson, *Paul, Judaism, and the Gentiles*, 179.

Watson concludes that it is "completely wrong to regard the phrase *sola gratia* as the key to Paul's theology."[34]

Lloyd Gaston, who in turn influenced John Gager, presents a more radical development of Sanders's basic position.[35] Both Gaston and Gager argue that Christian attitudes toward Judaism have conditioned our interpretation of Paul. They hold that Paul's emphasis on salvation by faith apart from works of the Law is directed solely to Gentiles and not to Jews because Jews were in a gracious covenant relationship wherein transgressions could be forgiven through the established means. Like Dunn, both Gaston and Gager argue that Paul criticizes the Jews because of national exclusivism that insisted Gentiles be obedient to certain aspects of the Mosaic Law.

This brief overview reveals some serious concerns with the New Perspective that will now be addressed. Luther would say that the pure Gospel is at stake. Although some may think this issue is a minor matter of scholarly debate and dialogue that has little impact on the church, it is nonetheless already filtering into several newer commentaries on Romans and Galatians. Because of this, the New Perspective is making its way into the pulpits and Bible classes of some congregations.

II. A CRITIQUE OF THE NEW PERSPECTIVE

The position of Sanders and those who have followed him has not gone unchallenged in the past two decades. Especially helpful are the critiques of Stephen Westerholm,[36] Thomas Schreiner,[37] Robert Gundry,[38] Frank Thielman,[39] Timo Laato,[40] Peter Stuhlmacher,[41]

---

34. Watson, *Paul, Judaism, and the Gentiles*, 179.

35. Lloyd Gaston, *Paul and the Torah* (Vancouver: University of British Columbia Press, 1987), and John G. Gager, *The Origins of Anti-Semitism: Attitudes toward Judaism in Pagan and Christian Antiquity* (New York: Oxford University Press, 1983).

36. Westerholm, *Israel's Law and the Church's Faith*, esp. 15–101 (see n. 1).

37. Schreiner, *Law and Its Fulfillment*, esp. 18–31 (see n. 26).

38. Robert Gundry, "Grace, Works, and Staying Saved in Paul," *Biblica* 66 (1985): 1–38.

39. Thielman, *From Plight to Solution* (see n. 6); see also Frank Thielman, "Law," *Dictionary of Paul and His Letters* (ed. Gerald F. Hawthorne, Ralph P. Martin, Daniel G. Reid; Downers Grove: InterVarsity, 1993), 529–42.

40. Timo Laato, *Paul and Judaism: An Anthropological Approach* (trans. T. McElwain; South Florida Studies in the History of Judaism 115; Atlanta: Scholars Press, 1995). This is a translation of the 1991 German edition.

41. Stuhlmacher, *Revisiting Paul's Doctrine of Justification* (see n. 7).

Donald Hagner,[42] A. Andrew Das,[43] Seyoon Kim,[44] Simon J. Gathercole,[45] and the significant two-volume project entitled *Justification and Variegated Nomism*.[46] The one assertion of the New Perspective that has received widespread welcome, even among its critics, is that the false caricatures of Judaism—some of which have been penned or proclaimed by Luther and subsequent Lutherans—as a purely merit-based and works-righteous religion have been challenged and corrected. Although there were many before Sanders who worked tirelessly to improve the understanding of first-century Judaism, Sanders deserves credit for making a visible impact on the subject among New Testament scholars.[47] Before challenging certain aspects of the New Perspective, Das offers this accolade:

> Sanders' work was fundamentally a corrective to New Testament scholarship that had been all too ready to malign first-century and rabbinic Judaism as legalistic. Consequently, he rightly emphasized the central and significant roles that God's election and mercy played in Jewish thought.[48]

Stuhlmacher gives a similar assessment, but he quickly notes that with this positive contribution have come significant negative by-products:

> The change in scholarly evaluations of ancient Judaism that E. P. Sanders brought about was an idea whose time had come. Unfortunately, this new picture of ancient Judaism was worked out at the expense not only of Luther's understanding of justification but also of the Pauline doctrine of God's righteousness and justification. Both are regrettable and should be corrected.[49]

There are six problematic aspects of the New Perspective that will be addressed below. First, the New Perspective tends to narrow

---

42. Hagner, "Paul and Judaism," 75–105 (see n. 8). This essay is a revision of Hagner, "Paul and Judaism—The Jewish Matrix of Early Christianity: Issues in the Current Debate," *Bulletin for Biblical Research* 3 (1993): 111–30.

43. A. Andrew Das, *Paul, the Law, and the Covenant* (Peabody, Mass.: Hendrickson, 2001).

44. Seyoon Kim, *Paul and the New Perspective* (Grand Rapids: Eerdmans, 2002).

45. Simon J. Gathercole, *Where Is Boasting? Early Jewish Soteriology and Paul's Response in Romans 1–5* (Grand Rapids: Eerdmans, 2002).

46. Volume 1, *The Complexities of Second Temple Judaism* (ed. D. A. Carsons, Peter T. O'Brien, and Mark A. Seifrid; Tübingen: Mohr Siebeck, 2001). Volume 2 on Paul is forthcoming.

47. W. D. Davies, *Paul and Rabbinic Judaism* (4th ed.; Philadelphia: Fortress, 1980 [1948 original]).

48. Das, *Paul, the Law, and the Covenant*, 12.

49. Stuhlmacher, *Revisiting Paul's Doctrine of Justification*, 40.

the referent of "Law," especially "works of the Law," in Paul to the identity markers of Judaism rather than the broader Mosaic Law that reflects a universal moral law. Second, the New Perspective downplays evidence of the significant role that works of the Law play in maintaining one's righteous status in the covenant within first-century Judaism, at least within some Jewish groups. Third, and closely related to the second problem, the New Perspective does not give sufficient attention to the significantly different anthropologies of first-century Judaism and first-century Christianity, the former often optimistic in its assessment of one's abilities to obey and the latter extremely pessimistic.[50] Fourth, many adherents of the New Perspective tend to downplay the demand for "perfect obedience" or evidence that some Jews believed some humans to be capable of such obedience. Fifth, the New Perspective fails to see that Paul's understanding of the Law and human anthropology as articulated in Galatians and Romans was not merely a continuation of Jewish teaching nor did it develop primarily out of the necessity of the Gentile mission, but this understanding came from Paul's Christophany that the Jesus of Nazareth who was crucified is YHWH. Paul's radical rereading of the Old Testament and his critique of Judaism in light of Christ is sometimes downplayed in recent research. Sixth, the New Perspective supports the understanding that justification is not as central to Paul's soteriology as mystical participation in Christ. These two aspects of soteriology in Paul's Epistles are too often pitted against each other in modern scholarship rather than appreciated for their interdependent and complementary relationship.

A. THE REFERENT OF "THE LAW"
AND "WORKS OF THE LAW" IN PAUL'S EPISTLES

It is important to acknowledge that the meaning of the word νόμος ("law") in Paul's letters is somewhat complex and certainly dependent on context. It can signify *Torah* in the sense of the instructive revelation contained in the Pentateuch or all of the Old Testament, the *Mosaic Law* given at Sinai (especially the *moral law* as summarized in the Decalog), or an *authority* or *principle* in a broad

---

50. "First-century Judaism" and "first-century Christianity" are umbrella terms that describe complex and diverse religious phenomena. These terms are used here with an understanding of the diversity within various Jewish or Christian groups, as well as with the awareness that Christianity has its roots in Second Temple Judaism.

and general sense.[51] A quick look at Romans illustrates this range in Paul's usage of νόμος. Paul quotes from several texts in Psalms, Proverbs, and Isaiah in Rom 3:10–18, then concludes that this is what "the Law [i.e., Old Testament] says" (Rom 3:19).[52] He goes on to state that "the Law [i.e., Pentateuch] and Prophets testify" to the Righteousness of God (Rom 3:21). A little later Paul states that the grounds for the lack of boasting is "through the law [i.e., authority or principle] of faith" (Rom 3:27; cf. "law of the Spirit" in Rom 8:2 and "the law of Christ" in Gal 6:2). This usage sets up the verbal contrast in Rom 3:27–28 between νόμου πίστεως (the "law of faith") and ἔργων νόμου (the "works of the Law"). The most frequent referent of νόμος by Paul is clearly the Mosiac Law that illustrates the life to be lived by those who trust in YHWH. For example, Paul uses it eleven times in Rom 2:17–27, and each time the referent is the entire Mosaic Law:

> [17] But if you bear the name "Jew," and rely upon *the Law*, and boast in God, [18] and know his will, and approve the things that are essential, being instructed out of *the Law*, [19] and are confident that you yourself are a guide to the blind, a light to those who are in darkness, [20] a corrector of the foolish, a teacher of the immature, having in *the Law* the embodiment of knowledge and of the truth, [21] you, therefore, who teach another, do you not teach yourself? You who preach that one should not steal, do you steal? [22] You who say that one should not commit adultery, do you commit adultery? You who abhor idols, do you rob temples? [23] You who boast in *the Law*, through your breaking *the Law*, do you dishonor God? [24] For "the name of God is blasphemed among the Gentiles because of you," just as it is written. [25] For indeed circumcision is of value, if you practice *the Law*; but if you are a transgressor of *the Law*, your circumcision has become uncircumcision. [26] If therefore the uncircumcised man keeps the requirements of *the Law*, will not his uncircumcision be regarded as circumcision? [27] And will not he who is physically uncircumcised, if he keeps *the Law*, will he not judge you who though having the letter of *the Law* and circumcision are a transgressor of *the Law*? (*my emphasis*)

---

51. See the discussion in Schreiner, *Law and Its Fulfillment*, 33–40. Das argues for a more uniform understanding that views all references as signifying the Mosaic Law; see Das, *Paul, the Law, and the Covenant*, esp. 228–32.

52. All the Scripture quotations in this essay are the author's own translation.

Although it was not the position of Sanders, the narrower iden-tification of "works of the Law" as Jewish identity markers has become a component of the New Perspective largely through the writings of James Dunn and N. T. Wright.[53] The basic argument is that Paul's concern with the Law was not required obedience to the wider Mosaic Law but the insistence that Gentiles obey key parts of the Law that served as Jewish identity marks, especially circumcision, Sabbath observance, and dietary laws. When Paul states that "by works of the Law no flesh will be justified" (Rom 3:20), this is understood to exclude the soteriological role of Jewish identity markers.

Paul, however, was not only concerned about the Jewish laws that were preventing Gentiles from being included in the people of God; he also was concerned about Jews and some Jewish Chris-tians who viewed their obedience to the broader Mosaic Law, or at least their intent to obey, as an aspect of their righteous status before God. This point is supported by the broad and inclusive scope of the condemnation that the Law brings on both Gentile and Jew according to Rom 1:18–3:20. This is made especially clear in Rom 3:19–20, the climatic verses of Paul's carefully sustained argu-ment:

> Now we know that whatever the Law says, it speaks to those who are under the Law, that every mouth be closed and all the world become accountable to God; because by the works of the Law no flesh will be justified in his sight; for through the Law comes the knowledge of sin.

The source of Paul's broad understanding of "works of the Law" is undoubtedly the Old Testament, for example, the repeated exhor-tation in Deuteronomy to "do all the words of the *Torah*" (28:58; 29:29; 32:46).[54]

It is well known that Luther argued for a broad understanding of "the Law" and "works of the Law" in his exegesis of Paul's Epistles. For example, the following summary offers a window into Luther's understanding of this topic.

> Thus for Paul "works of the Law" means the works of the entire Law. Therefore one should not make a distinction between the Decalog and ceremonial laws. Now if the work of the Decalog

---

53. For example, see Dunn, "New Perspective on Paul," 95–122; and Wright, *Climax of the Covenant*, 240–42.

54. See Gathercole, *Where Is Boasting?* 92–93.

does not justify, much less will circumcision, which is a work of the Ceremonial Law. When Paul says, as he often does, that a man is not justified by the Law or by the works of the Law, which means the same thing in Paul, he is speaking in general about the entire Law; he is contrasting the righteousness of faith with the righteousness of the entire Law, with everything that can be done on the basis of the Law, whether by divine power or by human.[55]

Why is a narrower understanding of "works of the Law" problematic when interpreting Paul's letters? Such an understanding shifts the focus of Paul's critique from the role the Law played in Jewish soteriology to Jewish insistence on a few specific identity laws. Although circumcision and dietary laws were certainly concerns that surfaced with several early Christian congregations, such concerns are symptomatic of a broader Jewish (and Jewish Christian) focus on the Law's role in soteriology. This assertion will be supported in the discussion of Jewish soteriology immediately below. Furthermore, the flip side of this first problem is that a narrower understanding of "works of the Law" undercuts Paul's teaching of justification solely by grace for Christ's sake through faith. If "works of the Law" is not understood to be inclusive of all the demands of God's Law, then the exclusive dependence on God's grace in Christ as Paul proclaims is diminished.

B. THE ROLE OF THE LAW IN THE SOTERIOLOGIES OF FIRST-CENTURY JUDAISM AND PAUL

Despite the New Perspective's corrective emphasis on grace and faith as key to entrance into the covenant within first-century Judaism, problems remain when the soteriological role given to the Law by some first-century Jews and Christians is downplayed or denied. Sanders postulates an artificial distinction between "entering" the covenant by grace and "staying in" by obedience, as if this distinction prevents obedience to the Law from diminishing salvation by grace in Judaism. However, there is a future, eschatological dimension to salvation in both Judaism and Christianity.[56] Therefore, if one "stays in" the covenant through obedience to the Law, this means that obedience to the Law still has a prominent soteriological role as one looks toward the eschatological deliverance. Gathercole explains it in this way: "So, the category that is often

---

55. LW 26:122.
56. See especially Gathercole, *Where Is Boasting?* 23–24.

missed is the role of works in 'getting into the world to come,' 'getting into the life in the future age,' or 'getting *there.*' "[57] In fact, the tendency would be to focus more on the obedience process of "staying in" the covenant until the eschaton than on the gracious election of how one first "entered." As Donald Hagner notes: "A covenantal nomism will only remain 'covenantal' where very deliberate and explicit measures are taken to guard it as such; there will otherwise be a natural human tendency towards legalism."[58] To put it more pointedly: Covenantal nomism is still nomism. Schreiner's critique includes the sensible comment of one of his colleagues: "If Judaism were not legalistic at all, it would be the only religion in history that escaped the human propensity for works-righteousness."[59] Christianity, obviously, has not escaped this propensity over the past two millennia.

This soteriological function of the Law is supported by a look at its growing role in Jewish groups during the Second Temple period. Hagner, once again, makes a helpful observation:

> In the postexilic period, beginning with the proto-typical scribe Ezra, there was understandably a turning to the law with a new intensity of commitment. The exile was widely perceived as the result of Israel's failure to keep the law. In this new development, which constitutes the beginning of Judaism, it is hardly surprising that the law assumed central importance. Judaism is, of course, in continuity with the Old Testament, and grace was not necessarily occluded by the heightened emphasis on the law. But that this was overshadowed by the new emphasis on the law seems highly probable to me.[60]

There is evidence of this emphasis in Jewish literature of the Second Temple and early rabbinic periods. Much of it has been analyzed afresh in recent years in reaction to the New Perspective.[61] A few

---

57. Gathercole, *Where Is Boasting?* 23–24.

58. Hagner, "Paul and Judaism," 88.

59. Schreiner, *Law and Its Fulfillment*, 115.

60. Hagner, "Paul and Judaism," 84.

61. Three recent publications are especially helpful presentations of this evidence. Second Temple literature is examined in the first volume of *Justification and Variegated Nomism* (see n. 46 above) and also in Gathercole, *Where Is Boasting?* (see n. 45 above). For a masterful examination of this theme in rabbinic literature—such as the Mishnah, Tosefta, Tannaitic Midrashim, and the Talmuds—see Friedrich Avemarie, *Tora und Leben: Untersuchungen zur Heilsbedeutung der Tora in der frühen rabbinischen Literatur* (Texte und Studien zum antiken Judentum 55; Tübingen: Mohr Siebeck, 1996).

examples will suffice to illustrate this emphasis.[62] An important aspect of obedience to the Law in Sirach and Tobit is almsgiving (Tob 4:7–9; Sir 29:11–13). Tobit goes so far as to state: "Alms deliver from death and shall purge away all sin: those who give alms and do righteousness will be filled with life" (12:9). The *Psalms of Solomon* contain texts, such as the one that follows, that testify to the weight given to righteous deeds at the final judgment: "The one who does righteousness stores up life for himself with the Lord. And the one who does wickedness is the cause of the destruction of his own soul" (9:5). The Wisdom of Solomon also contains evidence that obedience to the Law plays some role in gaining eschatological salvation: "Love is keeping her [Wisdom's] commandments; observance of her laws is the guarantee of immortality" (6:18). The *Testaments of the Twelve Patriarchs* contains much exhortation to observe the Law of God so one can experience salvation. The *Testament of Gad*, for example, states: "[T]he spirit of love works by the Law of God through forbearance for the salvation of mankind" (4:7). Obviously, one should not conclude from these isolated texts that Second Temple Judaism had no concept of grace; however, neither should one ignore the soteriological role that obedience to the Law had within some Jewish groups.

Furthermore, evidence of a soteriological function of the Law that is found in early Christian literature, especially in the New Testament, should not be ignored or marginalized.[63] For example, John 6:26–29 reflects a concern for "doing the works that God requires" among Jesus' Jewish opponents:

> [26] Do not work for food that spoils, but for food that endures to eternal life that the Son of Man will give you. [27] On him God the Father has placed his seal. [28] Then they asked him, "What must we do to do the works God requires? [29] Jesus answered, "The work of God is this: to believe in the one he has sent."

John records Jesus' radical reinterpretation of what "work" God is interested in: faith in the sent one, who is the Son. Paul's concern with "boasting" in the early chapters of Romans also reflects the soteriological function that was being given to the Law. Gathercole highlights the importance of this evidence: "It is that assurance of obedience, as the basis of final vindication by God, which Paul crit-

---

62. For further discussion of these examples and several others, see Gathercole, *Where Is Boasting?* 37–111.

63. See Gathercole, *Where Is Boasting?* 112–35.

icizes at such length in 2:1–5; 2:21–24; and 3:10–20, which is why it makes sense to speak of the Jewish 'boast' in 2:17, 23 as including reference to confidence on the basis of obedience."[64] Schreiner aptly summarizes the wisdom of including the Pauline evidence in any analysis of first-century Jewish soteriology:

> But it should be remembered that Paul was a Jew. He viewed his own theology as a fulfillment of the Old Testament (Rom. 1:2). His critique of Judaism (and even his own past) was in line with that of the prophets (Gal. 1:13–14; Phil. 3:2–11). This is no attack from outside Judaism but an intra-Jewish debate on the meaning of the Scriptures. Further, what Paul attacks is not Judaism per se but a fundamentally human problem. Human beings, since they are sinners, are prone naturally to worship the creature rather than the Creator (Rom. 1:23). One dimension of human idolatry is a perverted desire to boast in one's works before God so that one can earn merit in his sight.[65]

Some advocates of the New Perspective acknowledge that Paul presents Judaism as legalistic, but they argue that this is a misrepresentation. Räisänen, for example, bluntly states that Paul is wrong in his assessment of Judaism.[66] In this matter, the sage advice of C. K. Barrett is on the mark: "He is a bold man who supposes that he understands first-century Judaism better than Paul did."[67] This soteriological use of the Law to maintain one's own righteousness until the eschaton is what Paul finds wrong in Judaism, as well as in (Jewish) Christian congregations where this teaching has taken root. Moreover, there is no exegetical foundation for those who assert that there are different soteriologies for Jews and Gentiles according to Paul because Rom 2:13 poses a theoretical possibility, not a reality.[68]

This evidence helps us to see that the soteriological function given to the Law—not only the Gentile mission—was the situation that led to Paul's emphasis on righteousness by faith apart from works of the Law. After Paul encountered the crucified and risen Christ, he realized the huge problem people face when they begin

---

64. Gathercole, *Where Is Boasting?* 215.

65. Schreiner, *Law and Its Fulfillment*, 120.

66. Heikki Räisänen, "Legalism and Salvation by the Law," in *Die Paulinische Literatur und Theologie* (ed. S. Pedersen; Teologiske studien 7; Århus: Aros, 1980), 73.

67. C. K. Barrett, *Paul: An Introduction to His Thought* (Louisville: Westminster/John Knox, 1994), 78.

68. Hendrikus Boers, *The Justification of the Gentiles: Paul's Letters to the Galatians and Romans* (Peabody, Mass.: Hendrickson, 1994), esp. 220–24.

to view their works as playing *any* role in soteriology.[69] The righteousness of God in Christ received by faith not only allows us to enter a righteous status before God but this righteousness in Christ also solely maintains our righteous status before God. The works that we do, though considered important and encouraged by Paul, play no role in either *establishing* or *maintaining* our righteous status before God. It is noteworthy that Paul uses Abraham as the example of this in Romans 4 and Galatians 3 instead of Moses. Genesis 15 contained evidence of one who was righteous by faith alone in the promise of God prior to circumcision and long before the giving of the Mosaic Law.

What is the key purpose of the Law? It is noteworthy that Paul does not view the key purpose of the Law to be moral behavior. In Rom 7:8, he states: "Sin, finding opportunity in the command, wrought in me all kinds of covetousness." Paul argues that the Law does not have any direct role in soteriology but functions in service to it. The Law brings the knowledge of sin constantly to light so sinners see their utter and constant dependence on the grace of God both for entering and for staying in a righteous status before God to the eschaton: "Through the Law comes knowledge of sin" (Rom 3:20b); "For the Law brings wrath, but where there is no Law, neither is there transgression" (Rom 4:15); and "The Law entered in order that the transgression increase" (Rom 5:20). The Law condemns and crushes all illusions that righteousness before God can be obtained or maintained through obedience. From his own experience, Paul understands that this primary function of the Law had been diminished or ignored among many Jews and Christians.

Unlike the New Perspective, which rarely speaks of this function of the Law, Luther saw it as fundamental to preaching and important throughout the life of Christians, not only at the time of conversion. For example, he states:

> The time of the Law is when the Law disciplines, vexes, and saddens me, when it brings me to a knowledge of sin and

---

69. Those who understand that obedience to the Law plays some soteriological function in Paul point to his self-professed mission of bringing about the "obedience of faith" among the Gentiles (Rom 1:5; 16:26); see Mark Nanos, *The Mystery of Romans: The Jewish Context of Paul's Letter* (Minneapolis: Fortress, 1996), 38. Although there are several ways that this genitive could be understood, in the context of Romans it signifies "obedience that consists of faith" (see especially Rom 10:16). Against opponents who criticize his lack of emphasis on obedience to the Law, Paul points to his stress on the kind of obedience that God desires: faith.

increases this. Then the Law is being employed in its true use, which a Christian experiences constantly as long as he lives.[70]

For as long as we live in a flesh that is not free of sin, so long the Law keeps coming back and performing its function, more in one person and less in another, not to harm but to save. This discipline of the Law is the daily mortification of the flesh, the reason, and our powers, and the renewal of our mind (2 Cor. 4:16) . . . . Here there is still need for a custodian to discipline and torment the flesh, that powerful jackass, so that by this discipline sins may be diminished and the way prepared for Christ.[71]

C. THE EXTENT OF EXPECTED OBEDIENCE: "INTENT TO OBEY" OR "PERFECT OBEDIENCE"?

As noted above when introducing the New Perspective, Sanders and those who have followed him argue that early Judaism emphasized the importance of the "intent to obey" the Law, not the demand for perfect obedience. In short, it is argued that early Judaism did not believe that God demanded perfect obedience or that individuals were capable of such obedience. There is, however, literary evidence to the contrary on both issues.[72]

First, several Jews within both early Christianity and first-century Judaism emphasized God's demand for perfect obedience. Jesus states: "Be perfect, even as your Father in heaven is perfect" (Matt 5:48). James also expresses this explicitly in his Epistle: "For whoever keeps the whole Law and yet stumbles at just one point is guilty of breaking all of it" (Jas 2:10). As noted above, Paul's own testimony should not be ignored. Possession of the Law, hearing of the Law, and intent to obey the Law were not enough for Paul. He saw that the demand for perfect obedience was not being acknowledged by many of his fellow Jews and Jewish Christians, as is clear from these texts:

For it is not the hearers of the Law [οἱ ἀκροαταὶ νόμου] who are righteous ones before God, but the doers of the Law [οἱ ποιηταὶ νόμου] will be declared righteous. (Rom 2:13)

---

70. LW 26:341.

71. LW 26:350.

72. See especially the essay in this volume by A. Andrew Das; see also Das, *Paul, the Law, and the Covenant* (see n. 43).

Cursed is everyone who does not abide by all things written in the book of the Law by doing them [τοῦ ποιῆσαι αὐτά]. (Gal 3:10)

For no human being will be declared righteous before him on account of works of the Law [διότι ἐξ ἔργων νόμου οὐ δικαιωθήσεται πᾶσα σὰρξ ἐνώπιον αὐτοῦ]. (Rom 3:20)

Second, this biblical evidence for the demand of perfect obedience is augmented by evidence that some Jews in this period believed that some people indeed obeyed the Law perfectly and were not in need of God's merciful forgiveness.[73] For example, one finds this assertion amid the profound penitential outpouring of the *Prayer of Manasseh*: "Therefore you, O Lord, God of the righteous, have not appointed repentance for the righteous, for Abraham and Isaac and Jacob, who did not sin against you, but you have repentance for me, who am a sinner" (v. 8). The understanding that more than a few noteworthy Old Testament patriarchs obeyed the Law perfectly is reflected in *4 Ezra* 7:88–99. The author introduces an extensive discussion of the seven orders of the righteous in heaven with these words:

[88] Now this is the order of those who have kept the ways of the Most High, when they shall be separated from their mortal body. [89] During the time that they lived in it, they laboriously served the Most High, and withstood danger every hour, that they might keep the Law of the Lawgiver perfectly. [90] Therefore this is the teaching concerning them: [91] First of all, they shall see with great joy the glory of him who receives them, for they shall have rest in seven orders.

The demand for perfect obedience and the understanding that some have fulfilled that demand diminishes the claims of the New Perspective that such obedience was neither demanded nor understood to be possible in Judaism. Hugo Odeberg summarizes the significant difference between early Christians and those in Judaism who discounted the Law's demands for perfect obedience:

Pharisaism is indeed far more lenient in its appraisal of the moral life than is Christianity, and this is precisely because it attaches such great significance to the right attitude of the mind. One need not be unduly anxious because of one's sins against the divine will if one has once determined to do what is right. For

---

73. For further evidence, see Das, *Paul, the Law, and the Covenant*, 13–69.

God is merciful, indulgent, and gracious, and He Himself sup-
plies what may be lacking on the part of men seeking righteousness in the matter of fulfilling the moral duty. "If a man had the
intention of performing a duty, but was hindered therein, the
Scriptures reckon it as if he had performed it; this is the essential
meaning of the prophet Malachi's words 'them that thought
upon His Name' " (*Babylonian Talmud*, Berakhot 6a).[74]

D. THE CONTRASTING ANTHROPOLOGIES
OF FIRST-CENTURY JUDAISM AND PAUL

The accomplishment of perfect obedience reflects a particular
anthropology. Another issue, therefore, that must be addressed in
any discussion of Paul's understanding of the Law is the issue of
human anthropology after the fall into sin. Is man's will in total
bondage to sin or does it have some freedom? Timo Laato, a
Finnish Lutheran scholar, has challenged Sanders's position on the
role of the works of the Law in maintaining one's righteous status
with his 1991 dissertation that was later translated and published as
Paul and Judaism: An Anthropological Approach.[75] Laato argues that a
key difference between first-century Judaism and Christianity was
the anthropological presuppositions of their respective soteriologies
or, to put it simply, their respective understandings of man's nature
after the fall and the role that fallen nature is able to play in salvation. Laato's study of this subject concludes with this sharp contrast:
"Judaism embraced an optimistic anthropology with the principle of
human free will. Paul in contrast depended upon a pessimistic
anthropology with the dogma of human depravity."[76]

The pessimistic anthropology of Paul came after his conversion
and is most extensively expressed in Rom 1:18–3:20. Paul's pessimistic assessment of fallen man climaxes in Romans 3 with his
masterful weaving together of the testimony of various Old Testament texts into one vicious litany that indicts all humanity:

[9] What then? Are we better than they? Not at all; for we have
already charged that both Jews and Greeks are all under sin;
[10] as it is written, "There is none righteous, not even one;

---

74. Hugo Odeberg, *Pharisaism and Christianity* (trans. J. M. Moe; St. Louis: Concordia,
1964), 29.

75. Laato, *Paul and Judaism* (see n. 40). Timo Eskola, another Finnish scholar, has a similar critique; see *Theodicy and Predestination in Pauline Soteriology* (WUNT II.100;
Tübingen: Mohr Siebeck, 1998).

76. Laato, *Paul and Judaism*, 213.

[11] there is none who understands, there is none who seeks for God; [12] all have turned aside, together they have become useless; there is none who does good, there is not even one." [13] "Their throat is an open grave, with their tongues they keep deceiving," "the poison of asps is under their lips"; [14] "whose mouth is full of cursing and bitterness"; [15] "their feet are swift to shed blood, [16] destruction and misery are in their paths, [17] and the path of peace have they not known." [18] "There is no fear of God before their eyes." [19] Now we know that whatever the Law says, it speaks to those who are under the Law, that every mouth be closed, and all the world become accountable to God; [20] because by the works of the Law no flesh will be declared righteous in his sight; for through the Law comes the knowledge of sin.

Paul could not be more clear in spelling out his pessimistic understanding of humanity. However, such an Old Testament biblical view of man's condition was not what Paul grew up with as a Pharisee. One of the wells from which Laato draws his analysis of human anthropology is the significant work of another Lutheran scholar that Sanders and others have ignored: Hugo Odeberg.[77] A few years before the discovery at Qumran stimulated the study of Jewish literature and decades before Sanders raised our sensitivity to caricatures of Judaism, Odeberg's short, penetrating comparison of rabbinic Judaism and first-century Christianity sought to correct false portraits of Judaism, including the understanding that Judaism had been founded on an ethic of reward (merit) and punishment. Odeberg focuses on anthropology as the underlying problem that led Christians such as Paul to emphasize that works of the Law cannot play any role in soteriology.

> However, what at this point constitutes the decisive difference between Pharisaic and the Christian view is that the Pharisee believes that man has the freedom to choose between good and evil, between doing the will of God and acting contrary to it, and that man is capable of performing the good he has resolved to do; the Christian view is again that man in his natural state has the freedom to choose between different ways of conduct, and that he also has the ability to perform the deeds that he has chosen to do; but he cannot choose what is good, and whatever

---

77. Odeberg, *Pharisaism and Christianity* (see n. 74). This book is a translation of the original Swedish *Fariséism och kristendom* (Lund: Gleerup, 1943).

ways of conduct he may choose, he can never produce what is good, that is so long as he remains "the old man."[78]

Evidence of the Jewish understanding of free will after the fall is found in several Second Temple Jewish texts that date to the first century. Here are a few examples:

> Our works are subject to our own choice and power to do right or wrong in the works of our hands; and in Thy righteousness Thou visitest the sons of men. He that doeth righteousness layeth up life for himself with the Lord; And he that doeth wrongly forfeits his life to destruction; For the judgments of the Lord are given in righteousness to every man and his house. (*Psalms of Solomon* 9:4–5 [ca. 50 B.C.])

> For though Adam first sinned and brought untimely death upon all, yet of those who were born from him each one of them has prepared for his own soul torment to come and again each one of them has chosen for himself glories to come . . . . Adam is therefore not the cause, save only of his own soul, but each of us has become our own Adam. (*2 Baruch* 54:15, 19 [ca. A.D. 70–100])

> And therefore it is reasonably held that the mind alone in all that makes us what we are is indestructible. For it is mind alone which the Father who begat it judged worthy of freedom, and loosening the fetters of necessity, suffered it to range as it listed, and of that free will which is His most peculiar possession and most worthy of His majesty gave it such portion as it was capable of receiving. For the other living creatures in whose souls the mind, the element set apart for liberty, has no place, have been committed under yoke and bridle to the service of men, as slaves to a master. But man, possessed of a spontaneous and self-determined will, whose activities for the most part rest on deliberate choice, is with reason blamed for what he does wrong with intent, praised when he acts rightly of his own will. (Philo, *Quod Deus sit immutabilis* 10.45–47 [ca. A.D. 40])

> They [the Saduccees] maintain that man has the free choice of good or evil, and that it rests with each man's will whether he follows the one or the other. (Josephus, *Jewish War* 2.165 [ca. A.D. 100])

---

78. Odeberg, *Pharisaism and Christianity*, 60–61.

How could some first-century Jews have such an optimistic anthropology in light of the testimony of Genesis 3 concerning the fall into sin? Odeberg addresses this question directly:

> In as much as this soul is indestructible, Pharisaic Judaism is unable to comprehend the fall of man and even less the idea of original sin. The story of the Fall in Genesis is therefore regarded by the Pharisaic teachers merely as a typical example of the disobedience against God of which man under certain circumstances is guilty. They speak of evil impulses in man, which oppose the good impulse during his earthly sojourn. These evil impulses, however, are able only for a time to obscure the purity of the soul, the divine spark in man, but they can never extinguish it.[79]

Laato offers a similar assessment:

> This anthropological optimism did not fail when the reading cycle of the synagogue reached Gen. 3. The fall into sin worked neither a total loss nor a partial limiting of the free will and respectively the purity of the soul. Before and after eating from the tree of knowledge Adam and Eve had the same capability of obeying God. Human nature went through no delimitation of essence by sin. Gen. 3 does not describe what ever after must take place, but rather what then and later can take place. The rebellion in Paradise serves as *one* (well typical) example of disobedience.[80]

Paul has a significantly different understanding of Genesis 3. He understands Adam and Eve's actions to have placed the entire creation in bondage to sin. The most extensive expression of the effects of the fall is found in the Adam-Christ typology of Romans 5:

> [11] And not only this, but we also exult in God through our Lord Jesus Christ, through whom we have now received the reconciliation. [12] Therefore, just as through one man sin entered into the world, and death through sin, and so death spread to all men, because [in Adam] all sinned—[13] for until the Law sin was in the world; but sin is not imputed when there is no law. [14] Nevertheless death reigned from Adam until Moses, even over those who had not sinned in the likeness of the offense of Adam, who is a type of Him who was to come. [15] But the free gift is not like the transgression. For if by the trans-

---

79. Odeberg, *Pharisaism and Christianity*, 75.

80. Laato, *Paul and Judaism*, 75.

gression of the one the masses died, much more did the grace of God and the gift by the grace of the one Man, Jesus Christ, abound to the masses. [16] And the gift is not like that which came through the one who sinned; for on the one hand the judgment arose from one transgression resulting in condemnation, but on the other hand the free gift arose from many transgressions resulting in justification.

Most modern readers of Romans 5 assume that Paul was affirming a traditional Jewish understanding of the fall of Adam and its consequences for creation, though this is not the case. By the first century, there were various Jewish explanations of how sin came into the world: some blamed the fallen angels (e.g., *1 Enoch* 6–11), some pointed the finger at Eve (*Life of Adam and Eve* 18:1 and Sir 25:24), and many blamed it on Adam's reaction to the "evil inclination" supposedly created within him by God (*4 Ezra* 3:20–30). Paul explains the origin of evil based on Adam and Eve's disobedience as recorded in Genesis 3. He understands their action as not merely one individual example of man's sin but as that action in which all mankind was brought into utter and complete bondage to sin: "because all sinned" (Rom 5:12).[81] There is no more free will after this tragic event because now man is in a condition of sin and death from the moment of conception. Lutherans label this condition "original sin."[82]

This pessimistic anthropology that Paul describes does not vanish when one is joined to Christ through the reception of the Holy Spirit. It is important to see that Romans 7 follows the discussion of the baptismal union with Christ that frees the Christian from the dominion of sin as proclaimed in Romans 6. This freedom from sin's dominion must always be understood in light of the ongoing battle against the sinful nature that continues to exist within us, though this nature no longer dominates. Paul, therefore, counterbalances his presentation in Romans 6 with a discussion of this battle in Romans 7:

[19] For the good that I wish, I do not do; but I practice the very evil that I do not wish. [20] But if I am doing the very thing I do not wish, I am no longer the one doing it, but sin which dwells in me. [21] I find then the principle that evil is present in me,

---

81. For a helpful discussion of the challenges in translating and interpreting ἐφ᾽ ᾧ πάντες ἥμαρτον, see Cranfield, *Romans I*, 274–81, especially option iv on 274.

82. See AC II (K-W, 36ff.) and Ap. II (K-W, 111ff.). For further evidence of Luther's understanding of this condition, see "Bondage of the Will."

the one who wishes to do good. [22] For I joyfully concur with the law of God in the inner man,[83] [23] but I see a different law in the members of my body, waging war against the law of my mind, and making me a prisoner of the law of sin which is in my members. [24] Wretched man that I am! Who will set me free from the body of this death?

One root of the problems with modern scholarship's assessment of Paul's understanding of the Law lies in the fact that during the twentieth century there was a strong shift away from reading Romans 7 as Paul's assessment of himself as a justified Christian who continues to struggle with obedience of basic moral law because of the continued presence of his sinful nature inherited from Adam.[84] Unlike the New Perspective's emphasis that both first-century Judaism and Pauline Christianity taught that one's righteousness is *maintained* through attempted obedience to the Law, Paul actually teaches in Romans 7 that faith alone in Christ both *establishes* and *maintains* our righteous status. After Paul's depressing confession of this ongoing struggle in Romans 7, he triumphantly declares: "But thanks be to God who gives us the victory through our Lord Jesus Christ" (Rom 7:25). Michael Middendorf, in his extensive and careful exegesis of Romans 7, draws this concise conclusion concerning Pauline anthropology:

> Romans 7 reveals an aspect of Paul's theology which dare not be neglected. His main point is to illustrate why no one can, in any way, depend on their "doing" the Law either for earning (vv. 7–11) or maintaining one's righteousness before God (vv. 14–25). Through his use of the "I," Paul demonstrates precisely why he or any other person is unable to rely upon his own observance of the Law. It is because sin, which reigns in the flesh of unbelievers (6:14, 17, 22), is able to misuse the Law's commandment in order to provoke sin, to deceive, and to kill (vv. 7–11, 13). It is because sin, which continues to dwell in the believer's flesh and to work in his members (vv. 14, 17, 20), is able to prohibit him from doing the "good" the Law requires and he desires. As long as the believer remains in this world, there is that within him, namely his flesh which, corrupted by

---

83. "The inner man" (τὸν ἔσω ἄνθρωπον) should be understood in light of the union with Christ presented in Romans 6. This "man" is Christ who is "in" Paul (2 Cor 4:16; Eph 3:16; cf. Gal 2:20). Middendorf does not make this point in his otherwise fine exegesis; see *"I" in the Storm*, 106.

84. See the masterful and complete discussion of modern research in Middendorf, *"I" in the Storm*, 15–51.

sin, also leads one to do the evil "I hate" (vv. 14–23). Paul's own example affirms this is true even after a person has been declared justified from sin (6:7) through faith in Jesus Christ and, thereby, freed from the *lordship* of sin, death, and the Law.[85]

E. THE CHRISTOPHANY AS THE BASIS FOR PAUL'S CHANGED PERSPECTIVE ON THE LAW

Modern scholars are correct in noting that, unlike Luther, the apostle Paul was not burdened by his unworthy sinful condition before he came to know the righteousness of God in Christ. This is clear from his own autobiographical description in Philippians 3:

> [4] If any other man thinks he has reason for confidence in the flesh, I have more: [5] circumcised on the eighth day, of the people of Israel, of the tribe of Benjamin, a Hebrew born of Hebrews; as to the law a Pharisee, [6] as to zeal a persecutor of the church as to righteousness under the law, blameless.

Furthermore, many adherents of the New Perspective also hold that Paul's attitude toward the Law did not change significantly at his conversion but developed later as he was confronted with the mission to the Gentiles.

Paul's changed perspective toward the Law and his own righteousness, however, was the result of a realization on the road to Damascus that Jesus of Nazareth, who was crucified, is both Christ and Lord.[86] Paul understood that he had encountered the visible image of YHWH, much like the prophets of old.[87] This encounter led him to make significant changes in his understanding of both human anthropology and the role of the Law because Paul realized for the first time both the depth of sin that demanded the death of the Messiah as well as the blindness of those who thought they could be righteous apart from God's Righteousness, namely, Christ. As Stephen Westerholm states: "The cross of Christ imposed on Paul a more pessimistic view of human capacities than one normally encounters in Judaism."[88] Peter Stuhlmacher draws a similar conclusion:

---

85. Middendorf, *"I" in the Storm*, 262–63.

86. See especially Seyoon Kim, *The Origin of Paul's Gospel* (WUNT II.4; Tübingen: J. C. B. Mohr, 1981), and more recently Kim, *Paul and the New Perspective* (see n. 44).

87. For a discussion of how Paul's Christology was grounded in the Old Testament theophanic traditions, see Charles A. Gieschen, *Angelomorphic Christology: Antecedents and Early Evidence* (Arbeiten zur Geschichte des antiken Judentums und des Urchristentums 42; Leiden: Brill, 1998), 315–46.

88. Westerholm, *Israel's Law and the Church's Faith*, 221.

The apostle anchors his dialectical criticism of the law of Moses in his christology because at his conversion at Damascus he was enlightened by the realization that God's splendor on the countenance of the crucified and resurrected Christ eschatologically eclipsed the glory of the Sinaitic Torah (cf. 2 Cor 3:7–11; 4:6).[89]

Martin Hengel is another strong advocate for grounding Paul's changed perspective in the Christology that resulted from his conversion:

> In no way can it be demonstrated that the [Pauline] doctrine of the law and of justification grew only out of the conflict in Galatia. It has its source in the conversion of the Pharisaic scribe and the revelation that was received in this connection. Its basis was the Gospel that was received from the Risen Lord, that made Paul a missionary to the Gentiles, and that he had to defend consistently in various situations of conflict.[90]

Against the dominant conclusion of the New Perspective, it must be emphasized that the Gentile mission was not the determining factor in the expression of Paul's theology. Paul did not desire to bring the Judaism in which he had been raised to Jews and Gentiles alike. Instead, he wanted to bring to them the Judaism he knew after the Damascus Christophany in light of Jesus Christ's death and resurrection. Contrary to Stendahl and those who follow him, Paul experienced more than a call and commission to bring the Gospel to the Gentiles at Damascus. One of the places where Paul expresses the profound conversion and change that resulted from the encounter with Christ is Philippians 3:

> [7] But whatever things were gain to me [in my former understanding of Judaism], those things I have counted as loss for the sake of Christ. [8] More than that, I count all things to be loss in view of the surpassing value of knowing Christ Jesus my Lord, for whom I have suffered the loss of all things, and count them but rubbish in order that I gain Christ, [9] and be found in him, not having a righteousness of my own derived from the Law, but that which is through faith in Christ, the righteousness which comes from God on the basis of faith, [10] that I may know him, and the power of his resurrection and the fellowship of his

---

89. Peter Stuhlmacher, "The Understanding of Christ in the Pauline School: A Sketch," in *Jews and Christians: The Parting of the Ways, A.D. 70 to 135* (ed. James D. G. Dunn; Grand Rapids: Eerdmans, 1999), 170.

90. Martin Hengel, "The Attitude of Paul to the Law in the Unknown Years between Damascus and Antioch," in *Paul and the Mosaic Law* (ed. James D. G. Dunn; Grand Rapids: Eerdmans, 2001), 50.

sufferings, being conformed to his death; [11] in order that I attain to the resurrection from the dead. [12] Not that I have already obtained it, or have already become perfect, but I press on in order that I lay hold of that for which also I was laid hold of by Christ Jesus.

Although there certainly was development in Paul's theology—especially in his exegesis of the Old Testament—after Damascus, the Christophany and his subsequent Baptism was the decisive event that led to a profound change in Paul's understanding of sin, soteriology, and the scope of the Jewish mission.

F. THE CENTRALITY OF JUSTIFICATION IN PAUL'S SOTERIOLOGY

Since William Wrede and Albert Schweitzer, there has been an ongoing effort by scholars to pit justification and mystical participation against each other, with justification coming out the loser as a less important teaching of Paul that he formulated decades after Damascus in response to the Judaizers he encountered, especially among the church in Galatia.[91] Schweitzer wrote: "The doctrine of righteousness by faith is a subsidiary crater, which has formed within the rim of the main crater, the mystical doctrine of redemption through the being-in-Christ."[92] Beginning with Sanders, the New Perspective has downplayed the cosmic and forensic aspect of Christ's work. Stuhlmacher has been a strong voice calling for a corrective in New Testament scholarship that recaptures the cosmic scope of Christ's work as proclaimed by Paul.

> This apocalyptic breath of the doctrine of justification must not be diminished by limiting the gospel of God's righteousness to the message of the forgiveness of sins for individual sinners who confess Jesus as Lord and Savior. What is involved in the demonstration of God's righteousness through the atoning death of Christ and in his resurrection for the justification of many and in his ongoing activity as Lord, Advocate, Savior and Judge of the world is nothing less than the establishment of the right of God over the whole cosmos.[93]

---

91. Stuhlmacher, *Revisiting Paul's Doctrine of Justification*, 10. See further William Wrede, *Paul* (trans. Edward Lummis; London: Philip Green, 1907), and Albert Schweitzer, *The Mysticism of Paul the Apostle* (trans. William Montgomery; New York: Henry Holt, 1931).

92. Schweitzer, *Mysticism of Paul the Apostle*, 225.

93. Stuhlmacher, *Revisiting Paul's Doctrine of Justification*, 28.

The eschatological nature of justification is distorted by the New Perspective.[94] The end-time righteousness promised by the prophets has come in Christ. The background for Paul's understanding of δικαιοσύνη θεοῦ ("Righteousness of God") is surely to be found in the Old Testament, especially in Isaiah:

> [YHWH says:] "Listen to me, you stubborn-hearted, you who are far from righteousness. I am bringing *My Righteousness* near, it is not far away; and *My Salvation* will not be delayed. I will grant salvation to Zion, my splendor to Israel." (Isa 46:12–13, *my emphasis*)

> [YHWH says:] "*My Righteousness* draws near speedily, *My Salvation* is on the way, and my arm will bring justice to the nations. . . . Lift up your eyes to the heavens, look at the earth beneath; the heavens vanish like smoke, the earth will wear out like a garment and its inhabitants die like flies. But *My Salvation* will last forever, *My Righteousness* will never fail." (Isa 51:5–6, *my emphasis*)

> [YHWH says:] "Turn to me and be saved, all you ends of the earth; for I am God, and there is no other. By myself I have sworn, my mouth has uttered in all integrity a word that will not be revoked: Before me every knee will bow; by me every tongue will swear. They will say of me, '*In the LORD alone are righteousness and strength.*' " [Isaiah concludes:] All who have raged against him will come to him and be put to shame. But in the LORD all the seed of Israel *will be declared righteous* and be glorified. (Isa 45:22–25, *my emphasis*)

It is noteworthy that "Righteousness of God" is not an abstract concept or attribute of God in these texts; instead, it is a term that identifies God's saving action that will be revealed in the latter days in his Servant. Furthermore, Isaiah 45 demonstrates that the coming of this "Righteousness of God" will result in a changed status: The seed of Israel will be declared righteous.

Paul uses δικαιοσύνη θεοῦ in Romans in a similar manner. The "Righteousness of God" is God's end-time saving action in Christ that has resulted in a changed status: All sinners have been declared righteous (universal or objective justification). This changed status is a forensic or legal status grounded in God's action in Christ; it is not a moral status that is grounded in any manner in man. This

---

94. Stuhlmacher, *Revisiting Paul's Doctrine of Justification*, 42.

"Righteousness of God," this saving action in Christ that has resulted in the changed status of sinners, is being revealed in the Gospel. The Gospel is the power of God because in it the saving action in Christ that has changed the legal status of sinners before God is unveiled to create and sustain faith that receives the benefits of this action and status (individual or subjective justification). This means the distinction between justification and Christ-mysticism is erroneous because Christ-mysticism should be understood as a vital expression of individual justification. Therefore, justification (especially universal justification) is the *content* of the Gospel, not only a *consequence* of the Gospel. Furthermore, neither "Righteousness of God" nor "Gospel" should be viewed as abstract ideas or concepts; they are realities that are tangible and personal in Jesus Christ. Paul expresses this most pointedly in Romans 3:

> [21] But now apart from the Law the Righteousness of God has been manifested, being witnessed by the Law and the Prophets, [22] even the Righteousness of God through the faith[fulness] of Jesus Christ for all those who believe; for there is no distinction; [23] for all have sinned and lack the glory of God, [24] and [all] are justified as a gift by His grace through the redemption that is in Christ Jesus; [25] whom God displayed publicly as a mercy seat sacrifice in His blood through faith. This was to demonstrate His righteousness, because in the forbearance of God He passed over the sins previously committed; [26] for the demonstration, I say, of His righteousness at the present time, that He be just and the justifier of the one who has faith in Jesus. [27] Where then is boasting? It is excluded. By what kind of law? Of works? No, but by a law of faith. [28] For we maintain that a man is justified by faith apart from works of the Law. [29] Or is God the God of Jews only? Is He not the God of Gentiles also? Yes, of Gentiles also, [30] since indeed God who will justify the circumcised by faith and the uncircumcised through faith is one. [31] Do we then nullify the Law through faith? May it never be! On the contrary, we establish the Law.

Romans 5, especially verses 6–11, is the clearest and most abundant testimony to universal (or objective) justification in the Pauline corpus. Notice the repeated emphasis on God's action in Christ taking place before the receipt of the righteousness of God by faith. This emphasis is especially clear in Rom 5:6: "Yet Christ, while we were without strength, according to that [powerless] time, died for the ones who are ungodly." There was no righteousness in us, no godliness, that merited God's action on our behalf. Notice the present participle with temporal force ("while we were") in the genitive absolute construction (ὄντων ἡμῶν ἀσθενῶν) and the noun used to describe people in this state (ἀσεβῶν). This same truth is restated in Rom 5:8 with another genitive absolute construction: "While we were sinners [ἔτι ἁμαρτωλῶν ὄντων], Christ died on our behalf." Both of these verses stress that Christ's death is the source of universal justification. This conclusion is confirmed in Rom 5:9: "Therefore, all the more, because we have now been declared righteous in his blood, we will be saved by him from the wrath" (cf. Rom 5:18–19).

The language in Rom 5:10 shifts to the "reconciliation" (καταλλάσσω) word group. Notice the similar construction of these three statements:

While we were without strength, [Christ] died for the ones who are ungodly. (Rom 5:6)

While we were sinners, Christ died on our behalf. (Rom 5:8)

While we were enemies, we were reconciled to God through the death of his Son. (Rom 5:10)

These statements make it clear that Christ's death has brought about a changed status for *all sinners* (note that faith is not mentioned in these verses). The fact that these three statements are directly related to justification is made explicit in Rom 5:9 and its parallel structure to Rom 5:10:

Because we have now been declared righteous in his blood, we will be saved by him from the wrath. (Rom 5:9)

Because we have been reconciled, we will be saved by his life. (Rom 5:10)

The truth is clear: Because of the universal justification/reconciliation that took place at the cross, those who believe in Christ can be certain of salvation from God's wrath. Justification is central to understanding Paul's theology. Paul also uses reconciliation language in 2 Cor 5:19–20 to communicate the reality of justification:

In Christ God was reconciling [καταλλάσσων] the world to himself, not counting their trespasses against them [universal justification], and entrusting to us the message of reconciliation. So we are ambassadors for Christ, God making his appeal through us. We beseech you, on behalf of Christ, be reconciled [καταλλάγητε] to God [individual justification].

III. Conclusion

Several aspects of Paul's perspective on the Law, as well as Luther's interpretation of that perspective, that have been discussed lead to four important conclusions. First, the research of the twentieth century helps us to see that more care in descriptions of first-century Judaism—or better, the various Jewish groups or Judaisms of the first century—are necessary to overcome the false portraits that Jews were merely works-righteous people who did not believe in the grace of God and the importance of faith. To step forward and paint sixteenth-century Roman Catholicism with the same brush is also problematic. Certainly first-century Jews, as well as sixteenth-century Roman Catholics, believed in the grace of God and stressed the role of faith; neither emphasized that doing works of the Law apart from the grace of God is the way of salvation. Although Luther at times painted the theology of both groups in broad strokes that accentuated their essential differences from biblical teaching (e.g., "salvation by works"), nevertheless he recognized that grace and faith were foundational in the soteriology of the Judaizers at Galatia, as well as that of the Roman Church. This is clear from the reformer's statement that began this essay:

> The false apostles [at Galatia] preached the Gospel, but they do so with this condition [the necessity of works of the Law] attached to it. The scholastics do the same thing in our day. They say that we must believe in Christ and that faith is the foundation of salvation, but they say that this faith does not justify unless it is "formed in love."[95]

Luther's critique of his contemporaries does not deny the important role of faith in their respective soteriologies, but he condemns the addition of obedience to the Law as *necessary for salvation*. Luther sees this as a denial of Christ's completed work for all sinners:

> Therefore it is inevitable that the papists, the Zwinglians, the Anabaptists, and all those who either do not know about the righteousness of Christ or who do not believe correctly about it should change Christ into Moses and the Law and change the

---

95. LW 26:88.

Law into Christ. For this is what they teach: "Faith in Christ does indeed justify, but at the same time observance of the Commandments of God is necessary; for it is written (Matt. 19:17): 'If you would enter life, keep the Commandments.' " Here immediately Christ is denied and faith is abolished, because what belongs to Christ alone is attributed to the Commandments of God or to the Law.[96]

Second, a conclusion that must not be dismissed, however, is that neither first-century Judaism nor sixteenth-century Roman Catholicism stressed that salvation was by grace *alone* and through faith *alone*. Indeed, works of the Law played a significant role in their respective soteriologies, especially in *maintaining* one's righteous standing before God in the covenant until the eschatological judgment. The basic problem is synergism: the role man plays in receiving and maintaining a righteous status before God. Here is where Luther's reading of Paul's monergistic teaching is helpful. Luther's convictions concerning Christ's atoning sacrifice and man's total corruption played an important role in his convictions concerning salvation by grace *alone* through faith *alone*. His clarity on this issue deserves our continued advocacy:

> The true Gospel, however, is this: Works are not the ornament or perfection of faith; but faith itself is a gift of God, a work of God in our hearts, which justifies us because it takes hold of Christ as the Savior. Human reason has the Law as its object. It says to itself: "This is what I have done; this is what I have not done." But faith in its proper function has no other object than Jesus Christ, the Son of God, who was put to death for the sins of the world. It [Faith] does not look at its works and say: "What have I done? Where have I sinned? What have I deserved?" But it says: "What has Christ done? What has He deserved?" And here the truth of the Gospel gives you the answer: "He has redeemed you from sin, from the devil, and from eternal death." Therefore faith acknowledges that in this one Person, Jesus Christ, it has the forgiveness of sins and eternal life.[97]

Third, the foundational role that Christology played in Paul's changed perspective of the Law, human anthropology, and justification has been confirmed. Paul's tireless commitment to the Gentile mission grew out of the apocalypse of God's Righteousness, Christ

---

96. LW 26:143.
97. LW 26:88.

becoming sin for all men, that had taken place at the cross and was seen by the sinner Paul as he was blinded by God's Righteousness on the road to Damascus.

Finally, it is sometimes asserted that Luther went far beyond Paul by stating that Christians are "freed" from the Law and no longer need it. For example, Thomas Schreiner states: "Luther's comments on the topic [the moral law reflected in the Old Testament] were somewhat ambiguous, but one receives the impression that one is freed entirely from the law of Moses, even the moral law."[98] Mark Nanos also characterizes Luther as an advocate of a Law-free Gospel and cautions readers from falling into "Luther's trap."[99] This is a misconstrual of Luther's position. Certainly a Christian is "freed" from the moral law's condemnation by Christ's obedience to the Law, but the prominent use of the Ten Commandments in both of the reformer's catechisms, as well as his exegesis of the Old Testament, testify to the ongoing important function of the moral law as both a mirror and a guide in the life of the Christian. Luther expresses the importance of keeping the Law distinct from justification while not disconnecting it from sanctification in the following excerpt:

> "But the Law is good, righteous, and holy." Very well! But when we are involved in a discussion of justification, there is no room for speaking about the Law. The question is what Christ is and what blessing He has brought to us. Christ is not the Law; He is not my work or that of the Law; He is not my love or that of the Law; He is not my chastity, obedience, or poverty. But He is the Lord of life and death, the Mediator and Savior of sinners, the Redeemer of those who are under the Law. By faith we are in Him, and He is in us (John 6:56). This Bridegroom, Christ, must be alone with His bride in His private chamber, and all the family and household must be shunted away. But later on, when the Bridegroom opens the door and comes out, then let the servants return to take care of them and serve them food and drink. Then let works and love begin.
>
> Thus we learn to distinguish all laws, even those of God, and all works from faith and from Christ, if we are to define Christ accurately. Christ is not the Law, and therefore He is not a taskmaster for the Law and for works; but He is the Lamb of God, who takes away the sins of the world (John 1:29). This is

---

98. Schreiner, *Law and Its Fulfillment*, 16.
99. Nanos, *Mystery of Romans*, 337.

grasped by faith alone, not by love, which nevertheless must follow faith as a kind of gratitude. Therefore victory over sin and death, salvation, and eternal life do not come by the Law or by the deeds of the Law or by our will but by Jesus Christ alone.[100]

"Christ is the end of the Law" in the sense that he is the fulfiller of the Law's demands in order that sinners can be freely extended God's forgiveness in him (Rom 10:4). As a new creation in Christ through Baptism, the "Christ in us" delights in the original intention of the Law, namely, love toward God and neighbor. This *old* Lutheran perspective still offers much of value for understanding *Paul's* perspective on the Law.

---

100. LW 26:137–38.

BEYOND
COVENANTAL NOMISM
PAUL, JUDIASM, AND PERFECT OBEDIENCE

A. ANDREW DAS

In his 1977 *Paul and Palestinian Judaism*, E. P. Sanders identified a common pattern in the documents that he examined from Second Temple and Tannaitic Judaism.[1] He concluded that the Jewish people observed the Mosaic Law in response to a gracious God who had elected Israel for a covenant relationship and who had mercifully provided for transgression of that Law. Sanders labeled this pattern "covenantal nomism." He surmised that no one was expected to obey the Law perfectly to enjoy a right relationship with God. Paul exuded a confidence in Phil 3:3–11 that he was an exemplary Law-observant individual. As a former Pharisee, he clearly suffered no anxiety or pangs of conscience.

What, then, was Paul's difficulty with the Law? In the wake of Sanders's work, James D. G. Dunn, N. T. Wright, and others have championed the "New Perspective" on Paul and the Law and have rightly highlighted the intensely ethnic dimension to the apostle's reasoning. The difficulty the apostle to the Gentiles had with the Law revolved around its differentiation of humanity into Jew and non-Jew. The Gentiles would have to convert to Judaism and be circumcised to enter into a relationship with God. Paul recognized that God had never intended the Gentiles to be excluded from the chosen people. The old walls of ethnic hostility and division had

---

1. E. P. Sanders, *Paul and Palestinian Judaism: A Comparison of Patterns of Religion* (Philadelphia: Fortress, 1977).

been torn down as all people, whether Jew or Gentile, were incorporated into a new humanity identified solely by faith in the Messiah, Jesus Christ. The New Perspective interpreters, on the basis of Sanders's analysis of Judaism, have rejected the traditional premise that Paul's problem with the Law was simply that no one could satisfactorily do it.

Scholars have not generally recognized that one can accept the bulk of Sanders's analysis of Judaism without accepting the New Perspective premise regarding perfect obedience. The New Perspective trajectory from Sanders is not in itself a necessary one. Pauline interpreters have overlooked Sanders's own struggle with the "demand" of the Law in its regulations and strictures on the one hand and the "grace" of the covenantal framework on the other. Quite often, his analysis appears deliberately skewed to emphasize God's grace and mercy. Sanders minimized the Law's strict demand as one side of a tension between the embedded nomism and the gracious covenantal framework. In at least three of the bodies of Second Temple literature that Sanders analyzed, the Law actually enjoined perfect obedience of its commands. If it is true that the Jews often saw the Law as requiring strict, perfect obedience, then the key premise in the "New Perspective on Paul" would be wrong. An incorrect premise would explain why scholars so frequently experience difficulty explaining why Paul's issue with the Law revolved quite often around satisfying the Law's demands. A few representative passages, then, will underscore that the apostle's "plight" with the Law was not just a matter of ethnic exclusion but also its demand for rigorous obedience.

How could the apostle claim difficulty with doing the Law in the face of Judaism's own gracious framework and provision for failure? Paul, however, has radically redefined that gracious framework of election, covenant, and atonement in favor of a reconstructed framework of grace centering on the person of Christ. The transition into a new framework of grace has affected the embedded nomism. Paul's problem with the Law, then, was not only with its division of humanity and Jewish ethnic pride and presumption. The time is ripe for a "newer perspective" on Paul and the Law.[2]

---

2. For further discussion of such a "newer perspective," see A. Andrew Das, *Paul, the Law, and the Covenant* (Peabody, Mass.: Hendrickson, 2001).

I. REVISITING SANDERS'S EVIDENCE
FROM SECOND TEMPLE JEWISH LITERATURE

Sanders analyzed *Jubilees* and the Qumran literature in *Paul and Palestinian Judaism*. He reviewed Philo in an article that was published prior to the book. These Second Temple Jewish works are more directly relevant to the interpretation of Paul than the Tannaitic literature that originated after the catastrophe of the temple's destruction in A.D. 70. At that point in time, a radical reorganization of Jewish leadership and Jewish thought took place. *Jubilees*, the Qumran literature, and Philo all showcase the gracious dimension of Sanders's covenantal nomism. Despite an overarching gracious orientation, however, all three bodies of literature also affirm that God's holy Law was to be obeyed rigorously and perfectly.

A. *JUBILEES*

According to the second century B.C. Jewish document entitled *Jubilees*, all Israel was God's elect people (1:17–18, 25, 28; 16:17–18; 19:18; 22:11–12). Israel enjoyed a special covenantal relationship with God that was bequeathed from the patriarchs (6:17–19). The author praised God's gracious provision of repentance (1:22–23; 23:26; 41:23–27) and the sacrificial system (6:14; 50:10–11; 34:18–19) for failure to obey the Law. Because God's elect could be "righteous" even when not perfectly obedient, it would be easy to conclude that the Law did not demand strict obedience.

From the point of view of the author of *Jubilees*, however, the Mosaic Law *did* enjoin perfect obedience. The people's sins were never ignored but always addressed through a process of atonement and repentance. Perfection of conduct nevertheless remained the ideal. "All of his commands and his ordinances and all of his law" are to be carefully observed "without turning aside to the right or left" (23:16). In 5:19: "[God] did not show partiality, except Noah alone . . . because his heart was righteous in all of his ways just as it was commanded concerning him. And he did not transgress anything which was ordained for him." Noah, while the recipient of God's mercy (10:3), did "just as it was commanded" and was "righteous in all of his ways." "He did not transgress." Jacob was also "a perfect man" (27:17). Leah "was perfect and upright in all her ways," and Joseph "walked uprightly" (36:23; 40:8).

Although God granted mercy to the elect, the requirement of right conduct "in all things" (21:23) is still upheld and admonished through these exemplary models. Although Israel enjoyed an elect status, the Law must still be obeyed (1:23–24; 20:7). God told Abram in 15:3 to "be pleasing before me and be perfect." Abraham was then praised in 23:10 because he "was *perfect in all of his actions* with the Lord and was pleasing through righteousness all of the days of his life" (*my emphasis*). The author looked forward to the day when Israel would be *perfectly* obedient (1:22–24; 5:12; 50:5). Sanders conceded on the basis of these passages: "Perfect obedience is specified . . ."[3] He added: "As we have now come to expect, the emphasis on God's mercy is coupled with a strict demand to be obedient."[4] Although God offered provision for sin and failure, the ideal remained strict and perfect obedience of the Law.

Sanders preferred to resolve the logical tension between God's mercy toward the elect and the rigorous demands of the Law in favor of mercy because *Jubilees* could speak of sinners as those who were righteous by means of God's own provision for sin.[5] Sanders states: "Righteousness as perfect or nearly perfect obedience is not, however, the 'soteriology' of the author."[6] Although it is true that perfect or nearly perfect righteousness was not the soteriology of the author, the Law itself demanded just such an obedience. The problem with Sanders's analysis is that he often downgraded or soft-ened the strict demand of the Law, undoubtedly as a reaction to those who had described Judaism as a purely legalistic religion. As much as the author of *Jubilees* identified the Law as an ethnic iden-tity/boundary marker and as much as he spoke of God's mercy toward an elect and often sinful people (unlike the strict judgment of the Gentiles offered in 5:12–18; 23:31), the author maintained that God intended the Law to be obeyed without transgression.

B. THE QUMRAN LITERATURE

The Qumran community admonished its members to be perfect in their obedience of the Law.[7] The demand of the Law was strict and absolute (1QS 1:13–17; 5:1, 8, 20–22; CD 2:15; 15:12–14; 16:6b–8; 20:2, 5, 7). According to 1QS 3:9–11, the individual must

---

3. Sanders, *Paul and Palestinian Judaism*, 381.

4. Sanders, *Paul and Palestinian Judaism*, 383.

5. Sanders, *Paul and Palestinian Judaism*, 380–83.

6. Sanders, *Paul and Palestinian Judaism*, 382. Sanders also argues that *Jubilees* is not so strict because it affirms repentance and God's mercy; see *Paul and Palestinian Judaism*, 379. This confuses the legal demand itself with the larger framework of Judaism inclu-sive of God's election and mercy.

7. For example, 1QH 9 (=1):36: perfection of way.

"steady his steps in order to walk with perfection on all the paths of God, conforming to all he has decreed concerning the regular times of his commands and not turn aside, either left or right, nor infringe even one of his words."

Sanders rightly stressed the availability of a system of atonement for sin at Qumran (particularly right conduct). The men of the Qumran community upheld repentance as a means of rectifying the situation caused by sin before God. Far from mitigating the strict requirement of the Qumran *halakah* to be perfect in actions, however, the system of atonement confirmed it. Each sin had to be atoned for in some way so the individual could be restored to "perfect righteousness." Any sin rendered a transgressor impure and out of favor before God, as well as before the community, until that sin had been properly rectified. For example, CD 10:2–3 says: "No-one who has consciously transgressed anything of a precept is to be believed as a witness against his fellow, until he has been purified to return."

Even with these provisions for sin, Qumran members still expressed an intense self-awareness of sin in their hymnic material.[8] Far from finding perfect obedience a matter of due course, they struggled individually with living in a fully righteous manner before God. The author of 1QH 12 (=4):29–33 lamented falling short of the "perfect path" required by God. Community members looked forward to the eschaton when they would be "cleansed" of this tendency toward sin (1QS 3:21–23; 4:18–22; 11:14–15; 1QH 14 [=6]:8–10; 7 [=15]:15–17).[9]

Sanders underscored that a status of "perfect righteousness" flowed out of God's gracious relations with the elect community, for example, 1QH 12 (=4):37; 15 (=7):30; 19 (=11):29–32.[10] The requirement for legal perfection was always set within a context of gratuity. The reward was always the result of God's mercy, while punishment was always deserved.[11] Obedience was always the elect people's response to God's grace.[12] Although God was indeed merciful, 1QS 4:6–8 is unmistakably clear, contra Sanders, that God

---

8. Sanders, *Paul and Palestinian Judaism*, 273–84.

9. Sanders, *Paul and Palestinian Judaism*, 279–80, 283–84, 291.

10. Sanders himself points out the dilemma between the requirement of perfect obedience and the failure to live up to the standard; see *Paul and Palestinian Judaism*, 288–90. Sanders attempts to resolve the dilemma by arguing that the failure to live up to God's standard refers to man's condition *before God*. Perfection must come by means of God's grace and pardon.

11. Sanders, *Paul and Palestinian Judaism*, 293.

12. Sanders, *Paul and Palestinian Judaism*, 295–96.

would reward those who were obedient in their works: "And the visitation of those who walk in it [the counsels of the spirit] will be for healing, plentiful peace in a long life, fruitful offspring with all everlasting blessings, eternal enjoyment with endless life, and a crown of glory with majestic raiment in eternal light." Although God was a God of compassion and mercy, he still "pays man his wages" (1QS 10:17–18). 4QPsf 8:4–5 says: "[Man is examined] according to his path each one is rewar[ded according to his de]eds." 1QM 11:14: ". . . you shall carry out justice by your truthful judgment on every son of man." 1QpHab 8:1–3 says: "Its interpretation concerns all observing the Law in the House of Judah, whom God will free from punishment on account of their deeds and of their loyalty to the Teacher of Righteousness."

Alongside those texts that speak of God's mercy and forgiveness of sin (even at the judgment), there are passages that adhere to a strict judgment according to the standard of works.[13] Sanders resolved the tension by subordinating the passages that speak of all people being judged according to their works to those passages in which God judged the wicked according to works while judging the elect with mercy and grace, for example, 1QH 13 (=5):6; 14 (=6):9; 17 (=9):34.[14] Although many Qumran passages affirm a judgment according to mercy for the elect, such passages do not exhaust all the evidence. The covenanters could also affirm that God would judge all people, even those of the community, on the basis of what they had earned by their works. The two motifs must be allowed to remain in tension.[15]

---

13. Sanders, *Paul and Palestinian Judaism*, 291–94. Sanders minimizes this evidence while citing these passages.

14. Sanders, *Paul and Palestinian Judaism*, 294. Note that these references fall *outside* the *halakah* in the context of the hymnic material.

15. As Sanders himself admits with respect to the strict demand of the *halakah*: ". . . from the point of view of the *halakah*, one is required to walk perfectly. From the point of view of the individual in prayer or devotional moments, he is unable to walk perfectly and must be given the perfection of way by God's grace" (*Paul and Palestinian Judaism*, 288). Unfortunately, Sanders is not consistent on this point. Elsewhere he writes: "The various provisions for the punishment of transgression show with striking clarity the way in which the religion functioned. Commandments were given which a man was to obey. Perfect obedience was the aim, and, within the tightly ordered community structure, was not considered a totally impossible goal. Infractions were punished, and the acceptance of the punishment, together with the perseverance in obedience, led to full restoration of fellowship" (*Paul and Palestinian Judaism*, 286). On the one hand, perfect obedience was not "totally impossible," but on the other hand, the individual is

C. PHILO

In *De praemiis et poenis* 79–83 (especially 79 and 82, citing Deut 30:10), Philo said that it was not enough to hear or to profess the precepts of God's Law; one must actually do them. Individuals would be weighed in the scales (e.g., *De congressu eruditionis gratia* 164; *Quis rerum divinarum heres sit* 46). In *Quod Deus sit immutabilis* 162, one must not deviate to the right or to the left from the path God has prepared for humanity in the Law (*De Abrahamo* 269; *De posteritate Caini* 101–102; cf. *Legum allegoriae* 3:165; the "middle road" of *De migratione Abrahami* 146). Philo praised Abraham (*De Abrahamo* 192) because "he had not neglected any of God's commands." One's "whole life" should be one of "happy obedience to law" (*De Abrahamo* 5–6).[16]

At the same time, God "ever prefers forgiveness to punishment" (*De praemiis et poenis* 166). God granted to the Jews several means by which they could rectify the situation created by sin and violation of God's Law. Philo affirmed atoning sacrifice (*De specialibus legibus* 1:235–241; 1:188–190; 1:235–239). Only God could be sinless (*De fuga et inventione* 157; *De virtutibus* 177; *Legum allegoriae* 3:106.211).[17] The possibility of repentance flowed out of God's recognition of the human tendency to sin (*De fuga et inventione* 99, 105).[18] It was as if one were ill, with repentance being the only hope

---

"unable to walk perfectly." Sanders tries to resolve the contradiction by distinguishing between behavior monitored within the community, where perfect obedience is possible, as opposed to strict obedience before God, where such perfection is not possible. The problem, though, is that the Qumran material itself does not make such a neat distinction. The two motifs are simply not so easily harmonized. Perfect obedience was required by the *halakah*, and such obedience entailed all the Law, not only what was monitored. Yet the devotional material shows the struggles individuals had with that requirement and the need to rely on God's grace and mercy available to members of the community; see 1QH 12 (=4):37; 15 (=7):18–19; 1QS 10: 11; 11:2–3, 12–15. See further Bruce W. Longenecker, *Eschatology and the Covenant: A Comparison of 4 Ezra and Romans 1–11* (JSNTSup 57; Sheffield: JSOT Press, 1991), 25. New Testament scholars have been led by Sanders's discussion to assert that perfect obedience of the Law is, in fact, possible. According to the Qumran materials, though perfect obedience is required by the *halakah*, it is not necessarily possible.

16. I take the law of nature to be coordinate with the revealed, Mosaic Law. See especially Philo, *De vita Mosis* 2:52; Naomi Cohen, "The Jewish Dimension of Philo's Judaism," *JJS* 38 (1987): 169–70; and John M. G. Barclay, *Jews in the Mediterranean Diaspora: From Alexander to Trajan (323 BCE–117 CE)* (Edinburgh: T&T Clark, 1995), 172.

17. David Winston, "Philo's Doctrine of Repentance," in *The School of Moses: Studies in Philo and Hellenistic Religion* (ed. John Peter Kenney; Atlanta: Scholars Press, 1995), 32; and Jon Nelson Bailey, "Metanoia in the Writings of Philo Judaeus," in *Society of Biblical Literature Seminar Papers 1991* (Atlanta: Scholars Press, 1991), 140–41.

18. Winston, "Philo's Doctrine of Repentance," 32. Note how contrary this assumption is to the prevailing trend in Pauline scholarship to think that perfect obedience of the Law is attainable.

for a return to health (*De fuga et inventione* 160; *De Abrahamo* 26; *De specialibus legibus* 1:236–253). Sincere repentance blotted out the effects of sin as if the sin had never occurred (*De Abrahamo* 19; *De specialibus legibus* 1:187–188; *Quaestiones et solutiones in Genesin* 1:84; *De mutatione nominum* 124; *De somniis* 1:91).[19] God bestowed rewards and blessings "in honor of their victory" (*De virtutibus* 175). Those who repented, though, still bore the scars of their misdeeds (*De specialibus legibus* 1:103).

Although Philo affirmed Israel's special status as recipients of God's mercy and affirmed repentance as a means to remedy the situation caused by sin, he nevertheless commended the ones whose conduct was perfect. Those who remained sinless and unblemished were superior to those who must repent and so be healed of their illness (*De Abrahamo* 26; *De virtutibus* 176). Abraham achieved perfect obedience of the Law (*De migratione Abrahami* 127–130; *De Abrahamo* 275–276; *Quis rerum divinarum heres sit* 6–9).[20] Noah was "perfect" in virtue (*Quod Deus sit immutabilis* 117, 122, 140; *De Abrahamo* 34, 47). Interestingly, Philo immediately qualified the attribute of perfection for Noah (*De Abrahamo* 36–39). Noah only attained a perfection relative to his generation; he was "not good absolutely" (οὐ καθάπαξ). Philo then compared Noah's "perfection" with other sages who possessed an "unchallenged" and "unperverted" virtue. Noah, therefore, won the "second prize." Although Noah was to be praised for his achievement, Philo clearly commended the "first prize" of an unqualified virtue to his readers. Moses, for example, fell into that highest category. The lawgiver exemplified the attainment of the highest place of all (*De vita Mosis* 1:162; 2:1, 8–11; *Legum allegoriae* 3:134, 140; *De ebrietate* 94; *De*

---

19. Winston, "Philo's Doctrine of Repentance," 34; see also Bailey, "Metanoia," 140. On the necessity of sincerity, see Philo, *De fuga et inventione* 160.

20. The passage from *Who Is the Heir?* is representative both as an admonition to strive toward perfect obedience and as an expression of Abraham's attainment of that goal:

> When, then, is it that the servant speaks frankly to his master? Surely it is when his heart tells him that he has not wronged his owner, but that his words and deeds are all [πάντα] for that owner's benefit. And so when else should the slave of God open his mouth freely to Him Who is the ruler and master both of himself and of the All, *save when he is pure from sin* and the judgements of his conscious are loyal to his master . . . . The loyalty of Abraham's service and ministry is shewn by the concluding words of the oracle addressed to Abraham's son, "I will give to thee and thy seed all this land, and all the nations of the earth shall be blessed in thy seed, because Abraham thy father hearkened to My voice and kept My injunctions, My commands, My ordinances and My statutes" (Gen. 26:3–5). It is the highest praise which can be given to a servant that *he neglects none* [μηδενός] *of his master's commands. . . .*" (*my emphasis*)

sacrificiis Abelis et Caini 8). Philo commended Moses as a model of the perfection toward which his readers were to strive (*De vita Mosis* 1:158–159). Obviously, perfect obedience and sinlessness remained the ideal for Philo.

Philo maintained that the Jews, as an elect people, were to strive to live as virtuously and as perfectly as possible, as difficult as this might be. Even Enoch and Enosh were not able to live perfectly and without sin. On the other hand, God, a merciful God, recognized humanity's difficulty with sin and offered abundant grace and mercy to the repentant. Although the balance certainly weighed heavily toward mercy and forgiveness of sin in Philo, the Law still enjoined a perfect obedience toward which all people should strive.[21]

D. CLARIFYING A CRUCIAL DISTINCTION

While upholding the Law as a marker of Jewish ethnic identity, *Jubilees* commended Noah, Abraham, and others for their perfect obedience of the Law. Philo also spoke of certain "perfect" individuals. Similarly, the language of "perfect righteousness" at Qumran had a prescriptive force. Perfection was the standard by which the community members were to try to live. Whether by perfect exemplary models or by claiming that God demanded strict obedience, these documents evince a struggle with the Law's strict demand. In the words of Eleazar to his torturer, Antiochus, in 4 Macc 5:20–21: "The transgression of the Law, be it in small things or in great, is equally heinous; for in either case equally the Law is despised."[22]

Certainly the virtually ubiquitous broader perspective was that the Jews were a special people who had been favored by God and who had been granted a system to remedy the situation caused by transgression of God's Law. Nevertheless, Sanders minimized the fact that perfect conduct always remained the ideal. A distinction must be made between the Law considered inclusive of its gracious framework, in which one may fall short of perfect obedience, and the Law considered from the vantage point of its legislation, in which the demand is absolute. The distinction is critical.

One of the shortcomings of Sanders's analysis is that he does not consistently distinguish between the gracious system as a whole and

---

21. For a more detailed discussion of Philo, *Jubilees*, and the Qumran material, see Das, *Paul, the Law, and the Covenant*, 12–44. These pages also treat the Tannaim at length. The analysis is extended into the apocalyptic literature of the first century on pp. 45–69.

22. The rabbis did at times speak of the necessity of perfect obedience, for example, M. Abot 3:16; see Charles L. Quarles, "The Soteriology of R. Akiba and E. P. Sanders' *Paul and Palestinian Judaism*," *NTS* 42 (1996): 190.

the embedded legal demand. He wrote in his discussion of the Tannaim at one point: "Human perfection was not considered realistically achievable by the Rabbis nor was it required."[23] The rabbis "consistently passed up opportunities to require legal perfection."[24] Sanders was wrong to claim that the *halakah* never required perfect obedience. As he rightly urged elsewhere: "In their [the rabbis'] view, God had given all the commandments, and they were all to be obeyed alike. It would be presumptuous of man to determine that some should be neglected."[25] In fact, as Sanders states, ". . . the biblical commandments, while not necessarily more difficult to fulfill than the laws of some other societies, are nevertheless difficult or even impossible fully to obey."[26] He also acknowledges that "[a]lthough the term 'righteous' is primarily applied to those who obey the Torah, the Rabbis knew full well that even the righteous did not obey God's law perfectly."[27]

The apparent contradiction in Sanders's analysis was resolved by keeping the strict demand of the Law conceptually distinct from the larger framework of God's mercy and election of Israel. The rabbis could, therefore, speak of how rare it was for anyone to obey God's Law perfectly, that is, the Law's requirements considered in themselves. Yet perfect righteousness and blamelessness were quite achievable when inclusive of God's forgiveness, sacrifice, and atonement. This was not the same, though, as actually accomplishing all that the Law required. Although affirming with Sanders the importance of God's election and merciful regard toward the Jewish people, the Jews did maintain that the Law enjoins perfect obedience, contrary to the claims of New Perspective Pauline scholars. These interpreters certainly appear to have erred by dismissing in advance the likelihood that Paul also considered perfect obedience of the Law's strictures difficult, if not impossible.

II. PAUL AND PERFECT OBEDIENCE

All the gains of the New Perspective in incorporating the ethnic dimension of Paul's argument are not necessarily incompatible with the possibility that the apostle also understood the Law to require strict obedience and was not optimistic about humanity's ability to

---

23. Sanders, *Paul and Palestinian Judaism*, 137.

24. Sanders, *Paul and Palestinian Judaism*, 138.

25. Sanders, *Paul and Palestinian Judaism*, 112.

26. Sanders, *Paul and Palestinian Judaism*, 115.

27. Sanders, *Paul and Palestinian Judaism*, 203.

meet its standards.[28] By adopting a privileged Jewish ethnic identity through observance of circumcision, Sabbath, and food laws, one would simply be obliging oneself to follow Moses' Law in its entirety. Because Paul's Jewish contemporaries maintained that God's Law should be rigorously obeyed by its recipients, the possibility cannot be rejected in advance that strict obedience of the Law played a role in Paul's thinking as well. In passages such as Gal 3:10, Romans 2, and Romans 7, the problem with the Law appears to be the difficult or impossible demand it places on its adherents. These passages have proven problematic for New Perspective interpreters but are understandable in light of Jewish struggles with the Law's strict demand.

A. PERFECT OBEDIENCE: GALATIANS 3:10

Galatians 3:10 forms an enthymeme, a logical argument in which one of the premises is missing because the premise should have been obvious to the original readers.[29] The stated premise is: "Cursed is everyone who does not observe and obey all the things written in the book of the law."[30] Paul concludes: "All who rely on the works of the law are under a curse." The omitted premise necessary to complete the syllogism is: "All who rely on the works of the law do not observe and obey all the things written in this book of the law." People simply are not capable of doing all that the Law requires, thus they fall under its curse.

New Perspective interpreters have offered several explanations of this problematic passage's apparent reference to perfect obedience. N. T. Wright and James M. Scott think that Gal 3:10 addressed Israel's corporate fate and said nothing about individual disobedience of the Law.[31] In response, however, the fate of the nation as a corpo-

---

28. For a recent study exploring the ethnic dimension of Paul's thinking, see Terence L. Donaldson, *Paul and the Gentiles: Remapping the Apostle's Convictional World* (Minneapolis: Fortress, 1997).

29. Aristotle writes: "For if any of these [premises of an enthymeme] is well known, there is no need to mention it, for the hearer can add it himself" (*Rhetoric* 1.2.13 [13 57a], translation from the Loeb Classical Library). In *Rhetoric* 2.22.3 (1395b): "[N]or should [an enthymeme] include all the steps of the argument . . . it is simply a waste of words, because it states much that is obvious." See also *Rhetoric* 3.18.2, 4 (1419a); Epictetus, *Discourses* 1,8,1–4; Quintilian, 5, 14, 24; 5, 10, 3; and The *"Progymnasmata" of Theon*, III, 104–109 (trans. James R. Butts; Ann Arbor: University Microfilms International, 1986), 198–201.

30. Unless otherwise indicated, all Scripture quotations in this essay are taken from the NRSV.

31. N. T. Wright, *The Climax of the Covenant: Christ and the Law in Pauline Theology* (Minneapolis: Fortress, 1992), 147; James M. Scott, " 'For as Many as Are of Works of the Law Are under a Curse' (Galatians 3.10)," in *Paul and the Scriptures of Israel* (ed. Craig A. Evans and James A. Sanders; JSNTSup 83; Sheffield: JSOT Press, 1993), 214 n. 89.

rate whole cannot be abstracted from the conduct of its individual members. The sin of individual Israelites accrued to Israel as a whole. In Gal 3:10, Paul cited Deuteronomy 27, a chapter that does not address the corporate fate of Israel only. Deuteronomy 27:26 is the twelfth in a series of curses (27:15–26). Two of the twelve curses are explicitly identified as sins committed "in secret" (Deut 27:15, 24).[32] Four more curses involve sexual sins that would also be committed privately (Deut 27:20–24). Likewise, no one would move a boundary marker in public (Deut 27:17). And a blind man would never be able to testify that he had been led astray (Deut 27:18).[33]

Elizabeth Bellefontaine explained that when the Levites pronounced the curse and the community responded in affirmation during the ceremony envisioned in Deuteronomy 27, the community was guaranteeing that sins committed by individuals in secret would not bring about God's vengeance on the community as a whole (e.g., Achan in Joshua 7). God would curse the guilty criminal with the community no longer liable.[34] Deuteronomy 27:26 is situated in the context of a section concerned with the retributive divine curse that falls on individual lawbreakers for secret sins. Likewise, Deuteronomy 29–30 shifts easily back and forth between individual and corporate accountability. Although Wright and Scott have corrected the tendency to ignore the corporate dimension, the fate of corporate Israel must not be abstracted from the deeds of its individual members. The exile of Israel testified to the conduct of individual Israelites under the Law. Paul's own discussion alternates between corporate responsibility and individual accountability later on in Gal 5:25–6:10.

James D. G. Dunn offered yet another alternative to the reconstructed syllogism offered above. Like Wright and Scott, Dunn did not think that Paul was claiming in Gal 3:10 that the Mosaic Law must be perfectly obeyed. On the contrary, Paul uses the technical term "works of the Law" which, according to Dunn, referred to those works required by the Law that distinguished the Jews from Gentiles. These works included circumcision, Sabbath observance,

32. Elizabeth Bellefontaine, "The Curses of Deuteronomy 27: Their Relationship to the Prohibitives," in *A Song of Power and the Power of Song* (ed. Duane L. Christensen; Winona Lake, Ind.: Eisenbrauns, 1993), 260.

33. Bellefontaine, "Curses of Deuteronomy 27," 262.

34. Bellefontaine, "Curses of Deuteronomy 27," 267; see also Albrecht Alt, "The Origins of Israelite Law," in *Essays on Old Testament History and Religion* (trans. R. A. Wilson; Oxford: Basil Blackwell, 1966), 115.

and the food laws.[35] Under pressure from his critics, Dunn modified
his position: The phrase "works of the Law" referred to all that the
Law requires, but the primary focus of the expression was still on
those laws that acted as national and ethnic boundary markers.[36]
Either way, Paul had in mind, from Dunn's standpoint, particularly
those aspects of the Law that served as signs of Jewish ethnic identity. Galatians 3:10 could be paraphrased: "Those who rely on their
Jewish ethnic identity are under a curse." In Dunn's paradigm, Gal
3:10 pronounced guilty those who were relying on their ethnic heritage because they denied uncircumcised Gentiles a place in God's
plan in Christ. By insisting on the "works of the Law," such individuals were guilty of nationalistically excluding the Gentiles from
God's people.[37] Pauline scholarship is indebted to Dunn for underscoring how Paul considers the Law to be the unique possession of
the Jews (e.g., Rom 2:12). Romans 3:28–29 certainly associates
"works of the Law" with Jewish ethnic identity.

Acceptance of Dunn's alternative that the Law was the unique
and special possession of the Jewish people does not rule out that this
Law must also be obeyed strictly and in its entirety. Dunn pointed to
Gal 2:16 as an example of "works of the Law" referring to Jewish
ethnic identity, but Paul continues in Gal 2:21: "[F]or if justification
comes through the law, then Christ died for nothing." Paul's statement in Gal 2:21 parallels his claim a few verses earlier that no one is
justified by the "works of the Law." Likewise Gal 2:19: "For through
the law I died to the law, so that I might live to God." Paul's elaboration in the ensuing verses seems to have more to do with the Law
as a whole than with a focus on only a part of the Law.[38] Paul's point
is that the Law as such cannot justify. A better approach would begin
not with the boundary-marking features of the Law but with the
Law in its entirety: Obedience to the Law requires obedience of all
that it commands. This obedience would certainly include those

---

35. James D. G. Dunn, *Romans 1–8* (WBC 38A; Dallas: Word, 1988), lxxi–lxxii, 186–87,
190–94.

36. For example, see Dunn, "Paul and Justification by Faith," in *The Road from Damascus:
The Impact of Paul's Conversion on His Life, Thought, and Ministry* (ed. Richard N.
Longenecker; Grand Rapids: Eerdmans, 1997), 96–97.

37. James D. G. Dunn, *The Epistle to the Galatians* (Black's New Testament Commentary;
Peabody, Mass.: Hendrickson, 1993), 172; and James D. G. Dunn, *Jesus, Paul, and the
Law: Studies in Mark and Galatians* (Louisville: Westminster/John Knox, 1990), 231.

38. Against Dunn's view that the Jews misunderstood the Law in overly ethnic terms,
Heikki Räisänen objects on the basis of Galatians 3: "And it is altogether impossible to
read chapter 3 as an attack on just a particular attitude to the law. Why should the
death of Christ have been necessary to liberate men from an attitude of theirs?"
("Galatians 2:16 and Paul's Break with Judaism," in *Jesus, Paul and Torah: Collected
Essays* [trans. David E. Orton; JSNTSup 43; Sheffield: JSOT Press, 1992], 122).

aspects of the Law that distinguish the Jews from the Gentiles. An acceptance of what the Law requires of new converts in circumcision or food laws would signal a willingness to obey the whole Law. Thus Paul could move naturally from a review of his critique of Peter at Antioch to a discussion of the Law itself. Paul saw no point in forcing the Gentiles to live like Jews under the Law because the Law did not offer a right relationship with God (Gal 2:15–16).

Paul claims in Gal 3:10 that everyone who relies on "the works of the Law" is under a curse. Another clue that Paul's phrase "works of the Law" cannot be limited only to those aspects of the Law that distinguish the Jews as an ethnic people from the Gentiles comes from Paul's citation of Deut 27:26, a verse situated in a portion of Deuteronomy (chaps. 27–30) that condemns all sorts of legal violations—illicit sexual relations, misleading the blind, changing borders, following other gods, even withholding justice from widows and orphans. The summary verses in Deut 27:26; 28:1, 15, 58, 61; 30:10 consistently emphasize obedience of all that God commands in the Law. The language is comprehensive; the Law is an organic whole that must be obeyed in its entirety. Deuteronomy's focus is never limited only to those laws that distinguish Israel from other nations. Even in the verses that immediately precede Deut 27:26, the commands often involve sins committed individually in secret (27:15–26). In fact, the prohibitions of Deuteronomy 27 usually correspond with similar prohibitions elsewhere.[39] Deuteronomy 27:15–26 has simply extended the threatened curses to situations in which the sin takes place in private. Because Deut 27:26 concludes a section hardly concerned with prohibitions that distinguish Israel as an ethnic people, it is difficult to see why Paul's citation of Deut 27:26 in connection with "works of the Law" in Gal 3:10 should be limited only to those features of the Law that function as boundary markers for the people of Israel.

The Qumran manuscript 4QMMT offers a rare independent witness in Hebrew to Paul's phrase "works of the Law" (מעשי תורה). The Qumran phrase refers to all that the Law requires. Whenever an individual chose to depart from the community's understanding of God's Law on a particular point, that member had apostasized. From the community's perspective, to neglect any aspect of the

---

39. For example, compare Deut 27:16 with Exod 20:12; 21:17; Lev 19:3; 20:9. Compare Deut 27:17 with Deut 19:14; verse 18 with Lev 19:14; and Deut 27:19 with Exod 22:20–23; 23:9; Lev 19:33–34; Deut 1:17; 10:18–19; 24:17–18. See Bellefontaine's discussion for the remaining curses ("Curses of Deuteronomy 27," 256–68), as well as Gerhard Wallis, "Der Vollbürgereid in Deuteronomium 27, 15–26," *Hebrew Union College Annual* 45 (1974): 50–51.

Law would bring about the curses of Deuteronomy 27–30 and the need for separation (as Dunn himself showed). In other words, the "works of the Law" refers primarily to what the Law requires in general and in its entirety. Only secondarily does it focus on particular boundary-defining strictures. Dunn reversed the rightful emphases. Because the focus is primarily on the Law as a whole, the particular laws referred to by the phrase can vary from one conflict situation to another. By esteeming and obeying those laws, the community showed itself devoted to the entirety of God's counsel.[40]

The *Rule of the Community* at Qumran confirms this interpretation of 4QMMT. The *Rule of the Community* called members to "return to the law of Moses according to all that he commanded" (1QS 5:8). In 1QS 5:21, individuals were examined upon entry into the community with respect to their "works of the law," especially whether they had been careful "to walk according to all these precepts" (see also 1QS 6:18). The precepts included the "avoidance of anger, impatience, hatred, insulting elders, blasphemy, malice, foolish talk, and nakedness" (1QS 5:25–26; 6:24–7:18). Circumcision, observance of the Sabbath, and the food laws were, therefore, only the starting point. The Qumran parallels further suggest that Paul had more than just the ethnic or boundary-marking components of the Law in mind in Gal 3:10, which is best taken as a reference to the necessity of perfectly obeying the entire Law.[41]

B. THE CHALLENGE OF LAW OBSERVANCE: ROMANS 2 AND 7

Recent scholarship has become polarized on whether Paul's problem with the Law was the inability of people to obey its demands or its exclusion of the Gentiles—whether by a misunderstanding or ethnic pride. New Perspective and more traditional interpreters do not always recognize that it is a both/and relationship. The Law functions both to distinguish the Jewish people and to place on them a burden of obedience. The apostle sees absolutely

---

40. 4QMMT's heading indicates that it addresses "some of the works of the Law." "Works of the Law" must therefore go beyond those aspects in dispute within the document to include the entirety of the Law; see Ben Witherington III, *Grace in Galatia: A Commentary on St. Paul's Letter to the Galatians* (Grand Rapids: Eerdmans, 1998), 176–77. Joseph A. Fitzmyer has likewise noted the "broad outlook" of this document. Nothing suggests the restriction of the phrase only to certain boundary-marking aspects of the Law; see Fitzmyer, "Paul's Jewish Background and the Deeds of the Law," in *According to Paul: Studies in the Theology of the Apostle* (New York: Paulist, 1993), 23. Fitzmyer repeatedly emphasizes throughout his article that "works of the Law" at Qumran must be taken as those works that the Law requires in a general sense; see especially pp. 19–24.

41. For a critique of other attempts to explain this text in a New Perspective paradigm (including Sanders's own approach), see Das, *Paul, the Law, and the Covenant*, 145–70.

nothing wrong in a Jewish ethnic identity in Romans 2, provided one actually does all that the Law requires. It is not enough just to obey those aspects of the Law that distinguish a person as Jewish. Paul's rhetorical charges against the Jews in Rom 2:17–29 assume the difficulty even for Jews of doing all that the Law required. He makes that assumption explicit in Romans 7.[42]

Romans 7 laments human inability to do what the Mosaic Law requires of its adherents. While the Law is indeed "spiritual" (Rom 7:14) and "good" (Rom 7:16; see also vv. 22 and 25), the power of sin turns out to be far stronger than the desire to do what the Law commands.[43] People under the Law find themselves in the "wretched" position of being unable to do good; they do what they hate instead (Rom 7:15) because of the tyranny and power of sin (Rom 7:14, 17, 20, 24). Three times Paul cycles through an admission that the "I" is unable to accomplish what the Law demands (Rom 7:15–16, 18–20, 21–23). Paul finds one commandment epitomizing the futile struggle to obey the Law: "Do not covet." Of all the commandments, the prohibition against coveting exposes the problem of a sinful heart. The battle against sin penetrates to the inner core of human existence, that is, to secret, sinful desires and motives that stand in the way of obedience of God's holy Law.[44]

---

42. For a detailed exposition of Romans 1 and 2, see Das, *Paul, the Law, and the Covenant,* 171–91.

43. On sin as an enslaving power, see Rom 3:9; 5:14, 17, 32; 6:18. See also Robert C. Tannehill, *Dying and Rising with Christ: A Study in Pauline Theology* (Berlin: Töpelmann, 1967), 16.

44. "Do not covet" in Rom 7:7 is the most private and interior of the commandments. Philippians 3 says little or nothing about the possibility of an internal struggle with sin and desire and remains only at the level of a public, observable blamelessness. The only distinguishing characteristic of the Tenth Commandment from the others is its unique focus on interiority; see J. A. Ziesier, "The Role of the Tenth Commandment in Romans 7," *JSNT* 33 (1988): 47–48. Whereas most Jews would have no problem keeping the other commandments (murder, adultery, robbery, the Sabbath), it is the command not to covet that exposes the extreme difficulty of keeping the Mosaic Law; see Ziesier, "Role of the Tenth Commandment," 48. As Ziesier himself points out, Paul "almost certainly generalizes from it [the command not to covet]" ("The Just Requirement of the Law [Romans 8.4]," *Australian Biblical Review* 35 [1987]: 80). This point is developed at greater length by Douglas J. Moo, "Israel and Paul in Romans 7:7–12," *NTS* 32 (1986): 123; and J. G. Strelan, "A Note on the Old Testament Background of Romans 7:7," *Lutheran Theological Journal* 15 (1981): 23–25. Philo calls desire the fountain of iniquity from which all sinful actions flows (*De decalogo* 142–153, 173); for this reason God prohibited coveting. Four Maccabees 2:5–6 (in its context) claims that if one can control and limit sinful desires through reason, then one will be able to obey the Law in other ways as well. The Tenth Commandment could, therefore, epitomize the entirety of the Law (even as it does in Romans 7).

Michael Winger has drawn attention to Paul's use in Romans 7 of ἐντολή ("command").[45] Paul may have had in mind the command οὐκ ἐπιθυμήσεις ("Do not covet") in Rom 7:7. A second possibility is that Paul was referring to νόμος from the point of view of all of its commands.[46] In either case, Paul's choice of ἐντολή amid his discussion of νόμος places the emphasis squarely on the Law's command. The varied terminology that Paul uses to express the same point makes it clear that doing the Law is the key issue. He repeatedly uses three distinct synonyms eleven times in Rom 7:15–21: πράσσω (vv. 15, 19), ποιέω (vv. 15, 16, 19, 20, 21), and κατεργάζομαι (vv. 15, 17, 18, 20).[47] The "problem" or "plight" of the Law according to Rom 7:14–25 is that those who know what the Law demands are unable to "do" it. Paul turns in Rom 8:3–4 to the work of Christ as the solution to fleshly humanity's inability (τὸ ἀδύνατον) to do what God requires in the Law. Through Christ, the Law's "righteous decree" (τὸ δικαίωμα τοῦ νόμου) is fulfilled in believers.[48]

Absolutely nothing in Romans 7 indicates that Paul's problem with the Law is that it leads to national righteousness or ethnic pride.[49] On the contrary, possession of the Law is good as long as

---

45. Michael Winger, *By What Law? The Meaning of Νόμος in the Letters of Paul* (SBLDS 128; Atlanta: Scholars Press, 1992), 166–67.

46. Paul is certainly not using the word as a synonym for νόμος. Why would Paul vary his terminology for the Mosaic Law here and nowhere else?

47. This creates a powerful rhetorical effect; Ernst Käsemann, *Commentary on Romans* (Grand Rapids: Eerdmans, 1980), 202. John M. Espy's distinctions between the three terms seem overly subtle; see "Paul's 'Robust Conscience' Re-Examined," *NTS* 31 (1985): 184–85 n. 62.

48. E. P. Sanders admits that in Romans 7 "humans are depicted as unable to fulfill it [the Law] because of sin and the flesh" (*Paul, the Law, and the Jewish People* [Philadelphia: Fortress, 1983], 74). Sanders adds: "Its 'fault,' rather, is that it does not bear within itself the power to enable people to observe it" (*Paul, the Law,* 74–75). Sanders is then quick to qualify his comments on Romans 7. He says with respect to Pauline material outside of Romans 7: "[I]t is worth observing that in none of these passages does Paul argue that the law is too hard to be fulfilled adequately" (*Paul, the Law,* 78). Romans 7 is, therefore, the exception in which Paul does say that people are unable to accomplish the Law. The problem is that other passages confirm what Paul says in Romans 7. Apart from Gal 3:10, the necessity of doing the Law has been a motif in Romans 2–4, and these chapters pave the way for the critique in Romans 7. What seems obvious to Sanders in Romans 7 need not be a contradiction of what Paul says elsewhere. Paul will continue his critique in Romans 9–11; see Das, *Paul, the Law, and the Covenant,* 234–67. Contra Sanders (*Paul, the Law,* 78), there is nothing "extreme" about Paul's "presentation of human inability" here.

49. James D. G. Dunn inexplicably thinks that Paul's problem with the Law in Romans 7 must be understood in terms of the sin of "national righteousness," "national self-righteous judgment on others," or the "unself critical presumption of God's favor"; see Dunn, *Romans 1–8,* 352. The eschatological Spirit has liberated humanity "from that too narrowing understanding of the law's role" in terms of "pride in national identity" (*Romans 1–8,* 387). Where does Paul address a mistaken understanding of the Law in Romans 7?

one can translate possession of the Law into the concrete action that the Law demands. Winger explained that ἐντολή was never used in a way that would clearly demarcate Jews from Gentiles.[50] Paul sees the Law as setting forth a demand that must be successfully accomplished by the individual. Sin renders successful accomplishment of the Law impossible.[51]

D. "BLAMELESS" OBEDIENCE: PHILIPPIANS 3:3–11

Philippians 3:3–11 proves difficult for the thesis that Paul thought people were unable to accomplish what the Law required. Paul called his own observance of the Law "blameless." Sanders's analysis of Judaism can be credited with providing the necessary background to evaluate Paul's claim of "blamelessness." A recurrent motif in Sanders's analysis of Judaism was the consistent recognition that human beings fall short of God's will. With respect to the Tannaim, Sanders wrote: "Although the term 'righteous' is primarily applied to those who obey the Torah, the Rabbis knew full well that even the righteous did not obey God's law perfectly."[52] The biblical commandments "are nevertheless difficult or even impossible fully to obey."[53] "Human perfection was not considered realistically achievable by the Rabbis."[54] The *Sifra on Leviticus* related the incident in the Hebrew Scriptures of Nadab and Abihu as an example of human imperfection. Nadab and Abihu were killed by fire for an unholy offering of fire before the Lord, yet they were not exposed or humiliated in death.[55] The *Sifra* commented: "[H]ow much the more so [will God show pity to] other righteous persons." Abihu and Nadab were considered among the righteous, though their sin warranted punishment by death. "Righteousness" for a Jew never meant that one had been sinless and had done perfectly all that God commanded in the Law. The "righteous" were those who attempted to obey the Law in its entirety and sought atonement for their sin or failure.[56] The ultimate criterion was faith-

---

50. Winger, *By What Law?* 166–67.

51. For a more detailed discussion of Romans 7, as well as the evidence that νόμος should be taken as referring to the Mosaic Law throughout Paul's discussion, see Das, *Paul, the Law, and the Covenant,* 215–33.

52. Sanders, *Paul and Palestinian Judaism,* 203.

53. Sanders, *Paul and Palestinian Judaism,* 115; see also 137.

54. Sanders, *Paul and Palestinian Judaism,* 137.

55. *Sifra Shernini Mekhilta deMiluim* 22–27 (on Lev 10:1–5).

56. As Sanders puts its: ". . . the righteous are those who obey the Torah and atone for transgression" (*Paul and Palestinian Judaism,* 204). Or with George Foot Moore:

fulness to the covenant relationship. As Sanders summarized the views of the Qumran sect: ". . . from the point of view of the *halakah*, one is required to walk perfectly. From the point of view of the individual in prayer or devotional moments, he is unable to walk perfectly and must be given perfection of way by God's grace."[57]

The "righteous" were typically sinners who availed themselves of God's mercy and election even while falling short of the perfect measure toward which they were striving. Biblical figures are often characterized as "blameless" even when the biblical text admits their sins (2 Chronicles 15–17 [cf. the catalog of sins in chapter 16]; Luke 1:6, 18–20). Paul could admonish his own audience to be "blameless" (Phil 2:15; see also 1 Thess 3:13; 5:23; 1 Cor 1:8). With respect to Philippians 3, Paul's boast as a Jew included not only his Jewish identity but also his zeal for and accomplishment of the Law. The Law always involved the demand for rigorous obedience alongside its ethnic particularity.[58] Paul reflected the same tension in his writings: He could call himself blameless with respect to the righteousness of the Law yet still affirm that all people are sinners.[59] What Sanders had to say on this matter is more accurate and cannot be stressed enough: "It would be hazardous to suppose that Paul must have held one position as his true view, while using the other only for the sake of argument. He could quite easily have held both,

---

"Righteousness, in the conception of it which Judaism got from the Scriptures, had no suggestion of sinless perfection. Nor are the sins of the righteous all venial; the gravest moral lapses may befall them, as they did David. What distinguishes the righteous man who has fallen into sin is his repentance . . ." (*Judaism in the First Centuries of the Christian Era: The Age of the* Tannaim [Cambridge: Harvard University Press, 1927], 1:494–95).

57. Sanders, *Paul and Palestinian Judaism*, 305–12. He concludes from the data: "On the one hand, there is the sense of human inadequacy before God . . . no one can be righteous or perfect before God; no one, on his own, has 'righteous deeds.' On the other hand, there is the consciousness of being elect; thus some are righteous (*tsaddiq, yitsdaq*), but only by the grace of God" (*Paul and Palestinian Judaism*, 311–12).

58. Blamelessness with respect to the Law ought to be distinguished from perfect obedience. Perfect obedience is unerring success in doing all that God commands in the Law.

59. *Four Ezra* 7:68–69 expresses a skepticism about human ability to refrain from sin: "For all who have been born are entangled in iniquities, and are full of sins and burdened with transgressions. And if after death we were not to come into judgment, perhaps it would have been better for us." In *4 Ezra* 9:36: "For we who have received the law and sinned will perish, as well as our hearts that received it." R. Gainaliel could despair over the necessity of perfect obedience, while R. Akiba consoled him on the basis of a more merciful judgment based on a majority of deeds; see Quarles, "Soteriology." Elsewhere, the rabbis generally considered a variety of means effective for the atoning of sin. Therefore, Gainaliel's despair in M. Aboth is unusual. Most rabbis were confident that "all Israelites" have a share in the world to come. Gainaliel is valuable as an example of the requirement for "perfection of way" within the system as a whole.

without ever playing them off against each other so that he became aware that they are mutually exclusive."[60] R. Eliezer (*Sanhedrin* 101a) could assert that "there is none that is righteous" while on another occasion be surprised that he had committed a sin for which he had to suffer.[61] The key lies in the fact that Paul described his prior status as "blameless," but he never said that he was without sin as a Pharisee. To assume that being "blameless" was the same as being sinless and innocent of any violation of the Mosaic Law would be an error. The New Perspective interpretation of Paul and the Law has been wrong to cite Philippians 3 as proof that Paul did not have a problem with perfect obedience of the Law.[62]

IV. THE GRACIOUS FRAMEWORK OF JUDAISM AND PAUL

Considering the much more optimistic outlook on living in accordance with the Law among the Jews of his day, how is it possible for Paul to see doing the Law as problematic? E. P. Sanders demonstrated that the Law's demands were always embedded within the gracious framework of God's election and covenant, which Sanders called "covenantal nomism." Whenever one failed in the performance of the Law's demands, one could avail oneself of the sacrificial system, atonement, repentance, and thereby God's mercy. Sanders himself admitted, however, that Paul was no "covenantal nomist":

> Paul's "pattern of religion" cannot be described as "covenantal nomism," and therefore Paul presents an essentially different type of religiousness from any found in Palestinian Jewish literature. . . . Paul in fact explicitly denies that the Jewish covenant can be effective for salvation, thus consciously denying the basis of Judaism.[63]

It is unfortunate that Sanders's conclusion was not based on a detailed comparison of Paul and Judaism with respect to the categories he deemed central to first-century Judaism, namely, election, covenant, and sacrifice. Sanders proceeded on the assumption that

---

60. Sanders, *Paul, the Law*, 24.

61. The rabbis could be surprised that they had sinned to the point that they merited suffering or death; see *Mek. Nezikin* 18 [to Exodus 22, 22 (23)] and *Sanh.* 101a [on R. Eliezer].

62. On Philippians 3, see Das, *Paul, the Law, and the Covenant*, 215–33.

63. Sanders, *Paul and Palestinian Judaism*, 543, 551.

Paul's categories of thought were simply different from those of Judaism. Yet how do these crucial elements in Jewish thought fare in Paul the former Pharisee? If Paul had abandoned a system of Judaism that can be described as "covenantal nomism," what happened to the key aspects of that system in his thought?

Paul was not entirely comfortable with the notion of covenant. As Gal 3:15–17 makes clear, the concept of "covenant" had become too closely associated with the Mosaic Law among Paul's contemporaries. In a radical move, Paul divorced the Mosaic Law from the only covenant of value, the Abrahamic covenant.[64] In Gal 4:21–31, the apostle places the Mosaic covenant alongside slavery and bondage.[65] Likewise, in 2 Corinthians 3, Paul speaks of the old Mosaic covenant as a covenant of the letter and death. The Mosaic covenant no longer functioned as a gracious framework for the Law.[66]

Paul granted the election of the Jewish people. He looked to a day when "all Israel" would be saved. Nevertheless, the extensive critique of the "two covenant" or Sonderweg theory in Romans 11 has shown that the saving benefits of Israel's election must be realized through the faith in Christ that Paul speaks of in Rom 10:9–10. There will be no separate path to salvation for the Jews apart from their own Messiah (Rom 9:5). Paul's subsequent emphatic fourfold use of "all" ($\pi\tilde{\alpha}\varsigma$) in Rom 10:11–13 will permit no other interpretation.[67] Further, if faith in Christ is the decisive element in God's electing activity, the fact that the apostle calls Gentile Christians

---

64. Paul's deliberate use of the plural διαθῆκαι in Rom 9:4 is probably a nod to the Abrahamic covenant.

65. For a more detailed discussion of Gal 3:15–17; 4:21–31, see Das, *Paul, the Law, and the Covenant*, 70–76.

66. For a detailed exegesis of 2 Corinthians 3, see Das, *Paul, the Law, and the Covenant*, 76–94.

67. Reider Hvalvik, "A 'Sonderweg' for Israel: A Critical Examination of a Current Interpretation of Romans 11.25–27," *JSNT* 38 (1990): 87–107; Dieter Sänger, "Rettung der Heiden und Erwählung Israels: Einige vorläufige Erwägungen zu Römer 11,25–27," *Kerygma und Dogma* 32 (1986): 99–119; Erich Gräßer, "Zwei Heilswege? Zum theologischen Verhältnis von Israel und Kirche," in *Kontinuität und Einheit: Für Franz Mußner, hrsg. Paul-Gerhard Müller and Werner Stenger* (Freiburg: Herder, 1981), 411–29; E. Elizabeth Johnson, *The Function of Apocalyptic and Wisdom Traditions in Romans 9–11* (SBLDS 109; Atlanta: Scholars Press, 1989), 176–205; Heikki Räisänen, "Paul, God, and Israel: Romans 9–11 in Recent Research," in *The Social World of Formative Christianity and Judaism: In Tribute to Howard Clark Kee* (ed. Jacob Neusner, Peder Borgen, Ernest S. Frericks, and Richard Horsley; Philadelphia: Fortress, 1988), 189–92; Frank Thielman, *From Plight to Solution: A Jewish Framework for Understanding Paul's View of the Law in Galatians and Romans* (NovTSup 61; Leiden: Brill, 1989), 123–32; and Das, *Paul, the Law, and the Covenant*, 95–112.

God's "elect" (Rom 8:28–35) becomes comprehensible.[68] The election of Israel no longer offered any saving benefit apart from faith in Christ.[69]

One looks in vain for atoning sacrifice in Paul. Perhaps Paul's reference to the ἱλαστήριον in Rom 3:25 may be a reference to atoning sacrifice. On the other hand, a reference to the mercy seat on the ark of the covenant has been disputed. Many scholars now believe that ἱλαστήριον could be more accurately translated in general terms as a "propitiation" or "expiation."[70] Should one maintain the reference to the mercy seat, then Paul has reinterpreted the premiere means of atonement in Judaism in terms of Christ. As Peter Stuhlmacher concluded: "The cultic celebration of the Day of Atonement is abolished and superseded by virtue of this act of God, because the atonement granted definitively by God in Christ once and for all renders superfluous further cultic atonement ritual."[71] In effect, the gracious covenantal framework of Judaism has been reconceptualized in favor of a new framework of grace in the work of Christ.[72]

V. CONCLUSION

Sanders wrongly minimized the belief in Judaism that God intended for the Law to be obeyed strictly and in its entirety. Judaism maintained a balance between the need for strict obedience of the Law and the possibility of atonement and forgiveness for God's elect. But if the gracious framework of Judaism is denied salvific efficacy in Paul, it becomes comprehensible why he has a problem with doing

---

68. Paul regularly calls his Gentile Christian readers the "elect," a title previously used for ethnic Israel.

69. For a fairly detailed discussion of Israel's election in both Romans and Galatians in light of these letters' respective situations, see A. Andrew Das, *Paul and the Jews* (Peabody, Mass.: Hendrickson, 2003).

70. My own preference is "propitiation" but not because of Rom 1:18–3:20. "Propitiation" functions better in this context as a demonstration of "the righteousness of God." For a more extensive discussion of why ἱλαστήριον should not be understood as the "mercy seat," as well as for a more extensive discussion of atoning sacrifice in Paul, see Das, *Paul, the Law, and the Covenant*, 132–43.

71. Peter Stuhlmacher, "Recent Exegesis on Romans 3:24–26," in *Reconciliation, Law, and Righteousness* (trans. Everett R. Kalin; Philadelphia: Fortress, 1986), 104.

72. This is precisely the logic of Romans 3. After the denial of any saving privileges based on ethnic identity in Romans 2, Paul asks at the beginning of Romans 3 whether there is any advantage in being a Jew. He answers, "Much in every way." The Jews were entrusted with the oracles of God, and these oracles testify to their salvation in the Messiah Jesus Christ (Rom 3:21–26). At just the point where the covenantal nomist of Romans 2 would have faulted Paul for denying God's mercy and atonement in the equation, Paul presents Christ.

the Law. The Law's rigorous demands have come to the fore in the apostle's thinking and emerged as problematic. These demands have become problematic in a Pauline logic in which the only gracious framework was in Christ. Paul's solution to sin resided strictly in the work of Jesus Christ.

Paul discovered that the Law was not God's provision for sin (Gal 2:21; 3:21). If the sacrifices and atonement of the Law were of no avail in and of themselves, then the Law was reduced to the realm of human achievement and doing. God acted *in Christ* to save. If the Jewish Law were no longer the basis for God's justifying activity, then the Law could no longer serve to exclude the Gentiles from God's plan. With the denial of the gracious framework of covenantal nomism, the Law no longer acted as a sign of Jewish privilege; it entailed an enslaving obligation. It entailed "works" (Rom 4:4–5).

CHRIST AND THE LAW
IN THE LIFE
OF THE CHURCH AT GALATIA

ARTHUR A. JUST JR.

If we were to ask St. Paul what his major concern was in writing to the Galatians, what do you think he would say? This study will demonstrate that the issue of Christ and the Law in the daily life of the church at Galatia is at the heart of Paul's letter. He writes with passion about the Gospel of Jesus Christ because it is in danger of being lost among the Galatian congregations. After all, Paul's opponents preached another gospel: the Gospel plus something, which was the Law, particularly circumcision. Paul, therefore, writes to the Galatians as their pastor so they will understand the radical change that has taken place in them since the Spirit has entered their hearts at Baptism and they cried "Abba, Father" (Gal 4:6). As J. Louis Martyn suggests in his recent Anchor Bible Commentary on this Epistle: "Paul's pastoral concern is focused on providing the Galatians with *a map of the world in which they actually live*."[1] By helping the Galatians to understand the relationship between Christ and the Law, Paul provides them with "a map of the world in which they actually live." Therefore, Paul's letter to the Galatians is as much a pastoral homily as it is a fiery defense of the Gospel, and his defense of the Gospel is the foundation for his pastoral concerns.

Charles Gieschen, in an earlier essay in this volume, has described the issues that have arisen in the past thirty years among New Testament scholars concerning the interpretation of Paul's

---

1. J. Louis Martyn, *Galatians: A New Translation with Introduction and Commentary* (AB 33A; New York: Doubleday, 1997), 482 n. 41 (*my emphasis*).

understanding of the Law. The issue that leads Paul to address the Law, however, is *not* the Law; it is the Gospel. To be more specific, the issue is Paul's apocalyptic Gospel. Moises Silva makes this bold claim: "We cannot possibly grasp Paul's teaching on the law unless we understand his eschatology."[2] To interpret the Law in Paul's letter to the Galatians, we must read it through the apocalyptic events of Christ's incarnation, his death on the cross, and his resurrection from the dead, which have forever changed the cosmos, including the Law and especially the Law. It is at the cross where the Messiah and the Law collide: "For all who rely on works of the Law are under a curse . . . . Christ redeemed us from the curse of the Law, having become a curse for us, for it is written, 'Cursed be every one who hangs on a tree' " (Gal 3:10, 13).[3] There is no better place in the Pauline corpus to look at Paul's view of the Law through an eschatological lens than his homily to the Galatian congregations.

I. An Apocalyptic Gospel
in a Liturgical Setting: Galatians 1:1–5

Martyn has suggested that Paul's letter is "an argumentative sermon preached in the context of a service of worship—and thus in the acknowledged presence of God."[4] He goes on to say: "Paul is concerned in letter form to *repreach* the gospel in place of its counterfeit. Rhetorically, the body of the letter is a sermon centered on factual, and thus indicative, answers to two questions, 'What time is it?' and 'In what cosmos do we actually live?' "[5]

To answer these two questions for the Galatians, Paul reveals his view of both eschatology and the Law in light of Christ's incarnation and death in our behalf. Because of the Christ event, the time in which we now live is "eschatological time" and the cosmos in which we dwell is the "new creation."[6] That is why Paul needs to

---

2. Moises Silva, *Explorations in Exegetical Method: Galatians as a Test Case* (Grand Rapids: Baker, 1996), 169. Silva develops this theme in his two chapters "Eschatology in Galatians" and "The Function of the Law." I am also indebted to Martyn for this eschatological/apocalyptic view of Galatians, especially with respect to the Law.

3. Unless otherwise indicated, all Scripture quotations in this essay are taken from the RSV.

4. Martyn, *Galatians*, 21.

5. Martyn, *Galatians*, 23 (*my emphasis*).

6. This understanding of time and reality is captured well in the early Christian teaching concerning "the eighth day"; see Jean Daniélou, *The Bible and the Liturgy* (University of Notre Dame Liturgical Studies 3; South Bend, Ind.: University of Notre Dame Press, 1956), 262–86.

provide the Galatians and us with a map for this world in which the hearers of this Epistle now actually live. As visible in Gal 1:3–5, his letter opens with both eschatological and liturgical elements, providing the context in which to understand these two fundamental questions.[7]

1:3　　χάρις ὑμῖν καὶ **εἰρήνη** ἀπὸ θεοῦ πατρὸς ἡμῶν καὶ
　　　　κυρίου Ἰησοῦ Χριστοῦ

1:4　　τοῦ δόντος ἑαυτὸν ὑπὲρ τῶν ἁμαρτιῶν ἡμῶν,
　　　　ὅπως ἐξέληται ἡμᾶς ἐκ τοῦ αἰῶνος
　　　　　τοῦ ἐνεστῶτος πονηροῦ
　　　　κατὰ τὸ θέλημα τοῦ θεοῦ καὶ πατρὸς ἡμῶν,

1:5　　　　ᾧ **ἡ δόξα** εἰς τοὺς αἰῶνας τῶν αἰώνων, **ἀμήν**.

1:3　　Grace to you and peace from God the Father and our
　　　　　Lord Jesus Christ,

1:4　　who gave himself for our sins
　　　　to deliver us from the present evil age,
　　　　　according to the will of our God and Father;

1:5　　　　to whom be the glory for ever and ever. Amen.

As most commentators note, the opening to Galatians departs from Paul's regular pattern, except for the greeting of "grace and peace." Paul does not speak these words in isolation, as is his pattern, but he adds a phrase that encapsulates his apocalyptic Gospel. Why does he expand this greeting into a profound theological affirmation? The final verse of this opening greeting suggests an answer. By beginning with "grace and peace" and closing with a doxology and a final "Amen," Paul frames his statement on the atonement with liturgical language. Paul is inviting the Galatians, gathered for the eucharistic feast, to join him in an "Amen" to Christ's liberating death as they gather to worship God the Father for sending his Son "who gave himself for our sins to deliver us from the present evil age."

Grace and *peace* are to be understood in this liturgical context. Martyn states: *Grace* sums up "the whole of God's good news in Jesus Christ . . . that, quite apart from human activity . . . God has acted in Christ to bring all people into the 'space' (Rom 5:2) of the new creation in which he is making things right."[8] Grace defines the space, the cosmos, in which we now live, and that space is the new

---

7. Silva affirms this eschatological perspective in the greeting of this Epistle; see *Explorations*, 171–72.

8. Martyn, *Galatians*, 87.

creation in which Christ is present in his flesh, liberating his people from this present evil age. For sacramental communities, that space is at a table where fellowship with God and other believers, both Jew and Gentile, takes place in Christ who is present with his gifts of grace. The greeting of *peace* provides another apocalyptic perspective, as Martyn asserts: "In his use of the term 'peace' Paul speaks of the well-being of the *world*" that "lies in its being regrasped from the power of evil by God's deed in Jesus Christ . . . [this] happens in his apocalyptic battle against the forces of evil and sin . . . peace is to be understood as a confident cry of victory in the midst of God's battle of liberation."[9]

Grace and peace, therefore, are announced as realities for the Galatians in their gathering for worship. The Galatians are constituted in this space of grace and peace because of the greater reality that "our Lord Jesus Christ . . . gave himself for our sins to deliver us from the present evil age" (Gal 1:3b–4). This not only locates grace and peace in Christ's substitutionary atonement but also does so in the language of the new creation. Christ's death liberates us from an evil age in which we were enslaved and delivers us into a new age where "the world has been crucified to me, and I to the world" (Gal 6:14). The one who gave himself for our sins now says, in the words of Luke's institution narrative: "This is my body, which is being given on behalf of you [τὸ ὑπὲρ ὑμῶν διδόμενον]" (Luke 22:19 *my translation*). The body Christ gave on the cross on our behalf is now given to the Galatians in a eucharistic feast of body broken and blood poured out in which the space of grace is given as gift and the state of peace is experienced as health, wholeness, and salvation itself.[10]

II. THE LAW AND FAITH: GALATIANS 2:15–3:5

In this eucharistic setting in which Christ is present, Paul now *repreaches* the Gospel to the Galatians to answer the questions "What time is it?" and "In what cosmos do we actually live?" Both questions center in the "identity" of the Galatian congregations; that is to say, Paul answers these questions by proclaiming to these Gentile converts that they do not receive their identity by observing works of the Law but by Christ's faithful death in their behalf. This question of identity could not be more pertinent for our context

---

9. Martyn, *Galatians*, 88.

10. See Martyn, *Galatians*, 88.

because, like the Galatians, many of those for whom our preaching is intended—non-Jews who in this post-denominational world come to us without much Christian baggage—live in a religious milieu that interprets reality through the Law rather than through the cross of Christ.

The juxtaposition of Christ's death and the Law first occurs in Gal 2:15–3:5, which is also the first occurrence of the term ὁ νόμος ("the Law") in Galatians. The significance of this section of Paul's homily cannot be overstated. Graham Stanton describes it as "the nerve center of Galatians."[11] The "works of the law" occurs five times in eleven verses, and these "works" are contrasted with "faith," either Christ's faithfulness or the Christian's faith in Christ. Everything depends on Gal 2:15–16, perhaps the most theologically dense verse in the Pauline corpus.[12] The following diagram shows not only its chiastic structure but also provides a schema to present the major theological issues:

2:15 ἡμεῖς φύσει Ἰουδαῖοι καὶ οὐκ ἐξ ἐθνῶν ἁμαρτωλοί·
2:16 εἰδότες [δὲ] ὅτι
    a οὐ δικαιοῦται ἄνθρωπος ἐξ ἔργων νόμου
    b ἐὰν μὴ **διὰ πίστεως Ἰησοῦ Χριστοῦ,**
    c **καὶ ἡμεῖς εἰς Χριστὸν Ἰησοῦν ἐπιστεύσαμεν,**
    b' ἵνα δικαιωθῶμεν **ἐκ πίστεως Χριστοῦ**
        καὶ οὐκ **ἐξ ἔργων νόμου,**
    a' ὅτι **ἐξ ἔργων νόμου οὐ δικαιωθήσεται πᾶσα** σάρξ.

2:15 We ourselves, who are Jews by birth and not
        Gentile sinners,
2:16 yet who know that
    a a man is not justified **by works of the law**
    b but **through [faith of Christ]**
    c even **we have believed** in Christ Jesus
    b' in order to be justified **by [faith of Christ],**
        and not **by works of the law**
    a' because **by works of the law** shall no one be justified.

The main clause of the sentence and the center of the chiasm is "even we have believed in Christ Jesus" (καὶ ἡμεῖς εἰς Χριστὸν Ἰησοῦν ἐπιστεύσαμεν), a clear reference to our faith in (εἰς) Christ. Grammatically and structurally, faith in Christ is at the center of Paul's programmatic statement.

---

11. Graham Stanton, "The Law of Moses and the Law of Christ," in *Paul and the Mosaic Law* (ed. James D. G. Dunn; Grand Rapids: Eerdmans, 2001), 103.

12. Martyn, *Galatians*, 263.

But is faith in Christ at the theological center of his argument? Clearly the clauses surrounding "faith in Christ" deal with justification (δικαιόω) because Paul is stating in no uncertain terms that justification is not by "works of the law" (a and a' ἐξ ἔργων νόμου) but by faith (b διὰ πίστεως and b' ἐκ πίστεως). Although these clauses are familiar to us, let us look at these words with fresh eyes through Paul's eschatological perspective.

To begin, entertain for a moment a translation of the Greek verb δικαιόω, which we normally translate as "justify" or "declare righteous," with the following translation from Martyn: "God's *making right what has gone wrong.*"[13] What has gone wrong is clear to Paul as he writes to the Galatians. Humanity is enslaved in "the present evil age" to the forces of sin (Gal 1:4), the flesh (Gal 5:13), and the elemental spirits of the universe (Gal 5:25; 6:16). Luther's triad of sin, death, and the devil captures Paul's view of what has gone wrong in the cosmos.

But the question facing Paul, the Galatians, and his opponents is this: "How does God make things right?" Does God make things right through works of the Law? No! Does he make things right through Christ's faithful death in our behalf? Yes! Does he make things right through our personal faith in Christ? Yes! Paul's opponents are suggesting the first solution to our human plight: God is making things right by observance of God's Law. Paul writes this letter to the Galatians to reject this notion of justification. But the next two alternatives are worthy of our consideration as Lutherans because exploring the difference between them will help us affirm what we believe, teach, and confess about the relationship between grace and faith.

The issue is how to interpret the prepositional phrases διὰ πίστεως Ἰησοῦ Χριστοῦ and ἐκ πίστεως Χριστοῦ.[14] There is considerable debate today concerning the genitives Ἰησοῦ Χριστοῦ and Χριστοῦ. If we understand them as objective genitives, they would be translated as "faith in Jesus Christ" and "faith in Christ," referring to our faith that has Jesus, the one who gave himself on behalf of our sins, as its object. The accent here is on personal faith that receives the realities of Christ's atoning death and vindicating resurrection. This is the traditional understanding of this prepositional phrase and Luther's understanding as well. It contrasts nicely with

---

13. Martyn, *Galatians*, 250.

14. For a brief introduction to the debate, see Paul Pollard, "The 'Faith of Christ' in Recent Discussion," *CJ* 23 (1997): 213–28.

works of the Law, a contrast between human observance of the law or human faith, though human faith has a divine origin.[15] To put it in common theological terms, the accent here is on "subjective (individual) justification" accomplished through our faith in Christ.

However, if we understand these genitives as subjective genitives,[16] they refer to Christ's faith, namely, his faithful death on our behalf in which "he died faithfully for human beings while looking faithfully to God."[17] These phrases would then be translated with Jesus as the subject who has faith: "faith of Jesus Christ" and "faith of Christ." This understanding of faith provides a different perspective: We are declared righteous by God either by our observance of the Law or by Christ's faithful death in our behalf. Here *human* action is clearly contrasted with *divine* initiative. Our unfaithful observance of the Law is set against Christ's faithful action in which he "gave himself for our sins to deliver us from the present evil age." Here "objective (universal) justification" takes center stage, and Paul's apocalyptic Gospel is the focus of how God is making things right in a world in which things have gone extremely wrong.

Please note that this interpretation of the genitives in Gal 2:16 does not suggest anything as radical as, for example, that we are justified by works or by our experience or whatever. In fact, even if you understand this as Christ's faithful death in our behalf, our faith in Christ still stands at the center of the chiasm in Gal 2:16: "even we have believed in Christ Jesus."[18] To interpret this genitive as Christ's faithful death in our behalf allows the atonement for sin, God's apocalyptic invasion and rescue, to be that which is contrasted to

---

15. See Martyn, *Galatians*, 271.

16. Some refer to them as "authorial" genitives; see Martyn, *Galatians*, 251 n. 127. The work of Richard Hays had a profound impact in the past two decades toward reading these phrases as subjective genitives; see especially *The Faith of Jesus Christ: The Narrative Substructure of Galatians 3:1–4:11* (2d ed.; Grand Rapids: Eerdmans, 2002 [1st ed. 1983]).

17. Martyn, *Galatians*, 271.

18. Silva, who understands the genitives as objective (i.e., faith in Christ), still makes a point of accenting objective justification: "To recognize the apocalyptic overtones of this clause is not to undermine the traditional application of the verse, since in this very passage Paul is stressing the significance of faith for his own personal—yes, present—justification and that of his Jewish-Christian contemporaries. My point, however, is that this truth is set within the context of cosmic, eschatological realities. In other words, the 'subjective' experience of justification is not divorced from the 'objective' judgment at the end of the age. On the contrary, it is grounded in that final judgment, so that our sense of assurance (cf. Gal. 4:6–7) is not a psychological strategy that bypasses reality, but rather a proleptic manifestation of God's righteous verdict" (*Explorations*, 174).

the observance of the Law as the means through which God is making things right.[19] The accent, then, is on God's objective act in Christ on the cross and in his resurrection for the life of the world. To make this interpretation of this verse more explicit, we can translate the Greek text in this way:

A human being is not declared righteous
    a by works of the Law, but rather
    b by Jesus Christ's faithful death in our behalf
    c even we have believed in Christ Jesus so that we are
        declared righteous
    b' by Christ's faithful death in our behalf
    a' not by works of the Law

For maintaining that justification is not by works of the Law, Paul is being accused of being a sinner; that is, he is accused of living like a Gentile. This is why circumcision is so significant in the Epistle to the Galatians. Paul's opponents are suggesting to the Galatians that if they follow Paul in his views on justification, they are returning to their former existence, one in which they lived outside the *Torah*. To show that they are rejecting Paul's preaching, they need to be circumcised. The issue Paul now confronts is: "Whether the law is still in force, that is, whether it is 'torn down' or 'built up.' "[20] When Paul, therefore, says that "I through the Law died to the Law" (Gal 2:19), he is speaking heresy as a former Jew and Pharisee. To die to the Law is to be separated from it. The Law is what distinguishes a Jew from a Gentile, the holy from the profane.[21] The dative "to the Law" (νόμῳ) indicates one's direction toward something or someone. In his book *Dying and Rising with Christ*, Robert Tannehill writes that "this construction is used in connection with one's release from one lordship and entry into another, the dative indicating the lord in question."[22] Having died to the Law, through which he distinguished the sacred from the profane, Paul now lives to God (θεῷ) because he has been crucified with Christ (Χριστῷ). These two datives also indicate a change in lordship. Instead of the Law, it is now through Christ that Paul is able to distinguish the sacred from the profane.

---

19. Martyn, *Galatians*, 97.
20. Robert C. Tannehill, *Dying and Rising with Christ: A Study in Pauline Theology* (Berlin: Töpelmann, 1967), 57.
21. See further Martyn, *Galatians*, 256.
22. Tannehill, *Dying and Rising*, 57.

The questions "What time is it?" and "What cosmos do you live in?" take center stage again. The death of Christ is the eschatological event for Paul in which humanity is freed from powers of the old lord in the old aeon and put under the subjection of a new lord in the new aeon. The death of Christ is the pivotal event that separates these two aeons and brings about the apocalyptic change of death to the Law and life to God. But these two aeons overlap in the sense that the "present evil age" is the time when the old and new aeons are engaged in battle. The boundaries of the map of this embattled world in which Paul and the Galatians now live have been redrawn. It is no longer through the Law that one distinguishes holy from profane, that is, where God is making right what has gone wrong; rather, it is through Christ, and particularly through his death, that one now maps the world of God's holiness, the space of the new creation.

III. THE LAW, THE CROSS, AND BAPTISM: GALATIANS 3:11–14; 4:3–7

Why does Paul say that his death to the Law takes place through the Law? It is because of the role of the Law in Christ's crucifixion. Tannehill points to "Christ's subjection to the law" (Gal 4:3–5) and "endurance of its curse in his death (3:13) as background necessary to understand Christ's death through the law."[23] Galatians 3:10–14 is where Paul proclaims how Christ and the Law, the blessing of God and the curse of the Law, meet at the cross.[24] This is the only place in the Pauline corpus in which Paul uses the language of the "curse of the Law." He describes those who observe the Law to be "under the power of a curse." Martyn describes it this way:

> Reaching back to his apocalyptic interpretation of the Jewish-Christian atonement formula of 1:4a, Paul strikes a note that subsequently permeates the whole of the exegetical section of 3:6–4:7: the human dilemma consists at its base, not of guilt, but of enslavement to powers lying beyond the human being's control. As the quotation from Deut 27:26 will show, the first such power specified by Paul is a curse pronounced by the Law.[25]

---

23. Tannehill, *Dying and Rising,* 58–59.
24. Martyn, *Galatians,* 307.
25. Martyn, *Galatians,* 308.

Everyone is cursed by the Law, both those who attempt to keep the Law and those who do not, that is, both Jew and Gentile. By citing Hab 2:4 (the only place in the Old Testament where righteousness and faith occur together besides Gen 15:6, cited by Paul at the beginning of this section at Gal 3:6), Paul shows that what is clear is that "[h]e who through faith is righteous shall live" precisely because no one is justified before God by the Law. This life of the righteous is an eschatological one, begun by Christ through his atoning death and vindicating resurrection and continued in the church by Baptism and faith.

There is only one way out for everyone, one chance at rescue and liberation from the slavery of the Law's curse. This way out is by a power greater than the Law, and that power is the person of Christ, "who embodied the faith Paul has just contrasted with the law (v 12)."[26] F. F. Bruce notes that "the 'curse of the law' is the curse pronounced on the lawbreaker in Dt. 27:26."[27] If this is true, all who break the Law are cursed by the Law or made slaves to the Law. One supposes that if someone could live perfectly under the Law, then one would not have the Law pronounce a curse. Bruce refers to 2 Cor 5:21 and Rom 5:19 as evidence that Christ was the only one to live in perfect obedience to the Law; thus he was able to redeem us from the curse of the Law, placing himself under the ultimate result of the curse, namely, death. For us, Christ's faithfulness to his Father is so radical that he not only embodies faith but also in faith is lifted up on the tree of the cross so he might now embody the curse of the Law, becoming a curse for us. Second Corinthians is the most appropriate verse: "For our sake he made him to be sin who knew no sin, so that in him we might become the righteousness of God" (2 Cor 5:21). Bruce concludes: "[T]he curse which Christ 'became' was the people's curse, as the death which he died was their death."[28]

The sacrificial overtones here are unmistakable. Paul states that Christ redeemed us, "having become a curse for us" (ὑπὲρ ἡμῶν), using the ὑπέρ formula that links this passage with the self-sacrificial language of his opening greeting in Gal 1:4—"who gave himself for our sins" (ὑπὲρ τῶν ἁμαρτιῶν ἡμῶν)—and with his programmatic statement on the death of Jesus in Gal 2:20: "who loved me

---

26. Martyn, *Galatians*, 317.

27. F. F. Bruce, *The Epistle to the Galatians* (The New International Greek Testament Commentary; Grand Rapids: Eerdmans, 1982), 163–64.

28. Bruce, *Epistle to the Galatians*, 166.

and gave himself for me" (ὑπὲρ ἐμοῦ). Martyn describes the theological significance of this sacrificial language:

> [2 Corinthians] clearly reflects sacrificial language that was employed in ancient Israel. By laying his hands on an animal that was to be sacrificed a man transmitted his sin to it, the result being that the animal, having become sin, was itself called "sin" (*ḥet'*, often translated as "sin-offering"). . . . Sin is something that can be transferred from one person to another. . . . God transferred our sin to Christ, thus freeing us from its effect.

> By analogy it seems that in Gal 3:13 Paul does not intend to say that Christ fell under the Law's curse because he committed discrete transgressions. On the contrary, just as Christ embodied (and elicited) the faith spoken of by Habakkuk (Gal 3:11), so he embodied the Law's curse. When one looked at him, as he was being crucified (3:1), one saw the only juncture at which that embodied faith met that embodied curse in all its power.[29]

That the Gospel he preaches to these Gentile Galatians is an apocalyptic one Paul asserts at the theological center of his Epistle when he says that in the fullness of time God sent his Son (ἐξαπέστειλεν ὁ θεός) into this present evil age so he might redeem those who are under the Law. The connection between Gal 3:13, in which Paul asserts that "Christ redeemed [ἐξηγόρασεν] us from the curse of the law," and Gal 4:4–7 is the verb ἐξαγοράζω, which, in Galatians, means the "redeeming and liberating act of Christ."[30]

4:4 ὅτε δὲ ἦλθεν τὸ πλήρωμα τοῦ χρόνου,
ἐξαπέστειλεν ὁ θεὸς τὸν υἱὸν αὐτοῦ,
γενόμενον ἐκ γυναικός,
γενόμενον **ὑπὸ νόμον**,

4:5 ἵνα τοὺς **ὑπὸ νόμον** ἐξαγοράσῃ,
ἵνα τὴν υἱοθεσίαν ἀπολάβωμεν.

4:6 Ὅτι δέ **ἐστε** υἱοί,
ἐξαπέστειλεν ὁ θεὸς τὸ πνεῦμα τοῦ υἱοῦ αὐτοῦ
εἰς τὰς καρδίας ἡμῶν κρᾶζον·
ἀββα ὁ πατήρ.

---

29. Martyn, *Galatians*, 318.
30. See Martyn, *Galatians*, 370–73.

4:7 ὥστε οὐκέτι εἶ δοῦλος ἀλλὰ υἱός·
     εἰ δὲ υἱός,
     καὶ κληρονόμος διὰ θεοῦ.

4:4 But when the time had fully come,
     God **sent forth** his Son,
          born of woman,
          born **under the law**,

4:5   **to redeem** those who were **under the law**,
     so that we might receive adoption as sons.

4:6 And because you are sons,
     God sent the Spirit of his Son into our hearts, crying,
     "Abba! Father!"

4:7 So through God you **are** no longer a slave but a son,
          and if a son
          then an heir.

Galatians 4:4–5 is an interpretation of Gal 3:13, describing the incarnational and atoning aspects of Christ's work. Paul uses the same preposition with the Law (ὑπὸ νόμον) to describe Christ's birth (γενόμενον ἐκ γυναικός) under the power of the Law (γενό-μενον ὑπὸ νόμον) and the purpose (ἵνα) of his birth, namely, his redemption of those who are under the power of the Law (τοὺς ὑπὸ νόμον ἐξαγοράσῃ). Paul repeats the prepositional phrase "under the power of the law" (ὑπὸ νόμον) in these two verses to show the apocalyptic character of both Christ's incarnation and atonement. In Galatians, ὑπό with the accusative describes those things of the old aeon under whose power we are enslaved and from whom Christ has set us free in the new creation.[31] To be born under the power of the Law is to be born in the present evil age, and to redeem those under the power of the Law is to redeem them from one of the enslaving powers in which they live and from which they are set free.

Just as the Father sent his Son into the cosmos to redeem it, so now the Father sends (ἐξαπέστειλεν ὁ θεός) the Spirit of his Son into our hearts and we give the baptismal cry: "Abba, Father." The Galatians' birth and identity came through the Spirit of Christ, not through circumcision. Paul now interprets his baptismal practice for

---

31. E.g., "curse" (Gal 3:10); "sin" (Gal 3:22); "custodian" (law) (Gal 3:25); "guardian and manager" (Gal 4:2); "elemental spirits" (Gal 4:3); and "the Law" (Gal 3:23; 4:4, 5, 21; 5:18).

the Galatians, tying the apocalyptic event of Christ's incarnation with the pneumatic entrance of Christ's Spirit in them by water and Word in which their identity was formed in Christ. Paul's exegesis of the church's baptismal practice climaxes his exegetical argument by stating unequivocally that the Galatians' identity is "in Christ" because they have been baptized into Christ. They are now a part of the family of God as God's sons because the Spirit of God has invaded their hearts—baptismal language for Paul—and that Spirit of God "is now that of the crucified and resurrected Christ."[32]

IV. CHRIST AND THE LAW IN THE LIFE OF THE CHURCH: GALATIANS 5:14; 6:2

Because Baptism gives the Spirit of Christ to the Galatians, Christians now look at the Law through Christ and his Spirit. Ezekiel anticipated such an event: "A new heart I will give you, and a new spirit I will put within you; and I will take out of your flesh the heart of stone and give you a heart of flesh. And I will put my spirit within you, and cause you to walk in my statutes and be careful to observe my ordinances" (Ezek 36:26–27).[33] The problem, however, is that the baptized live simultaneously in the present evil age and in the new creation. This is the mystery of the overlap between these two ages, of *simul justus et peccator*.

That is why the baptized need a map of the world in which they actually live: the real world of the new creation. Paul, therefore, ends his homily by addressing what God's act of justification "looks like in the daily life of the church."[34] The church is engaged in apocalyptic warfare with "the flesh," what Martyn calls "a suprahuman power, indeed an inimical, martial power seeking to establish a military base of operations in the Galatian churches."[35] In this war of liberation, the church fights the power of the evil age with the Spirit of God's Son given in Baptism. The irony is that it is not "the flesh" that has declared war but Christ, through his invasion into this cosmos, and his Spirit, who has invaded us in Baptism and enlisted us in the fight. Paul gives pastoral advice to the Galatians through a series of eleven imperatives or hortatory subjunc-

---

32. Martyn, *Galatians*, 391–92.
33. The suggestion of Ezekiel comes from Martyn, *Galatians*, 391–92; he also suggests Jer 31:31–34 as another possible source.
34. Martyn, *Galatians*, 482.
35. Martyn, *Galatians*, 483.

tives in Gal 5:13–24 that begin with only the second positive reference to the Law in Galatians.[36]

5:13   ὑμεῖς γὰρ ἐπ᾽ ἐλευθερίᾳ **ἐκλήθητε**, ἀδελφοί·
μόνον μὴ τὴν ἐλευθερίαν εἰς ἀφορμὴν τῇ σαρκί,
ἀλλὰ διὰ τῆς ἀγάπης **δουλεύετε** ἀλλήλοις.

5:14   **ὁ γὰρ πᾶς νόμος** ἐν ἑνὶ λόγῳ **πεπλήρωται**,
ἐν τῷ·
ἀγαπήσεις τὸν πλησίον σου ὡς σεαυτόν.

5:13   For you were called to freedom, brethren;
only do not use your freedom as an opportunity
for the flesh,
but through love be servants of one another.

5:14   For the whole law is fulfilled
in one word,
"You shall love your neighbor as yourself."

The Law must now be seen within the new eschatological world
in which, through Christ, God is making things right in this present
evil age. What Paul wants the Galatians to see is how the Law, fulfilled in Christ, is lived out in this overlap of the ages through compassion, mercy, and love. Martyn puts it this way:

[Paul] speaks of a genuine war, a war of liberation that has been
commenced by the Spirit upon its arrival. And in this war the
Galatians are far more than mere spectators. Having the Spirit in
their hearts, they are soldiers who have been called into military
service by the Spirit. Placed in the front trenches of the Spirit's
war against the Flesh, they need a reliable map of the landscape.

For specific clues to the topographic details of the war in which
the Galatians are caught up, Paul refers them to the marks of the
two antagonists, the Flesh and the Spirit. And in listing those
marks (v 19–21a and 22–23a) Paul draws not on scripture, but
rather on a widely known Greco-Roman and Jewish tradition in
which a catalogue of *vices* is contrasted to a catalogue of *virtues*.
The result is a portrait of daily life that is appropriate to a group
of soldiers who are on a field of apocalyptic battle, and who are
led there not by a set of regulations, but rather by the power
that is certain to be the victor on that battlefield, the Spirit of
Christ . . . .

---

36. Of the thirty-two references to the Law in Galatians, only three are considered to be
positive: 3:24; 5:14; and 6:2.

In sum, then, at its core, 5:13–24 is not a prescription of the way the Galatians ought to behave, a series of exhortations focused on demands laid on human beings by the Law or by some other system of moral norms. On the contrary, this paragraph is fundamentally a description of the way things are, given the advent of the Spirit, its declaration of war against the Flesh, and its community-building power, already evident in the Galatian churches.[37]

The way things are in the new creation is that our lives are led by the Spirit, not the Law. To survive as the church in this present evil age, Paul reminds the church in Gal 6:2 that she must:

Ἀλλήλων τὰ βάρη **βαστάζετε** καὶ
οὕτως **ἀναπληρώσετε** τὸν νόμον τοῦ Χριστοῦ.

Bear one another's burdens, and
so **fulfill** the **law of Christ**.

No better reflection of what Paul means with this exhortation may be found than that in the Formula of Concord, Solid Declaration, Article VI on the "third use of the Law." This confession reflects the language of Paul in Galatians:

> [W]hen people are born again through the Spirit of God and set free from the law (that is, liberated from its driving powers and driven by the Spirit of Christ), they live according to the unchanging will of God, as comprehended in the law, and do everything, insofar as they are reborn, from a free and merry spirit. Works of this kind are not, properly speaking, works of the law but works and fruits of the Spirit, or, as Paul calls them, "the law of the mind" and "the law of Christ." For such people are "no longer under law but under grace" . . . .[38]

By loving our neighbors as ourselves and bearing their burdens, we show the Spirit's victory in us, in our flesh, where the apocalyptic battle is waging even now. Paul concludes his homily to the Galatians by harking back to his opening greeting to them: "But far be it from me to glory except in the cross of our Lord Jesus Christ, by which the world has been crucified to me, and I to the world. For neither circumcision counts for anything, nor uncircumcision, but a new creation" (Gal 6:14–15).

---

37. Martyn, *Galatians*, 483–84.
38. FC SD VI, 17 (K-W, 590).

BIBLICAL THEOLOGY
PERSPECTIVES

LAW IN A LAW-LESS WORLD

DAVID P. SCAER

All the essayists in this volume agree that the Bible superimposes external standards, a thesis not in tune with the contemporary "culture of excess" that finds little to no room for law.[1] Matters are complicated by postmodernism, which allows biblical injunctions a place in its systems only when they are regarded as self-imposed and never universal.[2] Despite various problems in the Victorian world of the nineteenth and early twentieth centuries, certain external behaviors were expected, especially of its leaders. Today these expectations rarely exist and moral freedom is everyone's entitlement. Only those freedoms that inflict irreparable damage to others are disallowed.

This free, open, and unrestrained "law-less" ethic is also at work in the church and is barely distinguishable from today's secular ethic. Many pastors live with the frustration that even professing Christians claim freedom in what they will believe and how they will live. Any doctrinal standard is viewed as "law," and requiring submission to it is regarded as "legalism." In a former time, churches set standards of faith and life for their members. Now this is often reversed and many churches adjust their standards for faith and life to fit the commonly accepted beliefs and behaviors of their members. What some Christians believe has little resemblance to the *official* faith professed by the churches to which they belong. Ethics mirroring common behavior have replaced the biblical idea

---

1. For example, see Robert H. Bork, *Slouching towards Gomorrah: Modern Liberalism and American Decline* (New York: Regan Books, 1996).

2. See Stanley Grenz, *A Primer on Postmodernism* (Grand Rapids: Eerdmans, 1996), and Gene E. Veith Jr., *Postmodern Times: A Christian Guide to Contemporary Thought and Culture* (Wheaton, Ill.: Crossway, 1994).

that the moral law in Holy Scripture is God's standard for behavior. Individual moral and religious autonomy is reflected in a more frequently heard claim that congregations are similarly autonomous and hence are sovereign in determining their worship forms and requirements for membership and admission to the Lord's Supper. Theology typically classifies sacraments with the preached Word as forms of the Gospel. Predecessor rites such as circumcision and Passover are often viewed as law because they were the divinely established parameters to mark the boundaries separating God's people from all other peoples. Ceremonial laws governing temple worship and sacrifice and the preparation and eating of foods are similarly viewed as insignificant, or at least peripheral, in Christian discourse. Some of the essays in this book take us down another path and show that through these customs God was acting graciously toward Israel. They were not arbitrary rubrics to prevent idle hands and hearts from going after idols.

The essays in this volume do not assess today's collapsing moral standards, but they take readers into the biblical world in which prophets and apostles were putting into place norms for a kingdom of priests on earth whose members were to relate with love first to God, then to one another. Today the church, or at least the true church, works to retard an internal moral disintegration among its members whose behaviors increasingly resemble those of the world. The prophets and apostles had the reverse task of putting into place moral and behavioral structures for communities that were emerging from a cruel world that knew not God or his Law.[3] Both Israel and the early church were people God had chosen as his own and in this they were unique from other peoples. The essayists carried out their assignments with an awareness of both the historic understanding that the Law's importance is often viewed as secondary to that of the Gospel and the recent antinomianism that has crept into the church under the guise of Christian freedom granted by the Gospel. They tread the tender soil of having to take into account traditional interpretations of the Law while taking exception to a growing antinomianism. It must be said, once again, that these essays do not pretend to do the task of systematic theology (also know as "dogmatics"), which directs commonly accepted principles to contemporary issues. Dogmatic conclusions about the Law, however, should be biblically defensible, and not only through typically

---

3. For the impact of Christianity on the Roman world, see Alvin J. Schmidt, *Under the Influence: How Christianity Transformed Civilization* (Grand Rapids: Zondervan, 2001).

cited "proof passages." Here these essays perform a service to dogmatics by examining the broad contours of the Law in the wider context of the biblical witness.

I. ANALYZING THE TITLE:
THE LAW IN HOLY SCRIPTURE

A perennial problem for a seriously confessional church and its seminaries is integrating the disciplines of biblical studies and systematic theology. In actual practice each of these disciplines is carried out in its own world of thought and with its own rules. Systematic theology is circumscribed by a church's confessions. Biblical theology draws on a wider range of scholarship and is in this sense the more ecumenical of the two disciplines. The essays for the 2001 Symposium on Exegetical Theology at Concordia Theological Seminary were presented under the title *The Law in Holy Scripture*, a biblical theme that has implications for Lutheran systematic theology at whose center is the Law-Gospel principle. This carries over into preaching. In homiletics classes, Lutheran seminary students are constantly reminded that their sermons must deliver a clear proclamation of the Law and the Gospel so listeners may be confronted with their moral depravity and then receive salvation in Jesus Christ.[4] Characteristically in this homiletical equation, the Law becomes God's *opus alienum* (foreign work) that he would rather not do but has to do because of man's fallen condition. In this kind of environment, the Law can hardly have a positive image.

Roots of the Law's negative image go back to the apostolic era. In the second century, Marcion, a priest with frustrated episcopal aspirations, neatly divided the Old Testament and New Testament into Law and Gospel respectively. He concluded that the older revelation with Law was inferior, had its own god, and was inapplicable to Christians who were to live only by the Gospel and worship the kinder, gentler deity revealed by Jesus.[5] Dispensationalism, the view that God provides different methods of salvation in different times, follows in Marcion's steps by holding that, in the Old Testament, salvation was by the Law and in the New Testament by the Gospel. This erroneous view is still dispensed in the popular Scofield Bible and is associated with Dallas Theological Seminary from whence it

---

4. See esp. C. F. W. Walther, *The Proper Distinction between Law and Gospel* (trans. W. H. T. Dau; St. Louis: Concordia, 1929).

5. For further discussion of Marcion, see E. C. Blackman, *Marcion and His Influence* (New York: AMS, 1978).

has gone on to influence some Neo-Evangelical Protestants.[6] In both Marcion and Dispensationalism, the Law served its purpose in the Old Testament era and was rendered inoperative by the Gospel. In contemporary terms, Marcion could also be called a "Gospel reductionist" because in his view only the Gospel qualified as a lasting word of God. Law had outlived its purpose with the coming of Jesus. In dogmatic terms, Marcion was also an antinomian (a person who opposes the Law), though not the first. Already in the apostolic era some understood Paul's definition of the freedom given believers by the Gospel as a license for immorality (cf. Rom 6:1; Gal 5:13).

Nor did antinomianism disappear with the Reformation. Before the Reformation was into its tenth year, a virulent form of antinomianism appeared in the attempt of the peasants to overthrow the already tottering structures of medieval society.[7] As Marcion had found fodder for his program in a misinterpretation of Paul's definition of the Gospel, leaders of the Peasants' War misused Luther's understanding of Gospel freedom as a pretense for a revolution against the ruling classes. A subtler but still theologically serious form of antinomianism appeared among some of Luther's followers, particularly Johann Agricola, who denied the Law had any function in the life of the redeemed within the church but belonged solely in the courthouse.[8] Law awakened an awareness of sin, which was Luther's position, but the Reformation antinomians held that after coming to faith, believers were exempt from its requirements. This was hardly the reformer's position. In the exposition of the Ten Commandments in his Small and Large Catechisms, Luther assigned a positive role to the Law. Article VI in the Formula of Concord on the "third use of the Law" set forth the classic Lutheran position concerning the function of the Law in Christian life, a position overtly supported by several of the essays in this volume.

Biblical scholars in the eighteenth and nineteenth centuries took an evolutionist approach to the relation of the Old and New Testa-

---

6. For example, see Charles Caldwell Ryrie, *Dispensationalism Today* (Chicago: Moody Press, 1965). Ryrie is a product of Dallas Theological Seminary.

7. See Martin Brecht, *Martin Luther: Shaping and Defining the Reformation, 1517–1532* (trans. James L. Schaaf; Minneapolis: Fortress, 1990), esp. 172. Luther was accused of inciting the Peasants' War because of his emphasis on the freedom of the Christian in the Gospel.

8. For further discussion, see F. Bente, *Historical Introductions to the Book of Concord* (St. Louis: Concordia, 1965), 162–63.

ments that had certain similarities to Marcion's evil and good gods.[9] That inferior Old Testament depictions of an avenging God evolved into the superior portrait of a loving God in the New Testament is a view held first by the Rationalists and then by Schleiermacher. Even today some biblical scholars assume an evolutionary hypothesis, namely, that underneath the Old Testament monotheism was a primitive polytheism that regarded the patriarchs as tribal gods. With his commands to love God and neighbor, Jesus is seen as the perfection of this trek to monotheism. Through a process of moral improvement, Old Testament Law was metamorphosed into the Gospel. Still another track to define the Law was taken by Karl Barth, who was arguably the most influential twentieth-century theologian. He reversed the classical order of Law-Gospel into Gospel-Law and claimed that the Gospel was the first and only word of God, but he absorbed the Law into his definition of Gospel and came to define it as demand.[10] Barth did not replicate Calvin or traditional Reformed thought on this issue, but he stood in the Reformed tradition of assigning the Law a higher place in the economy of the Christian life (sanctification) than Lutherans traditionally did. Although both Reformation traditions knew of the category of the third use of the Law, their definitions were hardly interchangeable. For the Reformed, God requires obedience to the Law, which is strange language for Lutherans.[11]

Along with taking into consideration a common history shared with other Christians, a topic such as the Law in Holy Scripture must also reflect on our own position as Lutherans and the resultant attitudes attached to this understanding. As mentioned above, in Lutheran theology, the Law comes on the scene as the enemy of the sinner; it is God's *opus alienum*. It is bad tasting medicine for the sinner yet necessary for his recovery, but this does not improve its disagreeable taste. Unlike Reformed theology, in which the Law drives

---

9. See Gerald Bray, *Biblical Interpretation: Past and Present* (Downers Grove: InterVarsity, 1996), 221–375.

10. See further Karl Barth, *Church Dogmatics* (Edinburgh: T&T Clark, 1936–1977).

11. For a full discussion of the third use of the Law in Reformed theology, see Jan Rohls, *Reformed Confessions: Theology from Zurich to Barmen* (trans. John Hoffmeyer; Louisville: Westminster John Knox, 1998), 200–206. At the heart of Reformed theology is a particular view of covenants. Adam lived within the covenant of works that was replaced by a covenant of grace when he fell into sin. Although the essayists in this volume address questions of historical theology only incidentally, the Old Testament contributors see God's gracious activities as beginning with the creation. It seems unlikely that a covenant of works fits into their understanding of *Torah*.

the hearer to Christ, in Lutheran theology the Law possesses an introductory role in preparing the hearer for the Gospel.[12]

None of the essayists deviate from Luther's understanding of the Law's function in uncovering sin in its hearers, which is also the Reformed position, but the question arises whether the word *Law* in every biblical occurrence deserves this negative image. Among Lutherans, Paul's definition of the Gospel as opposed to the Law becomes the trump card that takes every trick on a theological board, or so it seems. Several essayists in this volume demonstrate that the Hebrew word *Torah*, commonly translated "law," in many cases—maybe most—does not fit how Lutherans understand "law" in their Law-Gospel definition. *Torah* is the narrative of God's gracious activities among his people in which he himself was present. So in Lutheran terms, *Torah* as the document in which God is present, teaching his people and narrating his gracious deeds, is primarily Gospel. It is incarnational in a preparatory sense. Whoever listens to *Torah* listens to God.

II. WHAT ARE THE BACKGROUND ISSUES?

Titles for the various essays indicate which part of the biblical canon each contributor addressed in what is meant by *Law*. The three essayists who deal with the Old Testament treat it as a totality without concentrating on particular books. Daniel Gard calls this the diachronic approach in which the Old Testament is studied as total canon in the style of Brevard Childs. These essayists stress the salvific role of the Law for Israel. Two of the four New Testament contributors concentrate on Paul, one on Luke, and one on the sayings of Jesus in the Synoptic Gospels. Coming from different perspectives, each writer is agreed that the Scriptures assign positive functions to the Law for believers. Several make specific correlations with what is dogmatically known as the third use of the Law. These essays are not and do not pretend to be a critique on or a defense of past or present dogmatical positions and confessional views. Certain recent and current controversies, however, lie near the surface. If biblical studies are to have any real meaning for church life, they should not be done in a vacuum occupied by scholars alone but with an awareness of current issues.

Paul Raabe does precisely this in his essay by calling attention to the perennial Lutheran concentration on the Law in its function of

---

12. See Rohls, *Reformed Confessions*, 194.

accusing sinners. He takes issue with Werner Elert, who along with Paul Althaus and Herman Sasse was rightly regarded as one of the greatest and most influential twentieth-century Lutheran theologians. Raabe states that Elert "is patently false" in holding that "the 'law' throughout the Scriptures is always the law of retribution."[13] Elert drew his position from the often-cited confessional statement *lex semper accusat* ("the Law always accuses"), which was understood by Elert in an absolute and exclusivistic sense. This was hardly Melanchthon's intention, but of course this is what the debate is all about. Thus Law would have only an ancillary service in showing what calamities are in store for unrepentant sinners and by itself would have no positive function for Christian life. Some Lutherans following Elert soon concluded that the third use of the Law was an intrusion of Calvinism into Lutheran thought, and they were quick to take exception to Article VI of the Formula of Concord on the third use of the Law. In his defense, Elert must be understood in the context of his times. In the face of Barth's redefinition of the Gospel as ultimately an imperative, which Elert rightly saw as a confusion of Law and Gospel, Elert determined to maintain the traditional definition that required their separation, and that separation was at the heart of Lutheran theology. Elert's approach, however, allowed others to take the next step and deny a positive understanding of the Law in life.

This step is visible in the controversy over the Law and the Gospel that broke out in The Lutheran Church—Missouri Synod (LCMS) during the 1960s and 1970s.[14] Some LCMS theologians, later known as "Gospel reductionists," took Barth's view that the Gospel was the only word of God but refined it along with Elert's definition that the Law had only an accusatory function in Christian life. In holding that the Gospel was only the standard and criterion of what had to be believed in the Scriptures, they followed Barth; however, they used Elert's definition of Gospel to come to a minimalistic understanding of it as nothing else than a word of pure forgiveness. Barth defined Gospel as demand and so had subsumed Law into his definition of Gospel. In "Gospel reductionism," which was a Lutheran species of the Barthian definition, what did not fit under the category of the Gospel could be ignored and was. An immediate case in point was the ordination of women pastors.

---

13. See Paul R. Raabe's essay above, "Delighting in the Good Law of Yahweh," 68 n. 21.

14. See the historical introduction and analysis in Scott R. Murray, *Law, Life, and the Living God: The Third Use of the Law in Modern American Lutheranism* (St. Louis: Concordia, 2002).

Although such ordinations were disallowed by two citations in the Pauline corpus, these prohibitions were judged to be Law by the principle of the Gospel, hence they were nonbinding for church life. This and other prohibitions were abolished by the Gospel principle that constituted the heart and core of Paul's theology, so it was argued. Even if the passages cited could be interpreted to prohibit such ordinations, which the "Gospel reductionists" could grant in theory but not in practice, their Gospel principle rendered these and other biblical prohibitions inoperative. Proponents of "Gospel reductionism" labeled as legalists those who held that the Pauline injunctions against women's ordination remained in place. Christian life was lived according to the Gospel, not the Law, so they argued. In what was authoritative for the church or what had to be believed and accepted, this method pitted Gospel against Scripture and hardly fit Holy Scripture's own self-understanding as the narrative of God's salvific activities.

At issue is what is to be done with the Law, especially in light of Jesus Christ. Dean Wenthe and Daniel Gard argue in their essays that Old Testament believers did not see the Law as a foreign intrusion in their lives. Instead, it belonged to their election as God's people and was part of his gracious economy. Love of *Torah* is love for God himself who is present in *Torah* to teach his people. Placing the Scriptures and the Gospel in this adversarial relationship, as the "Gospel reductionists" did, took what was set down in ink on parchment as Law. If Gospel is the free unhindered oral proclamation, then the terms biblicism, literalism, and legalism became virtual synonyms. This theological program in which the Gospel was opposed to the Scriptures was unique and without a clear historical precedent, but its methods and results secured its place under the antinomian umbrella. Not only were the Law's threats and punishments made inoperative for believers by the Gospel principle but they also were its directives. This definition first led to allowing women to be ordained and is now used in some mainline churches to support the ordination of avowed homosexuals and to allow same-sex marriages. The argument goes that divergent lifestyles and practices may be prohibited by certain Scripture citations, especially Old Testament ones, but they are permitted by the Gospel that gives Christians freedom from the Law.

None of the essays specifically address these contemporary issues, but these current problems provide reasons for asking which biblical directives are binding on Christian life. Here is where the essays in this book provide a valuable service. They affirm that for the sinner as sinner, *lex semper accusat*, a position that is common in both Lutheran and Reformed thought, but they also confirm that the Law has a life apart from this function of locating and condemning sin. Christians can, do, and will fulfill the Law more and more, but perfect fulfillment will come only in the eschaton, as Dale Allison and Paul Raabe especially point out. If readers can agree that at the end time the Gospel will triumph, then they can agree as well that the final day also will be one of triumph for the Law, at which time it will be stripped of its accusatory functions and Christians will live in perfect accord. Triumph of the Law will be part of God's vindication. This hope was proffered by the prophets and realized in Jesus. In this hope his followers now live.

The essays collected in this volume are a daring, countercultural, and even counter-religious enterprise because they agree that the Law is both necessary and valuable for Christian life. Old Testament presentations show that *Torah* (the five books of Moses, also known as the Pentateuch) contains more than regulations Israel had to follow. It was the historical narrative that gave Israel purpose as God's people, as Dean Wenthe and Daniel Gard both stress. Law belonged to the fiber of their faith, religious practice, and nationhood. The New Testament essayists face other challenges, among which the first is whether Jesus opposed keeping the Law by pitting it against the Gospel. The question is whether the teaching of Jesus was an antinomianism of sorts in light of Jewish law. Should this view have any merit, it would mean that Jesus' opponents correctly recognized that he felt free to break the Law and that his mission included destroying the place of the Law in Jewish life. Both Dale Allison and Peter Scaer tackle this issue head-on and show that Jesus was Law observant, or *kosher*, not a revolutionary. Jesus' practices were in accord with the Judaism of his day, and he did not trump what the Law required with the Gospel. Jesus' everyday behavior provides no basis for a Law-less Christianity. Differences between Jesus and his Jewish opponents were not over the Law itself but how it was to be fulfilled and whether its fulfillment assured salvation. Another challenge faces the essayists who tackle a widely held opinion that Paul had a completely negative view of the Law, an understanding that is mistakenly seen as classically Lutheran and that has fueled antinomianism in mainline Protestant churches. Peter Scaer notes how Luke shows Paul to be respectful of the Law, even Jewish ceremonial law. Although both Charles

Gieschen and Arthur Just emphasize the accusatory function of the Law upon the sinner in Paul, both also note that Paul's focus on Christ's action in freeing us from the Law's condemnation allows Christians to value the Law as both a mirror and guide (the second and third uses of the Law).

Not unexpectedly at a symposium sponsored by a Lutheran seminary, eight of the nine essayists belong to this confession. With degrees awarded by universities such as Notre Dame (3); Michigan (2); Durham, UK (1); and Union Theological Seminary in Virginia (1), they do not advance predetermined or sectarian agendas. These exegetes are familiar with the methods and research of biblical scholarship even as their vocation is carried out in service to the church. Although Dale Allison, who was the keynote speaker for the symposium, is an internationally known biblical scholar, he also teaches within and for the church at Pittsburgh Theological Seminary. The hope of each of the essayists, I surmise, is that they will be heard by those who shape the church's life.

III. A CLOSER EXAMINATION OF INDIVIDUAL ESSAYS

Only by surveying the Old Testament's understanding of the Law is it possible to ask whether Jesus and his followers were Law observant and what this means for Christians today. First among the Concordia Theological Seminary's own presenters was its president, Dean Wenthe. In his essay, "The *Torah* Story: Identity or Duty as the Essence of the Law," Wenthe observes that in practice the Law is often detached from Israel's history and presented as if it were a collection of Kant's moral imperatives. Each reader will have to decide whether this censure is personally applicable. The Law was not a collection of "dos and don'ts" (Kant's moral imperatives); it was an integral part of Israel's history. The psalmist whom God has chosen, therefore, can delight in the Law of the Lord because it reveals God's gracious actions on behalf of Israel and the world. Law for the psalmist and other Old Testament writers consisted of more than directives governing behavior; it was the entire revelation God had given Israel, including guidance for a people who showed forth their identity in worship and life.

Paul Raabe is the author of the Obadiah commentary in the distinguished and widely used Anchor Bible series.[15] As is obvious from the title of his essay, "Delighting in the Good Law of Yahweh,"

---

15. Paul R. Raabe, *Obadiah* (AB 24D; New York: Doubleday, 1996).

Raabe affirms Wenthe's positive appraisal of the Law, but he puts the emphasis on *Torah* as instruction or teaching, a theme found in both Old and New Testaments. With Dean Wenthe, Daniel Gard, and Arthur Just, Raabe sees this emphasis developed in Lutheran theology in the third use of the Law. Law was not impersonal mandate, but the person of Yahweh amid his people as their teacher. Because the Law provided atonement and sacrifice as remedies for its abrogation, Raabe notes that it never had moral perfection in view. Within these remedies, Raabe finds the place for Christ's death that is the final and complete atonement for breaking the Law. As mentioned above, Raabe takes strong exception to those Lutherans for whom the Law's sole function is accusatory; however, he affirms that the Law does accuse those to whom it is addressed who then fail to live according to its directives. To this dilemma a solution is provided in the messianic King, who rules in perfect righteousness, and in Yahweh's servant, who suffers not for his sins but for those of others. Here is the basis for New Testament theology in which Jesus is presented as the servant-king and his followers as people who actually begin to fulfill God's Law, though never perfectly. Perfection does not belong to this age but to the eschaton, a point also stressed by Allison.

Daniel Gard, in his essay "The Law and Freedom in the Old Testament," understands Law as a reflection of God himself. God relates the Old Testament understanding of Law to Christian life today. For Gard, the Law constitutes Israel's identity as God's people. A gracious God gives Law to Israel, and this distinguishes them from all other peoples, a theme introduced in Wenthe's essay. Through the Law, God's attributes are reflected in the lives of his people. As ill-fated as were the attempts of the Pharisees to carry out the holiness regulations of the temple in their homes and villages, their endeavors showed that they understood that the Law was related to God's essence and that its regulations were not arbitrary, what Wenthe compared to Kant's moral imperatives. Even cultic laws were not capricious, but each carried in its own way the message of salvation. For example, offering the firstborn son back to God prepared the way for God sending his own Son. In this sense, God was fulfilling his own Law. On the one hand, Gard calls attention to modern antinomianism, which has no use for the Law, and on the other hand, he calls attention to modern legalism, which seeks to impose the Old Testament as civil law in the secular state. Here Gard is clearly alluding to the North American situation. In teaching *Torah* and presiding at worship, New Testament pastors are the successors to Old Testament prophets who were also priests. Gard defines the third use of the Law as providing definition to the Christian life, and within this definition, Christians have the freedom to do what they are in fact through union with Christ. Christian sanctification originates in God's holiness.

Dale Allison is especially well known for his work in the invaluable three-volume International Critical Commentary on Matthew.[16] His essay, "Jesus and the *Torah*," addresses the question of how Jesus related to the Judaism of his day. Although Allison does not provide contemporary reasons for his essay, one can be found in twentieth-century liberation theology, which gave some biblical scholars an opening to portray Jesus as a revolutionary who broke the Law at every turn. Such is the work of John Dominic Crossan.[17] At the other end of the spectrum are scholars who, perhaps in an attempt to relate to their Jewish contemporaries, see Jesus entirely within the terms of the Judaism of his day. This view means that Jesus and his contemporaries had no real differences about the Law and thus had to be opposed to each other for other reasons. Prominent among scholars with this view is E. P. Sanders, whom Charles Gieschen and A. Andrew Das challenge in their essays.[18] Allison approaches the question of whether Jesus was Law observant (Sanders) or not (Crossan) by locating passages from the Gospels that support both views. Was Jesus a conservative, Law-abiding, *kosher* Jew or a radical, even revolutionary, prophet or peasant?

Allison examines what appear to be competing moral imperatives in the Gospels, especially in regard to Sabbath keeping, and concludes that Jesus' practices were within the boundaries of what the rabbis accepted. Even the rabbis recognized that healing on the Sabbath did not break the Law because showing mercy took precedence. As Allison says: "[O]ne imperative can trump another imperative."[19] Another example of conflicting commandments is Jesus' requirement that his followers disregard their parents to pursue the kingdom of God, as he himself did in disassociating himself from

---

16. W. D. Davies and Dale C. Allison Jr., *A Critical and Exegetical Commentary on the Gospel according to Saint Matthew*, 3 vols. (ICC; Edinburgh: T&T Clark, 1988–1997). See also Dale C. Allison Jr., *The New Moses* (Minneapolis: Fortress, 1993).

17. See J. D. Crossan, *The Historical Jesus: The Life of a Mediterranean Jewish Peasant* (San Francisco: Harper, 1991).

18. See especially E. P. Sanders, *Paul and Palestinian Judaism* (Philadelphia: Fortress, 1977).

19. See Dale C. Allison Jr.'s essay above, "Jesus and the *Torah*," 78.

his family. In requiring primary allegiance, Jesus was acting in accord with the interpretation of the rabbis that commands of the Second Table of the Law were subordinate to those of the First Table, a principle inherent in the Law itself. Conflict exists not in the Law, which is perfect, but in its application in an imperfect world. A seminary curriculum would do well to offer a course in ethics that gives serious considerations to Jesus' behavior in light of contemporary rabbinical ethics. Law allowing for divorce is an example of an accommodation to the human condition, but the eschaton is dawning in Christ when the Law will be effective in the heart and concessions will no longer be needed. Sacrifices and festivals will have outlived their purposes, and laws covering clean and unclean will be revised.

On the question of whether Jesus was Law observant, Allison offers what can only be seen as a conclusive argument that he was. For example, the women wait until the Sabbath is over to anoint his dead body. His followers must have followed his example and observed the Sabbath in the same way as other Jews did. If Jesus was a revolutionary who taught his followers to be revolutionaries, as some scholars claim, they would have had no qualms in breaking the Sabbath to anoint his body. Although this is not noted by Allison, in reporting that Jesus' opponents approached Pilate on the Sabbath to place a guard at the tomb, Matthew cleverly pictures Jesus' enemies as the real Sabbath breakers (Matt 27:62–66).

In his essay, "Luke, Jesus, and the Law," Peter Scaer tackles a more specific problem in analyzing how Luke pictured Jesus and Paul in their fulfilling of the Law. Whereas Allison derived a composite picture of Jesus and the Law from all the Gospels, Scaer limits his topic to Luke, but both address the same basic question of whether Jesus was a conservative (kosher) or a radical in regard to keeping the Law. Scaer then asks the same question of Paul in Acts. In presenting his evidence, Allison keeps his cards close to his chest so only at the conclusion is the reader informed that Jesus was not the radical that some prominent scholars claim him to be. Allison lets himself (and the reader) be drawn or even dragged along by what he discovers so one suspects that he was as surprised by his conclusions as we are. Scaer begins by showing that already in the infancy narratives and throughout the Gospel, Jesus is Law observant; however, *Law* for Luke is Jewish custom without morally binding authority for the Gentiles. Luke's Law-observant Paul is no different. Luke's "Law as custom" approach allows Scaer to conclude that the Paul who emerges from the pages of Acts does not contradict the apostle's own self-understanding in the Epistles. To come to this conclusion, Scaer addresses the same question that Allison did in defining Jesus' attitude to the Law. Allison locates disparate passages in all four Gospels, while Scaer follows Luke's order in his Gospel and the Book of Acts. Characters in the infancy narrative (Zechariah, Elizabeth, Mary, Joseph, Simeon, Anna) are all Law-abiding Jews who on that account are respected citizens in their corner of the Roman Empire. God-fearing Gentile readers, however, know from the outset that these Jews are acting according to the custom, thus these things will not be expected of them as Christians. Jewish customs will not be imposed on the Gentiles, but Jesus and the Jews associated with him are hardly revolutionaries.

Scaer agrees with Allison that Jesus is Law observant and never breaks the Law. Allison comes to this conclusion by comparing Jesus' behavior with that of the rabbis. Scaer arrives at the same place by examining Luke's editorial comments, which provide a theological rationale for Jesus' actions. Take the case of the Jews accusing the disciples of breaking the Sabbath regulation by gathering grain. At the heart of Luke's presentation is Jesus' defense by means of a comparison to David eating the priestly bread. First, Jesus is like David and hence Messiah, so he is entitled to do this. Second, mercy takes precedence over rules, an essential part of Allison's argument that one commandment trumps another. Finally, Jesus is the Lord of the Sabbath and, therefore, not subject to its regulations. Whereas Allison argues that Jesus took advantage of the exceptions the Law itself allowed, Scaer argues that Jesus closed the exceptions or loopholes in the Law and perfected it.

Scaer's essay continues beyond Jesus by showing from Acts that the community that grew up around Jesus followed common Jewish practices. For some time scholars have noted that the firebrand Paul of Galatians who hates the Law is not the Law-abiding figure in Acts who submits himself to Jewish regulations. In Acts, Paul does the same thing for which he condemns others. Out of principle he refuses to circumcise Titus (Gal 2:3) but reverses his position in regard to Timothy (Acts 16:3). In Jerusalem, Paul keeps the laws of purification, but he condemns Peter for following Jewish rules for eating. With the evidence from the Epistles apparently contradicting that from Acts, some scholars believe that discovering the "historical Paul" is as elusive a task as finding the "historical Jesus." In determining Paul's true character, many scholars favor the Epistles and discount Luke's picture of him as fiction.

Scaer, however, does not see two Pauls that are at odds with each other. Luke's Paul in Acts knows of the compromise regulations adopted by the Council of Jerusalem to settle differences between Jewish and Gentile Christians, and he abides by them (Acts 15). He complies with the regulations not because of custom but for apologetic and diplomatic reasons. For Luke, the Law's significance is fading, but for the sake of others, Jesus and his followers such as Paul fulfill its regulations. Mosaic Law is the best summary of divine Law, but there is no one-for-one equation between them. Most important for Luke's understanding of the Law is that Jesus fulfills it. Whereas Raabe showed that Law in the Old Testament contained within itself a need for fulfillment and perfection, Scaer shows that Luke finds this fulfillment and perfection in Jesus.

There seems to me to be a correlation between Luke's and Luther's worlds in regard to what liturgical rules or customs from the Roman liturgy were to remain in force or could be practiced among the Lutherans. In both cases, as the older era was gradually pushed aside by a newer one, men had to address how this could be done with the least pain. After Luther's death, the Augsburg and Leipzig Interims were imposed by the Roman Catholic party, but without Lutheran participation they hardly qualified as compromises. Of course, our own times are not immune to similar conflicts about what we must not do and what we may be allowed to do. Scaer shows how Jesus and his church, who could compromise on some issues but not others, can still serve as our guide.

At the beginning of this chapter, I attempted to show the historical and dogmatic importance of the Law in Holy Scripture. In his essay "Paul and the Law: Was Luther Right?" Charles Gieschen provides reasons from the world of biblical scholarship for tackling the topic. E. P. Sanders took issue with Luther's negative assessment of Judaism and the Law, which Sanders claims has permeated biblical studies since the Reformation. In other words, Luther created a caricature of Judaism from which New Testament scholars were not able to emancipate themselves until now. Sanders argues that obedience to the Law in the Judaism of Jesus' day was not a condition for salvation, but it was the response of those whom God had elected and placed in the covenant. Sanders sees Paul in a similar light. He does not take issue with the idea that Paul focused the Law into the life of the Christian to uncover sin; instead, Paul took over from Judaism the view that the fulfillment of the Law was the response of faith. Antagonism between Jews and Christians, according to Sanders, did not originate in their opposing views about the Law but in the Christian claim that Jesus was divine. Of course, both are reasons the Jews used to execute Christ.

James Dunn nuanced Sanders's position and argued that Paul's real problem was not with the Law but with requiring certain national identity markers of Gentile converts. This view applied a double standard, one for Jews and another for Christians. Because Jews were required to do things and prohibited from doing other things from which Gentile Christians were exempt, animosity between the two groups arose. Certainly Dunn understands the human spirit, which easily recognizes the lack of fairness in an uneven application of regulations, but whether this is the real reason for Jewish-Christian animosity is another matter.

Gieschen is pleased that both scholars have worked to remove caricatures of Judaism as a thoroughly works-righteous religion, a view to which Luther may have contributed, but he notes that both Sanders and Dunn have not correctly understood first-century Judaism. To remain in the covenant, Jews were required to fulfill the Law or at least to have the intent to do so. Because a perfect fulfillment of the Law was impossible, even according to its own terms, as Gieschen points out, fulfillment hardly could have been a requirement for remaining in the covenant. Law was never assigned such an important salvific role. Although Luther and some of his followers may not have fully appreciated Judaism's broader and positive view of the Law, the reformer caught the major thrust of Paul's argument that Jews and others did not and could not possess the perfection that the Law required. Certainly the intent to fulfill the Law could not be substituted for the actual fulfillment. Jewish possession and knowledge of the Law was not enough to assure salvation.

A. Andrew Das, whose doctoral dissertation perused this topic of Paul and the Law, goes beyond Gieschen's broader introduction and critique to probe the topic of perfect obedience of the Law in first-century Judaism.[20] Unlike the wave of New Testament scholars who have bought into the New Perspective and argue that Paul really was not speaking against Jewish understandings of the Law, Das helps us to be sure that Paul understood his first-century Jewish

---

20. See A. Andrew Das, *Paul, the Law, and the Covenant* (Peabody, Mass.: Hendrickson, 2001).

context better than many modern scholars. His essay, "Beyond Covental Nomism: Paul, Judaism, and Perfect Obedience," shows that Das has read E. P. Sanders carefully and has gone back to the Jewish literature that Sanders used to show how Sanders minimized the demands for perfect obedience that the Law makes. In short, Das helps the reader to see why Paul stressed that though the Law is good and valuable, it is not the basis for God's justifying activity.

In his essay "Christ and the Law in the Life of the Church at Galatia," Arthur Just develops an understanding of Law and Gospel that fits the traditional Lutheran understanding but does so in a nontraditional manner by positing one world governed by the Law and another governed by the Gospel. The Galatians already had taken up residence under the Gospel, but by succumbing to the imposition of Jewish regulations, they were slipping into the older reality ruled by the Law. A new world had come into existence through Christ's death and resurrection, which are on that account regarded as apocalyptic events. Christians already are living in the eschatological time that is governed by divine grace and now the Law can only be understood through the cross. Following an argument by J. Louis Martyn that Galatians was originally a fiery sermon delivered by the apostle, Just recognizes certain phrases in the Epistle are taken from the liturgy (such as "amen" and "grace and peace").[21] This reflects Just's longtime dual interest in liturgics and biblical studies, and his conclusion, which I also share, is that the New Testament documents arose from and were written for use in church worship. *Grace* and *peace* are, however, more than liturgical words; they are realities for believers emerging from Christ's substutionary atonement.

Just makes use of the conclusions of a recent debate concerning the interpretation of the word *faith* in a passage such as Gal 2:16: "[Y]et who know that a man is not justified by works of the law but through *faith [of]* Jesus Christ, even we have believed in Christ Jesus, in order to be justified by *faith [of]* Christ, and not by works of the law, because by works of the law shall no one be justified."[22] In both cases, there is good reason, Just argues, to see these as references to Christ's faith. Thus the meaning would be that our salvation comes from trusting Christ's faithfulness for us in undergoing

---

21. See J. Louis Martyn, *Galatians: A New Translation with Introduction and Commentary* (AB 33A; New York: Doubleday, 1997).

22. For an introduction to the debate, see Paul Pollard, "The 'Faith of Christ' in Recent Discussion," *CJ* 23 (1997): 213–28. Unless otherwise indicated, all the Scripture quotations in this essay are taken from the RSV.

death by a cross. Christ's own faith has a salvific effect for believers. This faith required putting himself under the Law's curse. This view reinforces justification as an action outside of ourselves and not dependent on us. In dogmatical terms, this is called objective or universal justification.

Just highlights the Pauline teaching that all are born into the evil age under the Law, but by Baptism, Christians are given the Spirit and born into a new world. Problematic for Christians is that they live simultaneously in the evil age and in the eschatological age of the new creation. This mystery is expressed in dogmatic language with *simul justus et peccator*. Christians are caught in a war between the two opposing worlds of the flesh and of the Spirit, a war caused, ironically, not by demonic powers but by Christ's coming into the evil world. In this new existence, the Law is transformed into the law of Christ that requires Christians to bear the burdens of others, a conviction that is at the heart of the Formula of Concord's understanding of the third use of the Law. Of all the essayists, Just most closely approximates Luther, probably because the reformer also drew heavily on Galatians for his views on the Law.

IV. CONCLUSION

Jesus is the one in whom we find the understanding and definition of the relationship between the Law in the Old and New Testaments. He stated:

> Think not that I have come to abolish the law and the prophets; I have come not to abolish them but to fulfil them. For truly, I say to you, till heaven and earth pass away, not an iota, not a dot, will pass from the law until all is accomplished. Whoever then relaxes one of the least of these commandments and teaches men so, shall be called least in the kingdom of heaven; but he who does them and teaches them shall be called great in the kingdom of heaven. (Matt 5:17–19)

The "iotas" and "dots" of the *Torah* are not threats against those who do not fulfill its regulations, but Jesus is asserting his intention to fulfill every word and letter in the Old Testament, not only this or that prediction. All is accomplished in Jesus' crucifixion, a new era dawns, and heaven and earth quite literally pass away (Matt 27:45, 50–54). Jesus embraces and takes Moses and all the prophets into himself and transfigures and transubstantiates the Old Testament into the New. Jesus is incarnate *Torah*. The Old Testament

Scriptures become alive and permanently preserved in Jesus. Apart from him the veil of Moses stays in place. The "commandments" that are not to be relaxed are not the commandments of the Old Testament but *his* commandments, which subsume and surpass those of the Old Testament.

The essays of this volume address the topic of the Law in Holy Scripture from several angles and in light of twentieth-century theological developments in Christendom, particularly among Lutherans. They are worthy of careful consideration within the wider church, as well as among biblical scholars and theologians. Several essays stress the important theme that the ethical demands of the Law must always be understood in light of God's gracious and saving action, especially as revealed in Jesus Christ. As long as we remain in the evil world, the Law will continue to be God's *opus alienum* as it accuses and convicts all as sinners. Christ, however, in his death and resurrection fulfilled the Law. Christians are already living in the new era ushered in by Christ. In this world the Law has begun to be seen as God originally intended. It is this understanding of the Law that is needed by the church as she daily confronts a lawless world.

The Third Use of the Law in Light of Creation and the Fall

Piotr J. Malysz

The proper distinction between Law and Gospel was, without much exaggeration, the most fundamental theological decision of the Reformation. The Formula of Concord calls it "an especially brilliant light which serves the purpose that the Word of God may be rightly divided and the writings of the holy prophets and apostles may be explained and understood correctly."[1] Embracing more than this hermeneutical process, the distinction lies at the very foundation of the doctrine of justification by grace through faith, or any other article of faith for that matter. It serves to preserve the integrity of Christ's atoning sacrifice while at the same time ensuring due condemnation of unbelief.

Although the nature of the Gospel seemed quite clear to all those involved in the elaboration and application of the Law-Gospel distinction, the character and the place of the Law in relation to the Gospel remained subject to much dispute and discord. Some of the debates continued well into the twentieth century, only to leave the issue muddier than ever. Among them an especially prominent place is occupied by the lengthy discussion concerning the so-called third use of the Law.

Rather than offer an evaluation of the historico-theological data, this study will demonstrate that no satisfactory presentation of the third use of the Law can be given without an overt reference to

---

1. FC SD V, 1 (Tappert, 558).

creation and the fall. It will begin by synthetically delineating the role of the Law—with special focus on the third use—as it has been traditionally understood in Lutheran theology. After certain unresolved problems have been identified, our discussion then will proceed to deal with the complex question of anthropology in the context of creation, which eventually will form the basis for the proposed adjustment in the concept of the third use of the Law.

I. THE THIRD USE: WHENCE AND WHERE TO?

Even a cursory glance at the New Testament will reveal a strong emphasis on Christian living. Believers are encouraged to "live a life worthy of the calling you have received" (Eph 4:1).[2] As God's beloved children, they are to be "imitators of God," living "a life of love, just as Christ loved us and gave himself up for us as a fragrant offering and sacrifice to God" (Eph 5:1–2). The richness of expression is quite staggering. For the most part, however, the emphasis is conveyed through admonitions whose sense of immediacy reflects the crucial link between Christian life and Christ's atoning sacrifice on the cross as its source and driving force.

The admonitions are, of course, quite similar to, not to say identical with, the demands of the Law. One need look no further than the Ten Commandments for comparison. Although the mode of expression remains largely the same, what makes these New Testament admonitions markedly different is their relationship to salvation. Whereas the demands made by the Law present themselves as a means to a goal (Luke 10:25–28), the apostolic injunctions are clearly the result of that goal. Put differently, what requires attainment under the Law has now been accomplished apart from it. Of course, the accomplishment of salvation under the Law, though objectively possible, remains an unattainable goal in view of the reality of human sin. Hence the Law can only make accusations as it hurls one into despair and makes one yearn for respite.

Dogmatically, it has become customary to refer to this accusatory function of the Law as its second use (*usus elenchticus*). "*Lex semper accusat*" runs Philipp Melanchthon's oft-quoted adage, underscoring the soteriological significance of the Law in confronting the sinner.[3] The mechanics are somewhat complex. The Law holds out a promise of salvation. Deceived by sin, the sinner

---

2. Unless otherwise indicated, all the Scripture quotations in this essay are taken from the NIV.

3. See Ap. IV, 38, 128, 285, 319 (Tappert, 112, 125, 150, 156).

attempts to reach this goal, but no sooner does he make such an attempt than he finds himself under divine judgment. Naturally, when it comes to external behavior, it is quite possible to conform to the Law's demands.[4] This function of preserving social structures is known as the Law's first use (*usus politicus*). But the Law hardly aims at what is external; rather, it must reach the inner self to make the outside change meaningful. At this point, the sinner's heart—bent on self-justification—is forced to recognize that it invariably defies the Law and would only accept it out of a vested interest, which—if one is honest—is no acceptance at all. Two possibilities open up here: Either the self-deception continues, in which case the human heart "despises the judgment of God in its smugness,"[5] or the Law penetrates into the self-acknowledged sinner's being and engulfs him in despair. If the latter is the case, humans react by hating and fleeing from the judgment that God, through the conscience, passes on them.[6] In a last-ditch effort to prevent the disintegration of the self, humans will try desperately to construct some semblance of security only to realize that relief is short-lived.[7] It is at that moment, when there are no more straws to clutch at, that the sinner is ready to be pulled out of the depths of anguish by the Gospel, which proclaims the accomplishment of the sinner's salvation by Christ.

From then on, the Law takes on an entirely new dimension. What makes this crucial difference is faith, as the Lutheran Confessions affirm: "After we have been justified and regenerated by faith . . . we begin to fear and love God, to pray and expect help from him, to thank and praise him, and to submit to him in our afflictions. Then we also begin to love our neighbor because our hearts have spiritual and holy impulses."[8] This spiritual desire to live according to God's Law comes spontaneously, insofar as the Christian is a redeemed and renewed being. As a new creation in Christ, the new man is attuned to the Law, which he now gladly accepts as "the immutable will of God according to which man is to conduct himself in this life."[9] In this way, though believers "are never without law, they are not under but in the law, they live and walk in the

---

4. Ap. II, 12 acknowledges this by stating that "philosophical or civic righteousness . . . is subject to reason and somewhat in our power" (Tappert, 102).

5. Ap. IV, 34 (Tappert, 112); cf. Ap. II, 24 (Tappert, 103).

6. Ap. IV, 34 (Tappert, 111–120); FC SD V, 10 (Tappert, 559–60).

7. Ap. IV, 212 (Tappert, 136).

8. Ap. IV, 125 (Tappert, 124).

9. FC SD VI, 15 (Tappert, 566).

law of the Lord, and yet do nothing by the compulsion of the law."[10] Sin, however, is still a powerful reality in the life of the Christian, even more so than in the life of an unbeliever. In fact, the Christian life is one of constant struggle with temptation and failure. Consequently, believers need the Law to be taught to them so, on the one hand, the Law will continue its work of accusation and, on the other hand, the Law will continue to ensure "that they will not be thrown back on their own holiness and piety and under the pretext of the Holy Spirit's guidance set up a self-elected service of God without his Word and command."[11] This latter use has been customarily labeled "the third use of the Law" (*tertius usus legis*). Pointing back to the atonement as the source of its motivation, this use rests on the Christians' new identity in Christ through faith and admonishes them to "conduct yourselves in a manner worthy of the gospel of Christ" (Phil 1:27).

This is how, in broad outline, the work of the Law is usually presented in Lutheran theology. Setting aside the technical questions of how a formal concept of the third use developed,[12] one is, nevertheless, led to ask how the third use relates to the other two. To put it yet another way, why are Christians now to keep the much-hated Law from whose curse they longed to be liberated? Following Melanchthon, the Formula of Concord interprets the Law as the immutable will of God, affirming simply that "it is God's will, ordinance, and command the believers walk in good works."[13] It states, in addition, that good works, though not a part of faith, invariably

---

10. FC SD VI, 18 (Tappert, 567).

11. FC SD VI, 20 (Tappert 567).

12. None of the Lutheran Confessions prior to the Formula of Concord mentions a third use of the Law. The designation first appears in the 1535 edition of Melanchthon's *Loci Theologici*. This is not to say that the Confessions consider the issue of good works performed by the unregenerate to be insignificant. On the contrary, while emphasizing the sole importance of faith in justification, to the explicit exclusion of the Law, the Apology adds that "the keeping of the law should begin in us and increase more and more. But we mean to include both elements, namely, the inward spiritual impulses and the outward good works" (Ap. IV, 136 [Tappert, 126]). It then states that in this spirit the Lutherans actually "teach . . . not only how the law can be kept, but also that God is pleased when we keep it" (Ap. IV, 140 [Tappert 126]). In the same vein, one need look no further than Luther's exposition of the Decalogue in his catechisms to find out how important a function he ascribed to the teaching of the Law in Christian life. This is hardly belittled by his stress on the Law's function to reveal sin and wrath in the antinomian disputations of the 1530s. Thus, formal differences aside, it is reasonable to assume that both Melanchthon and Luther taught the third use of the Law, though Luther never used the term and in the Lutheran Symbols it appears only in the Formula of Concord.

13. FC SD IV, 7 (Tappert, 552); cf. FC SD V, 17 (Tappert, 561) and FC SD VI, 15 (Tappert, 566).

flow from faith.[14] They are necessary: first, because such is the divine will; second, because they secure temporal blessings; and third, because they indicate, though do not preserve, salvation.[15] Although undoubtedly correct, this answer does not seem to satisfy the question why—in an apparently arbitrary fashion—God actually wills that believers do good works, why he should reward them with temporal blessings, and why the works of the Law should be an indication of salvation.

No satisfactory answer can be given to the above questions as long as the third use of the Law is seen as a mere flipside of, and as derived from, the second use. The latter mistake is easily made, and Lutheran theology has, by no stretch of the imagination, remained invulnerable to this fact. The Law accuses prior to the gift of salvation; the Law guides afterward. This scheme is only reinforced by the fact that in the believer's life both the second and third uses are present.[16] Thus the third use of the Law is frequently little more than the second without a "sting," with salvation serving as a catalyst. What results is an undesirable internalization of the Law.[17] To illustrate: The Law's accusation has its locus in the God-initiated self-reflection of the soul; good works follow the Gospel as a consequence of rebirth and the soul's spontaneous conformity to God's will; for no apparent reason—despite their imperfection—these good works are the believing individual's way of procuring temporal blessings but not salvation; and, finally, as an inseparable outcome of inner faith, good works are an outer indicator of salvation. The soul thus becomes the seat of God's dealings with humankind. There is no broader context, other than the private divine-human relationship—the immutable and eternal will of God as it reaches man in his conscience—that could justify the significance of the Law in Christian life. Consequently, it is difficult not to walk away with the impression that, for believers, good works are an issue of morality, of appreciation of the gift of salvation, with the

---

14. FC SD IV, 12 (Tappert, 553). See also AC XX, 29 (Tappert, 45); Ap. IV, 275 (Tappert, 148).

15. FC SD IV, 14–36 (Tappert, 553–57). See also AC VI (Tappert, 31–32); AC XX (Tappert, 41ff.); Ap. IV, 141, 189, 200, 214 (Tappert, 126, 133, 134, 136).

16. See FC SD VI, 9 (Tappert, 565).

17. A similar point has been made by Friedrich Mildenberger, *Theology of the Lutheran Confessions* (ed. Robert C. Schultz; trans. Erwin L. Lueker; Philadelphia: Fortress, 1986), 170.

Gospel followed by the Law, which now must be conformed to, albeit in a nonthreatening manner.[18]

By contrast, a glance at the New Testament admonitions, commonly understood to be the Law in its third use, will reveal that we are dealing not merely with the opposition of the unredeemed state to the state of redemption but also, if not primarily, with the state of redemption treated as a return to the pre-fall creation. For example, in his Epistle to the Ephesians, the apostle Paul reminds his addressees that they are something other than what they used to be: "[Y]ou were once darkness, but now you are light in the Lord" (5:8). This means that a change has occurred, a renewal in which darkness has given way to light. One need only think of the divine "Let there be light" in this context (Gen 1:3). In Galatians we find an even clearer statement: "[W]hat counts is a new creation" (6:15). However, the most emphatic witness to this creationally construed transformed identity of those who are now in Christ can be found in Paul's second letter to the Corinthians: Believers are "a new creation; *the old has gone, the new has come!* All this is from God, who reconciled us to himself through Christ" (2 Cor 5:17–18, *my emphasis*).

Because the essence of the new creation lies in the healing of the broken relationship between God and man (*reconciliation* and *restoration*), Christian life must not be interpreted in isolation from the old, pre-fall, creation. To take the atonement seriously requires that everything that can be said about those who are now in Christ necessarily reflects the primal *wholeness* and the unspoiled fellowship that Adam and Eve had with God. Not without deeper theological motivation is Christ portrayed as the counterpart of Adam.[19] What all this means is that redemption can no longer be seen in individualistic terms; rather, it should be placed in the context of the entire creation as it awaits liberation "from its bondage to decay" and participation in "the glorious freedom of the children of God" (Rom 8:21). In this light, as will be demonstrated below, the third use of the Law, as well as the second, actually derives from the first, which is the foundational use, though the importance of the second use cannot be overestimated. Accordingly, to arrive at a creational interpretation of the *tertius usus legis*, we must now turn to the anthropology of creation.

---

18. That this is a real fear is especially evident in Lutheran preaching, with its debilitating indecision concerning how to preach sanctification.

19. Rom 5:12–21; 1 Cor 15:45.

II. God's Image: The Riddle of Humanity

Among all the various questions that arise out of human experience, some of the most baffling ones—surprisingly so—concern self-experience. In one way or another, all people face Hamlet's dilemma:

> What a piece of work is a man! How noble in reason! How infinite in faculty! In form and moving how express and admirable! In action how like an angel! In apprehension how like a god! The beauty of the world! The paragon of animals! And yet, to me, what is this quintessence of dust?[20]

Much as we would like to see ourselves as the noble product of our own mental and physical capacities, we are constantly confronted by our baseness on the ethical plane and by our insignificance in the categories of science. Paradoxically, the more we learn about ourselves and the world that surrounds us, the more undesirable affinity we seem to find between us and the rest of the universe.

The foundation of our claim to uniqueness is crumbling. First, as ethical beings, we never cease to face the overpowering ambiguity of our dealings with others and theirs with us. As we interact with one another, the ultimate, though often not verbalized or even realized, goal is the preservation of our security as both individuals and groups. Human life is a struggle to maintain and guard the sources of our security at all costs. We define ourselves in terms of what makes us secure because it provides a necessary point of reference and, in so doing, prevents the disintegration of our being. But this process is true not only of human interaction. Closely related is our often thoughtless exploitation of creation's resources, as well as our use of them to assure an advantageous position among members of our own race. Second, in light of today's sciences—from genetics through psychology to ethnology—it is questionable whether a clear-cut distinction between humans and the rest of animate creation can at all be established on the basis of creation-internal data.[21] A powerful testimony to humanity's unparalleled intellectual capacity, science has at the same time undermined our uniqueness within our world. Scientifically, it has been shown that humans are part and parcel of their environment, distinguished from it not by certain

---

20. William Shakespeare, *Hamlet*, Act II, Scene II, line 242.

21. Note in this connection Luther's first thesis from his "Disputation Concerning Man, 1536": "Philosophy or human wisdom defines man as an animal having reason, sensation, and body" (LW 34:137).

unique intrinsic characteristics but merely by the degree to which they possess them.

Thus the question why we are the way we are and what it is that makes us *human* remains more elusive than ever.[22] Still, it remains legitimate to ask whether all there is to human beings is a specific set of mathematically, physically, chemically, or biologically definable properties; namely, can the essence of the human be reduced simply to one's empirically ascertainable composition, to sheer matter, and to mere struggle for preserving the particular atomic structure we know as the human being? It remains legitimate to ask whether it is only by force—exercised both ethically and through science—that our uniqueness can be established and maintained.

It is in this context of incomprehensibility and resignation that the question of meaning is inevitably raised, first of humanity and then of all existence. This question is raised because meaning is felt to be lacking.[23] The awareness of this problem is not absent from the Bible. The psalmist asks, "[W]hat is man that you are mindful of him" (Ps 8:4). It must not be overlooked, however, that, in contradistinction to the questions posed from within human experience, this one implies a relationship beyond human experience. *The theological definition of humanity presupposes involvement on God's part.* Humanity can be defined only from the outside, by understanding itself from the perspecive of God's mindfulness. Only by referring outside of ourselves can the questions that originate within the world be given meaningful answers.

Nowhere in the Bible is man's uniqueness shown more clearly than in the creation account (Genesis 1–2). Man was brought forth on the last day of God's creative activity. Unlike the rest of the created realm, he was fashioned from the dust of the earth by the Creator himself (Gen 2:7), made in God's very image and likeness (Gen 1:26–27). It is this image that determines human distinctiveness, a testimony to the dignity and worth of the person. Although it does not render man substantially divine, it underlies human subjectivity: Man is not a mere object within creation but an acting and responsible subject (Gen 1:28–30). Although there is agreement among

---

22. Pastoral constitution *Gaudium et spes* [§ 12] captures the dilemma perceptively: "But what is man? He has put forward, and continues to put forward, many views about himself, views that are divergent and even contradictory. Often he either sets himself up as the absolute measure of all things, or debases himself to the point of despair" (Austin Flannery, ed., *Vatican Council II: The Conciliar and Post Conciliar Documents* [rev. ed.; Boston: St. Paul Books & Media, 1992], 913).

23. Eberhard Jüngel, *The Freedom of a Christian: Luther's Significance for Contemporary Theology* (trans. Roy A. Harrisville; Minneapolis: Augsburg, 1988), 44–45.

theologians concerning this raw biblical data, in the history of dogma the problem of the makeup and the role of the *imago Dei* has been rather complex. Even a brief overview of all the interpretations would by far exceed the scope of this essay. We shall, therefore, limit ourselves to an exposition of only several pertinent points and the dilemma to which they lead.

Humans were originally created holy and perfect, with an intimate knowledge of God. This state of original righteousness was, according to the Lutheran Confessions, characterized not only by a life of attentiveness to each other's needs but also, in the first place, by "fear of God, faith and love toward him."[24] In other words, "original righteousness was intended to involve not only a balanced physical constitution, but these gifts as well: a surer knowledge of God, fear of God, trust in God, or at least the inclination and power to do these things."[25] The Confessions identify this righteousness expressly with the image of God.[26] At the same time, while it is recognized that the fall brought about the loss of original righteousness coupled with a thoroughgoing corruption of human nature, man's humanity was not destroyed. Man has not lost—at least not completely—his subjectivity, his rational capacities, or his sense of responsibility. He remains a *human* being whom God desires to renew in his image and likeness (cf. Col 3:10).

Several approaches have been put forth to account for this apparent discrepancy. Roman Catholic theology, following the anthropocentric scholastic tradition, introduces a distinction between the image and likeness of God. The image, associated with human reason, remains in humans after the fall. What is lost is the likeness, identified with original righteousness, which, as a super-added gift (*donum superadditum*), has no bearing on man's essential humanity. Correspondingly, original sin has not, in any real sense, corrupted man's entire nature by rendering its powers inoperative and opposed to all things godly. According to Roman Catholic theology, original sin has only "wounded" and "weakened" human nature, making it inclined to sin, but it has not destroyed man's humanity. With their humanity essentially intact, all people have retained some capacity for God.[27] By contrast, taking seriously the exclusive centrality of the cross, the Protestant tradition does not

---

24. Ap. II, 16 (Tappert, 102).

25. Ap. II, 17 (Tappert, 102).

26. Ap. II, 18 (Tappert, 102–3); FC SD I, 10 (Tappert, 510).

27. *Catechism of the Catholic Church* (New York: Doubleday, 1995), 114 [§ 405].

share this optimistic view of sin. It considers the position that original righteousness was not an integral part of man's constitution, as well as the opinion that human nature remains essentially intact after the fall, to be anthropologically determined and unbiblical.[28] Consequently, Protestant theology sees no reason to introduce what is an exegetically unjustified distinction between "image" and "likeness." Unfortunately, by recognizing the fact that even after the fall human beings retain their subjectivity, Protestant theology now has to speak of the *imago Dei* in a wider and proper sense, with only the latter being totally obliterated.[29]

In a somewhat modified form, this distinction played a significant role in one of the most interesting theological debates of the twentieth century—the debate between Emil Brunner and Karl Barth concerning nature and grace.[30] Brunner proceeds from the premise that sin has not abolished man's personhood. He asserts that even as a sinner man remains a human being; namely, man remains one that is accountable and rational, thus also capable, albeit in a passive way, of revelation. This Brunner attributes to the presence of the *humanum*, the *formal* image of God, in sinful humanity.[31] As a responsible agent, man possesses some knowledge of the divine Law derived from creation and is thereby able to recognize his sin. In other words, the Law, as a product of God's creative activity, enables humans, though in a highly deficient way, to gain some insight into God and to see themselves in relation to him. This knowledge, however, is so distorted that any trust in God prior to grace is, of course, out of the question.[32] However, once divine grace reaches out to the sinner, the restoration of the material image of God begins, which gives rise to true knowledge of and trust in God.

---

28. What is now the position of Protestantism can be traced to the early church; for example, see Athanasius, *De incarnatione* 7.4.

29. For example, see Francis Pieper, *Christian Dogmatics* (St. Louis: Concordia, 1950), 1:518–20.

30. The debate came to a head in 1934 with the publication of Emil Brunner's treatise *Natur und Gnade*, which was followed by Barth's fierce rejoinder *Nein!* An English translation of both is found in *Natural Theology* (trans. Peter Fraenkel; London: Geoffrey Bles, Centenary Press, 1946).

31. The formal *imago*, according to Brunner, is "nothing less than the entire human, rational nature, the immortal soul, the capacity for culture, the conscience, responsibility, the relation with God, which—though not redemptive—exists even in sin, language, the whole cultural life" (*Natural Theology*, 41).

32. Brunner states: "[T]he *imago* is just sufficient to enable man to know God but not to know his How, to urge him towards religion, without, however, making a true religion possible for him" (*Natural Theology*, 42).

Opposed to Brunner's immanent-structural conception of humanity is Barth's transcendental-relational understanding. For Barth, any knowledge of God, however incomplete and imperfect, is, nevertheless, real knowledge that cannot be irrelevant to salvation. Two criticisms are offered at this point. First, Barth agrees that the identity of the sinner before and after the act of faith remains the same; yet the transformation that occurs is so radical that it can only be the work of God alone, without anything in man to prepare him for grace. Second, Brunner's definition of the formal *imago*, contends Barth, places beyond the pale of humanity those "children of Adam" who do not exhibit sufficient rationality, responsibility, and ability to make decisions. According to Brunner's standard, they must be unfit for grace.[33] In sum, for Barth there is in the sinner no point of contact for divine grace, no capacity for God, however broadly or narrowly understood. It is solely through the relation of God to man that the latter, in faith and under grace, becomes a *human* being, recreated in the image of God in radical discontinuity from his sinful existence.

The above is, of course, little more than a sketch of the contours of the debate, a sketch aimed to illustrate a significant discrepancy. Because as a sinner man retains his subjective nature of a responsible agent while no longer possessing the original righteousness, which is identified with the *imago Dei* in which he was inherently created, we are faced with the question whether after the fall one should and can continue to speak about the humanity of the sinner. The above overview also shows that in both Roman Catholic and Protestant theologies, extending well into the twentieth century, the predominant interpretation of the image/likeness of God has been focused on man's inherent powers and capabilities. Luther's own understanding is only too typical:

> In the remaining creatures God is recognized as by His footprints; but in the human being, especially in Adam, He is truly recognized, because in him there is such wisdom, justice, and knowledge of all things that he may rightly be called a world in miniature. He has an understanding of heaven, earth, and the

---

33. Barth states: "Is the revelation of God some kind of 'matter' to which man stands in some original relation because as man he *has* or even *is* the 'form' which enables him to take responsibility and make decision in relation to various kinds of 'matter'? Surely all his rationality, responsibility and ability to make decisions might yet go hand in hand with complete impotency as regards *this* 'matter'! And this impotency might be the tribulation and affliction of those who, as far as human reason can see, possess neither reason, responsibility nor ability to make decisions: new-born children and idiots. Are they not children of Adam? Has Christ not died for them?" (*Natural Theology*, 88–89, *Barth's emphasis*).

entire creation. And so it gives God pleasure that He made so beautiful a creature.[34]

Although this interpretation is not necessarily wrong, it seems to be lacking. As we have shown, to understand the image of God as man's capacity for God must lead in two directions: either to its exclusion from among the essential components of human nature, as is evidenced by the Roman Catholic construal of the likeness of God as a superadded gift, or to a dilemma in regard to what exactly constitutes humanity, requiring that we speak of an image of sorts prior to the act of faith and the image proper in the context of faith.

Contrary to this immanent-structural understanding, Barth is correct in seeing the *imago* as a transcendental-relational concept. The image finds its essence not in man by himself but in the act of God relating to humanity. Consequently, the image is not a device tuned to receive a variety of divine waves for the benefit of one's intellect. Rather, it is, as the Apology of the Augsburg Confession puts it, "a wisdom and righteousness . . . implanted in man that would grasp God and *reflect* him."[35] This being the case, to be human is not to have some capacity for God but to have God relate to oneself and to reflect his being in oneself. As will be shown, only this approach can resolve the discrepancy concerning the humanity of believers and unbelievers. First, however, it is in order to inquire into the being of God, whose relationship to us and whose reflection in us have been determined to be constitutive of humanity.

III. GOD'S BEING:
THE TRAGIC MISINTERPRETATION

Considered merely in light of divine omnipotence, God's act of creation *ex nihilo* remains somewhat of a mystery. If God is all-powerful, he obviously did not need as many as six days to bring the world into being. The easiest way of explaining this conundrum would be by appealing to some voluntaristically construed decision of the inscrutable divine will. This, however, would be to miss the point of what revelation actually is. Through the act of creation, God reveals his own being. From this perspective, one cannot but notice the

---

34. "Lectures on Genesis, 1535" (LW 1:68). The age of Lutheran Orthodoxy notoriously interpreted the *imago* as the perfection of intellect. The overview offered by Heinrich Schmid is quite revealing; see *The Doctrinal Theology of the Evangelical Lutheran Church* (3d ed.; trans. Charles A. Hay and Henry E. Jacobs; 1875; repr., Minneapolis: Augsburg, 1961), 217–31.

35. Ap. II, 18 (Tappert, 103, *my emphasis*).

deliberation, symmetry, and order exhibited in the six-day account. What initially appears "formless and empty" (Gen 1:2) soon becomes characterized by an unprecedented level of complexity and organization. But order—ranging from laws regulating the motion of stars to those governing human life—is hardly the point of it all. It is merely a means to a goal. And the goal is the creation of man in the image of God.

What is significant about Adam is that he alone becomes the locus of God's self-sharing. In Adam, God reveals himself as self-giving, as *love*. Through creation, he who already perfectly and sufficiently affirms otherness within himself—as Father, Son, and Holy Spirit—freely reaches out to another. In other words, man is the only creature willed by God for its own sake.[36] Such is the nature of love. It affirms another not because of a vested interest but freely and disinterestedly, for the other's sake. It finds the other beautiful and interesting. And God's love, as it finds beauty and a source of interest in the other, truly creates the other to be beautiful and worthy of interest. Thus, surveying his creative work, God was able to conclude approvingly: "[I]t was very good" (Gen 1:31). The divine self-sharing manifests itself, in the first place, in the act of creation, but it goes much further. Man receives God's blessing as he is told to "be fruitful and increase in number" (Gen 1:28). All that God has created is now entrusted to man to rule over and to subdue (Gen 1:28). What this means is that creation is God's gift to be used in a meaningful and responsible way. Finally, God shares with man his own being. The latter not only has a direct and personal experience of his Creator but also is himself created to reflect the being of God.

Man is created with a capacity to love and to reciprocate love. Like God, man has the ability to go beyond himself. In the same way that God affirms otherness within himself, man, too, is made to affirm another so the two "will become one flesh" (Gen 2:24). Furthermore, he is endowed with the capacity to affirm creation; man finds meaning in his responsible and God-like stewardship. As one commentator put it: "[W]hile [man] is not divine, his very existence bears witness to the activity of God in the life of the world."[37] In other words, just as God finds Adam and Eve worthwhile in and of themselves, humans also are to find God's gift of creation worth-

---

36. See *Gaudium et spes* [§ 24] 925.

37. Nahum M. Sarna, *Genesis* (JPS Torah Commentary; Philadelphia: Jewish Publication Society, 1989), 12.

while in and of itself. Creation is not to be abused. Humans are created to love God, fellow men, and God's gift of creation. By definition, they are *social* and *vocational* beings, relating to others in such a way as to further their good through God-appointed means. In so doing, they surrender their being in all its individualism only to gain it back in, with, and through the being of another. Only by receiving and giving can they realize their humanity. Only thus can they be human beings.

It has already been indicated that love consists in self-giving. Naturally, there can be no love under coercion. Thus, with its origin in the divine love, human existence is one of freedom. God did not create automatons. He created beings that were beautiful, interesting, and worthwhile for their own sake. He created them with the capacity, of their own free will, to reflect the love received. A loving relationship by nature implies an option for un-love. Love as self-giving implies the possibility of rejection. It is in this context of what love is that the presence in the garden of the tree of the knowledge of good and evil finds its purpose. To Adam and Eve is entrusted all that God has created with the exception of one tree, of which they are expressly forbidden to eat. In negative terms, the tree presents itself as an alternative to God's love; it makes the possibility of choosing un-love, or self-love, a real one. In positive terms, it underscores the free and self-giving character of the divine-human relationship, pointing to the centrality of love in the constitution of man. From man's perspective, it makes love possible. Finally, it points to the fundamental significance of trust as an inseparable aspect of love. Adam and Eve know their creator intimately in his self-sharing. All they are and all that they have comes from him. It would seem there surely is a sufficient basis for trust. Despite this, they give credence to the serpent's deceitful promise. Their action is incomprehensible but all too familiar.

The fall is often portrayed as a transgression of what seems to be an otherwise arbitrary command. We already have demonstrated that the command is far from arbitrary. Neither is it meant to stress the importance of divinely established order, as if God's self-giving were a mere show. The command is not there to put man in his place and show him who is really in charge. On the contrary, it is there to complete his humanness in its capacity for love and freedom. Interpretations that view the command in arbitrary or legalistic terms fail to do justice to the complex mechanics of sin, placing a disproportionate emphasis on its moralistic aspect rather than understanding it in the context of God's being as love and of what this love actually is. The essence of the fall lies not so much in the violation of God's command, not even in the breach of trust, though it is this breach that unequivocally places all responsibility and guilt on man. Rather, the fall, and with it all sin, consists in a misinterpretation and rejection of the being of God. Again, this misrepresentation is to be seen not so much in the attempt to make God into a liar as in the denial of God's being as love (Gen 3:1–4). When the serpent promises to Eve that she and Adam "will be like God, knowing good and evil" (Gen 3:5), he does more than portray God as fundamentally dishonest and untrustworthy. In the first place, the serpent makes the man and the woman believe that divinity consists in power and secret knowledge instead of the so-familiar love that gives to the other all that it has. It is this misrepresentation that leads Adam and Eve to forget that they already are like God! The consequences could hardly be more disastrous.

Rooted in man's failed attempt to accord himself what he understands to be divine status, sin is by nature un-relational and counter-relational, thus it is without doubt un-Godlike. It goes against everything that humans were supposed to be as subjective creatures endowed with God's own image. Numerous characterizations and analogies could be evoked here to illustrate the deceitful and destructive nature of sin. For our purposes, we will focus on isolation, enslavement, and inability to trust and love.

Sin is isolation because it severs man's ties with everything around him. By attempting to be like God, man separates himself from God. He forgoes the gift of freedom in favor of self-established and self-centered independence. He also separates himself from creation. A usurper of divinity, man can no longer accept himself as part of creation, resenting his God-given function as the recipient of divine gifts and blessings and as the steward of the created realm. He finally separates himself from his fellow humans beings. This he does, first, by avoiding responsibility and trying to shift the blame. But even without these efforts, separation would be inevitable. By violating God's trust, man has now become painfully aware that the same could be done to him; his own act has brought him to the realization that it lies within human capacity to abuse another's self-giving. This is a terrifying and unbearable thought.

As an inability to trust, isolation leads to enslavement. Because the sinner cannot rely on others, fearing his trust will be violated, he is forced to rely on himself alone. Like a black hole, he cannot go beyond his own event horizon. His self-proclaimed independence has, in reality, turned him into a prisoner of himself. First, it has made him a slave to the lie that it is possible to be like God on one's own terms, that one owes what one is only to oneself, that one can make oneself into what one wishes to be in defiance of the relational aspect of being. It cannot be otherwise. As lack of trust, sin makes one shortsighted. Man can see no further than himself, and, instead of finding the meaning and purpose of humanness in mutual self-giving, he continues to search for it within himself. Without anybody or anything to fall back on, he is doomed to this endless and futile pursuit of "godhood."

Of course, Adam and Eve had no intention to destroy their relationships. They sought, however, their reconstitution. God's essence, misconstrued as consisting of power and secret knowledge, seemed to them a threat to their own being. Because their trust in God had been undermined, receiving from another appeared, in their eyes, to be a sinister means of control that had to be shed at all costs. Their nature, as they saw it, could only be preserved through a similar exercise of control. Thus sin is also enslavement to *imperium*—control and, if need be, violence—as a means of preserving one's integrity. Adam and Eve destroyed their relationships not only by fearing a violation of their trust on another's part but also by chronic suspiciousness of God's self-giving, seeing in it an attempt to confine them into reciprocation, to exert control over their independence. Human life has thus become a struggle for control as a means of survival.

This, in turn, has brought about the enslavement of man to creation. Man has abandoned his God-appointed role as creation's steward and endeavours to place himself above the created order as God's equal. But as a creature, man can only claim equality with and independence from God by violently lording it over creation, not merely because this is the way he now understands God's being but also because he recognizes his dependence on creation, which is God's work, and thus his dependence on God himself. Exploitation of God's things gives an illusion of power. In this way, creation is necessary for man as a means of self-assertion. The continued increase of his control over the created realm, including other human beings, creates the impression of approximating divinity. Put differently, to preserve his integrity, man must enslave. Paradoxically, this only deepens human dependence on the now-hostile creation. Man is both *enslaved* and *enslaver*.

The isolation and enslavement of sin underscore that it is a debilitating inability to love and trust, which "like a spiritual leprosy, has thoroughly and entirely poisoned and corrupted human nature."[38] As such, sin undermines everything that human nature was created to represent. Instead of allowing oneself to receive another in his self-giving, and thus to gain oneself, the sinner attempts his self-realization by going in the opposite direction, to the inside. Sin, to use Luther's dictum, makes man into a *homo incurvatus in se ipsum*.[39] This "turning in on oneself" is the inevitable price of the trust-destructive misinterpretation of God's being and also of failing to acknowledge one's humanity in its relational richness. In other words, the price of the knowledge of good and evil is the recognition of oneself as evil. Man cannot know evil without at the same time seeing it in himself, in his lovelessness and distrust.

The tree from which Adam and Eve were forbidden to eat was not, contrary to their expectations, a vehicle of secret wisdom. The knowledge originated within man together with the deed, with his choice of un-love, with his rejection of God's self-giving. It came on the heels of man's attempt to be like God, in which the former isolated himself from his Creator and other human beings, abandoning his unique position within the created realm as the recipient of God's love and blessing. It came with man turning in on himself and the resultant collapse of his being.

It is now with great difficulty that man preserves his integrity. He can do so only by a violent, self-centered, and self-enslaving exercise of supremacy. Therefore, in so doing, man not only knows evil in himself but also actively propagates it. Consider the dreadful ambiguity that underlies all human desire to be creative. Ethically speaking, even the best of human works are tainted by vested interests, resentment, or distrust. Moreover, from the scientific perspective, man's harnessing of creation's resources exposes his potential for self-destruction and thirst for power, as much as it shows his ingenuity.

Finally, much as he may wish to avoid or ignore it, man meets with disintegration throughout his life only to be confronted by it conclusively at the point of death. The all-consuming presence of death reveals that creation without its steward has gone wild; it dies both from lack of proper care and from the abuses it suffers at the hand of man. Creation has become the devil's playground. Man,

---

38. FC SD I, 6 (Tappert, 509).
39. Cf. "Lectures on Romans, 1515–16," LW 25:291, 313, 345.

having separated himself from the life-giving love of God, faces the same destiny as the creation he was so hasty to abandon in pursuit of self-realization. In isolation from God, man is dust and to dust he must return (Gen 3:19). In a word, life without love and trust is deadly; it not only kills the isolated and enslaved human being but also spreads death around despite and because of human attempts to avoid the inevitable. As Jesus says: "Whoever tries to keep his life will lose it" (Luke 17:33).

IV. UNDERSTANDING THE THIRD USE OF THE LAW IN LIGHT OF THE FIRST

As self-inflicted solitary confinement, sin has completely destroyed the relational aspect of man's being. At this point, we must go back to our question concerning the sinner's humanity. We have shown that any interpretation of the image of God that views the latter as a perfection of the intellect, enabling man to know God and to be attuned to his will, leads to a serious discrepancy. On the one hand, we are confronted with the theologically inevitable conclusion that sinful man, through his opposition to everything that is God's, is no longer human. On the other hand, we cannot but acknowledge the fact—both experiential and scriptural—that even sinners remain rational, responsible, and subjective creatures. In addition to the discrepancy, if our humanity were truly determined by an inherent intellectual capacity for God, we would be forced to conclude that some people are, therefore, unfit for grace because they lack the necessary point of contact. Over against this immanent-structural conception of humanity, we have opted instead for a transcendental-relational understanding. An inobservant reader might respond that, by admitting the destruction of man's relationality, we have ended up with exactly the same dilemma. Because sin is an un-relational and counter-relational turning in on oneself, we can no longer speak of the sinner's relationally construed humanity. This, however, could not be further from the truth.

Recall that, contrary to man's own futile attempts at self-defini-tion, we have suggested that a definition of humanity, if it is to be all-inclusive and enduring, can only come from the outside. This outside connection is found in none other than the image of God. Let us repeat some of our earlier conclusions. The theological def-inition of humanity presupposes involvement on God's part. To be human is not to have some capacity for God; rather, it is to have

God relate to onself and to reflect his being in oneself. Divine involvement is decisive. Without it, there would be no image. Note that the two are related far more closely than mere cause and effect. The fact that God goes beyond himself and creates man as a creature worthwhile in itself determines the content of the *imago Dei*. Creation, especially that of man, reflects the being of the Creator; in creating humans as subjective and free entities with the capacity to reciprocate divine love, God is fundamentally consistent with himself. In creation, he reveals himself as love. Thus it is the nature of God, the very nature that has brought them into being, that humans are to reflect as those created in God's image. Because God relates to them, it likewise belongs to human nature to reach out and to offer themselves to fellow human beings in acts of love. The model to emulate is God's giving of himself together with his gift of creation. Creation as a gift to man is not only a reflection of divine love, on account of which it is beautiful and interesting and worthy of care, but it also is a means of human self-giving. Man is to use creation for the promotion of life, a goal that receives God's unqualified blessing (Gen 1:28). In short, the image of God implies not only social interaction but also responsible stewardship of creation's resources. To repeat: Humans, because they are created in the image of God, are by nature social and vocational beings.

With the *imago Dei* so understood, sin—though it has obliterated man's relational being, isolating, enslaving, and incapacitating him for love and trust—has not deterred God or prevented his involvement in creation, particularly in human life. In the words of the apostle: "[I]f we are faithless, [God] will remain faithful, for he cannot disown himself" (2 Tim 2:13). It is this fact of God's continued relationship to creation, his overwhelming and steadfast love for the world, and his desire that sinners should turn from their wicked ways and live that still determines our humanity (John 3:16; Ezek 33:11; 1 Tim 2:4). Put differently, God's mindfulness prevents man's immediate dissolution into dust. It keeps original sin under control and extrinsically mitigates its radicalness.

Although man has done everything to destroy his being, God lovingly continues to uphold this being in an external way. He does so, first, by persistently creating life amid death, which Adam's sin has brought into creation. "He causes his sun to rise on the evil and the good, and sends rain on the righteous and the unrighteous" (Matt 5:45). By creating life, God preserves—albeit in an external manner—the structures of society, which in turn facilitate the promotion of life.[40] For example, despite its many structural ambiguities and the ease with which it can be misused, language continues to be a means of communication. Human interaction, challenging as it may be, is possible. Now, however, language is but a weak shadow of the inherently creative Word with which God brought creation into being.[41] Further, governments ensure that justice should prevail and wrongdoing meet with appropriate punishment, though they can only do so with great difficulty, facing an even greater temptation to abuse the powers vested in them.

Through structures such as these, especially the family, God's life-giving and life-preserving presence in creation is a real presence. For this reason, Luther does not hesitate to call holy not only the works of order themselves but also those who perform them, as he states: "Even the godless may have much about them that is holy without being saved thereby."[42] This means that man's failure to carry out these functions, or his deficient fulfilment thereof, still serves the divine purpose. Thus not only respectable members of the community but also the corrupt and the wicked, by virtue of living within God's sphere of action, wittingly or unwittingly yet always inevitably carry out the works by which this sphere is defined. God's creating activity continues despite and against sin, as God uses even human blindness and ignorance to advance his life-creating goal. "The will of the Creator," observes Gustaf Wingren, "runs like an undercurrent beneath the stream of human works, and is not disturbed even when the surface is ruffled."[43] As the reader will have recognized, this is what Lutheran theology calls the first, or political, use of the Law, which is now only a remnant of the original relationality built into creation.

The first use of the Law is a mere vestige because, first, that order within creation is now being preserved one-sidedly—by God alone. Originally, order was a clear expression of divine self-giving, with creation's deliberate structure and symmetry underscoring

---

40. Eberhard Jüngel observes that Cain, the first murderer, is the one who becomes the founder of the first city; see *Justification: The Heart of the Christian Faith* (trans. Jeffrey F. Cayzer; Edinburgh: T&T Clark, 2001), 11.

41. That language, because of human sin, is only a shadow of what it once was can be inferred from Jesus' statement: "I tell you the truth, if anyone says to this mountain, 'Go, throw yourself into the sea,' and does not doubt in his heart but believes that what he says will happen, it will be done for him" (Mark 11:23). I am indebted to Charles St. Onge for drawing my attention to this verse in this context.

42. "Confession Concerning Christ's Supper, 1528," LW 37:365.

43. Gustaf Wingren, *Creation and Law* (trans. Ross Mckenzie; Philadelphia: Muhlenberg, 1961), 96.

God's love for man and understood by man as such. Prior to the fall, order was interpreted by man not only as an expression of God's disinterested affection but also as an expression of God's very being. It was an indicator of human dignity because man was accorded a place of honor within that order. Now order is only external. True, as we have indicated, it still expresses God's loving involvement, but it is neither reciprocated nor understood for what it truly is. Man's sin has made him deaf and blind to God's offer of love.

Further, the first use of the Law is only a remnant of the thoroughly relational character of the primal creation because in this function the Law is now permeated with deadly ambiguity. In sin, man has separated himself from creation, including fellow human beings. Instead of the much-craved Godlike (though, in fact, un-Godlike) independence, this attempted self-extraction from within creation has only led to man's enslavement to its structures. Humans radically depend on creation for the pursuit of what they understand to be divinity. They are unable to create *ex nihilo*. As Eberhard Jüngel points out: "Sin wants to be creative itself. It does not want to receive the good that God gives. It wants to be the giver."[44] Thus the creativeness of sin must lead to the abuse and destruction of God's creation. Humans can only build their security by controlling and violently subjugating everything around themselves. All they do always has the benefit of the self in view. This should hardly be surprising. Because the shortsighted sinner cannot accept God's gift of humanity, it is imperative that he construct his own humanity or disintegrate. In other words, the ambiguity of human interaction, evident in the Law's first use, results from the desperate and violent attempts to establish one's own identity over against what is God's in the context of a quest for godhood. And we are all well aware of that. Good works are defiled by ulterior motives as we try to procure another's favor or perhaps count on reciprocation; relationships fall short of vulnerable openness, marred by the fear of breach of trust; knowledge—harking back to the misconstruction of God's being by Adam and Eve—is never neutral but is power; language separates and destroys as easily as it unites; and governments must be subject to strict control because power corrupts.

By positing the humanity of the sinner as a consequence of God's steadfast and loving involvement in creation despite the obliteration of the *imago Dei*, it may seem that we are falling into Brun-

---

44. Jüngel, *Justification*, 113.

ner's relativization of the knowledge of God. Consider the implications of the divine involvement in creation and of the human endeavor to establish one's own identity in opposition to God's humanity-constitutive relationship to man. If God's involvement and desire to establish a meaningful relationship with his wayward creature can indeed be discerned through whatever structure there remains in creation, that would mean that man must have some knowledge of God. If that were the case, then it would hardly be explicable why humans should persist in their stubborn pursuit of self-definition and godhood. Not only that, the radical nature of the Gospel would be seriously undermined if it lay within the natural power of the sinner to turn back to God and to acknowledge his preservation of creation's order as loving involvement.

Rather than deny the possibility of natural revelation altogether—an option favored by Karl Barth—this problem can find a solution in the context of our discussion of sin. We already have mentioned shortsightedness as one characteristic of sin. To be shortsighted, however, is not to be blind. The apostle himself says that "since the creation of the world God's invisible qualities—his eternal power and divine nature—have been clearly seen, being understood from what has been made, so that men are without excuse" (Rom 1:20). The solution to the dilemma is to be found in the misinterpretation of God's being that lies at the root of sin. It is this misinterpretation that prevents sinners from seeing, though they have sight (Matt 13:13). Having misconstrued God's nature in terms of power, control, and secret knowledge, Adam and Eve were no longer able to trust God, seeing in his self-giving only an attempt to keep them in submission. Deceived by the serpent's manipulative use of language, they began to doubt the divine self-giving. How could they not if God had seemingly withheld an essential part of his being, if he seemed to have deceived them?

Consequently, the ambiguity of creation's law structure comes only secondarily from man's self-centered use of it. First, such ambiguity results from man's misconception of creation's order as God's means of exerting tyrannical control. Humans accept the divine law only insofar as it promotes their welfare. Beyond that, they react with suspicion and rebellion or, more important, they may try to use God to advance their status. If the latter is the case, they will attempt, in their self-centeredness, to propitiate God, to obligate him by their own devious works, to be favorably inclined toward them. In this act they not only defy God's nature by misinterpreting it, they actually trample his being underfoot, thinking God himself could be used in the human pursuit of divinity.

Finally, the first use of the Law is a vestige of the original relational structure of creation because the latter is now hostile and inimical. Without its steward, creation has fallen prey to the devil and has become subject to death. At the hands of man, creation suffers constant abuse, being treated as a necessary springboard to godhood. Because God remains involved in it, however, creation has not suffered total disintegration. Outwardly there is a semblance of order, though it is only a glimmer of the original relationality built on God's love for man and man's for God. For the sinner, this order can be nothing but a burden. Humans not only find themselves submerged in it but also see their dependence on it in terms of an unpleasantly stifling confinement. Because they are part of creation, forever trying to extricate themselves from its bonds, yet dependent on it for their life and well-being, creation's structure forms a powerful indictment of man. If he is honest with himself, he will realize that his own "godhood" is incapable of establishing and preserving a completely new order for the ages. Thus in his own struggle against creation, man sees himself indisputably accused of being a negligent steward, a puny god without a definite identity, a usurper, and a failure.

Note that in this accusatory function, derived from the sinner's relationship to creation, we can discern the foundation of the second use of the Law. Once reinforced, the accusation will lead either to continued self-deception or, if man recognizes his weakness, it will cause him to attempt to assure his status in relation to God by means of works and propitiatory measures. In building his own security, man is able to and will go much further than the abuse of creation; he will not shy away from using God to uphold his own prideful and self-centered individualism.

Misuse aside, the goal of the accusation is, of course, that man will despair of himself as demigod and God-maker and acknowledge that all he is and has comes from God, who, despite human sin, in love continues to relate to man, upholding the latter's life and humanity. Man must recognize, to quote Gustaf Wingren, "that our relationship to God is given in and with life itself. It can never, properly speaking, be created or established from man's side, as though there had been a time after a man's birth when this relationship was not yet established. Man cannot live without living from God."[45]

---

45. Wingren, *Creation and Law*, 20.

In this way, the second use of the Law, though central as far as salvation is concerned, is, in fact, only a necessary outcome or a corollary of the first use of the Law. It has its origin and rationale in the vestigial character of the *usus politicus*. It derives its force from God's unilateral preservation of creation's order, from the ambiguity of the first use, as well as from its inimical and hostile character. The second use is driven solely by the reality of sin because it is against sin—against man's failed self-extraction from his God-given position of honor—that it is directed. The second use of the Law can, therefore, never be the goal nor can it represent all that there is to the Law. It begins in aberration and aims at combating the aberration. The real goal, however, is the restoration of creation's structures based on mutual love. This goal is brought to fruition in the third use of the Law.

The third use of the Law is none other than the first use without the latter's plaguing vagueness and hostile undercurrents, without its alien character. It is a return to creation in its primeval beauty, with order being maintained not merely externally but also internally through the bond of love and trust between a self-giving God and a reciprocating and socially and vocationally self-giving man. This radical change has been made possible by the reality of redemption. God's continued self-giving reached its apex and most perfect manifestation in his offering of himself to man in the most intimate of ways—by becoming man and sharing in humanity (Heb 2:14).

Note that the incarnation is fundamentally consistent with God's preservation of the whole creation and thus with his very being; it is an extension of God's loving presence. What is of significance is that God the Son was "made like his brothers in every way . . . yet was without sin" (Heb 2:17; 4:15). Christ became a man perfect in his humanity, with the fullness of its God-given relational potential, only to take on himself our isolation and enslavement. This Jesus then conquered by trustingly offering himself both to God and to his fellow men, even to the point of death. Thus amid life's ambivalence, Christ exposed with utmost clarity the deceptive nature of sin, based as it is on a fundamental denial of God's nature as love. Through seeming powerlessness, Christ revealed the power of divine love, which alone has the capacity to triumph over isolation and enslavement by unflinching, total, and unconditional self-giving. Consequently, in Christ, the despairing sinner again perceives the astounding faithfulness and the life-bestowing love of God that reach beyond each individual to all of creation. More than that, in Christ, the sinner becomes a *human* being by being restored and recreated in his capacity to reciprocate the no-longer-ambiguous divine love and to reflect it in loving relationships with fellow human beings and in one's stewardship of God's gifts. In other words, in Christ, divine love once again becomes human love.

Through Christ's incarnation, death, and resurrection, God's love for all humanity eventually becomes the love that intimately reconstitutes, restores, and defines humanity's essence. In this way, the seemingly individual character of the divine-human relationship is firmly and inseparably embedded in the renewal of all creation because it necessarily reestablishes bonds of love within creation. The third use of the Law, through its creationwide scope, shows that "human nature, being a human, consists solely in being justified by faith."[46]

As we have shown, the third use of the Law must be seen in the context of the universal first use if it is to be something more than arbitrary legalism that comes after the Gospel and is then ineptly justified by an appeal to the mysteries of God's will. The Law, as a meaningful reflection of creation's structure, though it is misinterpreted by the sinner, remains at its foundation an expression of God's love, the same love that has freely brought creation into being and shared itself with the creature. In this context, some of the questions raised earlier—why God actually wills that believers do good works, why he should reward them with temporal blessings, and why the works of the Law should be an indication of salvation—naturally find their answers. *To be human means to have God lovingly relate to one and to reflect this love by relating to fellow humans through the gifts one has received from God.* On account of the Christ event, all creation is now in labor pains as love is being restored into the fabric of our being, as the Law again becomes the essence of our humanity instead of an externally controlling tyrant (Jer 31:33–34). Through Christ's cross, one now sees God's faithfulness to and love for his creatures evident amid the ambiguities of creation. This is the Gospel.

V. CONCLUSION

This paper began with the identification of a number of problems posed by the treatment of the third use of the Law in Lutheran

---

46. Oswald Bayer, "The Doctrine of Justification and Ontology," *Neue Zeitschrift für Systematische, Theologische and Religionsphilosophie* 43 (2001): 46.

theology. In one way or another, they are all related to an individu-
alization and privatization of the Law, whereby its work becomes
restricted to atomized divine-human relationships. This individual-
ization is an unwanted outcome of the otherwise rightful elevation
of the second (accusatory) use to salvific preeminence. Without the
terrors of conscience the second use of the Law engenders, man
would never abandon his attempts at self-salvation. The second use
shows to man the dubious character of his works.

In this context, however, it is difficult to understand why, once a
believer, the individual must continue to live by the hateful Law and
do good works. It does not do to appeal to the seemingly arbitrary
will of God. Such arbitrariness flies in the face of divine revelation
as a disclosure of God's being. Consequently, deeper theological
motivation has been sought for why God actually wills that believers
do good works, why he should reward them with temporal blessings, and why the works of the Law should be an indication of salvation.

Taking our cue from the Scriptures, where redemption is portrayed in creational terms, we have suggested that these questions,
which cannot find satisfactory answers if the *tertius usus legis* is seen
as a derivative of the second use of the Law, can be explained once
the third use is given creationwide scope. This has, naturally,
directed us to the rather neglected first, or political, use of the Law,
the goal of which is to preserve social structures. Despite its apparent salvific irrelevance, we have discovered that this external use is a
vital remnant of the once-internal order of the pre-fall creation.

To understand this close affinity between the first and third uses
of the Law, and thus also the meaning of redemption, we have given
serious consideration to the anthropology of creation and the fall.
Only by inquiring into the nature of God the Creator, as it is
reflected in the creature he fashioned in his own image, can one
understand the constitution of humanity. Without this, the Law is
made arbitrary at best and meaningless at worst. Once, however,
creation and the fall are taken into account, it becomes possible to
appreciate the Law as God's continuing willingness to deal with his
rebellious creature as an expression of his love, which—though dis-
astrously misconstrued—has not been annihilated by human sin.
Against this background, both the first and the third uses of the Law
can be interpreted in terms of God's creationwide presence, the
goal of which is to restore wholeness in the world. The close relationship of the first and third uses of the Law underscores the piv-

otal character of Christ's atoning sacrifice without the lingering impression that the latter's validity will be undermined by an arbitrary legalism.

Both externally and internally, the Christian is at peace with God. Because Christ became "sin for us" to atone for our sin (2 Cor 5:21), sin is no longer a defining factor in the life of the Christian (though, of course, it is still present in the life of believers on this side of the grave). The curtain separating humanity from the holy has been destroyed. Restored wholeness is now the characteristic of the divine-human relationship. It is this wholeness—whereby God faithfully and self-givingly relates to man and whereby man reciprocates God's love and in love offers himself to other humans through the gifts he receives from his Creator—that constitutes our humanity.

ANCIENT LITERATURE INDEX

MODERN AUTHORS INDEX

CPSIA information can be obtained
at www.ICGtesting.com
Printed in the USA
LVOW08*0037030418

572028LV00005B/26/P